TRANSPLANTED FAITH

LAURA HERN

Transplanted Faith

By Laura Bichler Hern

Copyright © 2012 by Laura Bichler Hern

Published by TreasureLine Publishing

The views expressed in this work are solely those of the author. Some names have been changed to protect identities.

ISBN: 978-1-61752-118-8

Also available in eBook publication

PRINTED IN THE UNITED STATES OF AMERICA

❦

In memory of David Bichler.
The love of my life.
My soul mate.
My friend.

You always told me, "We will not be apart if,
in our hearts, we love the Lord Jesus Christ."
I will see you again, my love, when God decides it's time.

❦

Laura is an amazing friend and excellent writer. She is
a woman of God whose love for life is clearly shown in
her descriptive and unique writing techniques. Her
words lead you into a place where you feel that you are
actually there. Her book is about loving and losing and
then finding the strength and hope to carry her
through that grief. I recommend her book to men and
women of all ages and backgrounds.
Jean Smith ~ Director of Care & Prayer Ministries
Trinity Lutheran Church, Spring, TX

༄༅

Laura's book was so inspirational. I felt like I was on
their journey with them. I experienced all the ups and
downs they went through. They held onto their faith in

spite of the crushing blows they received and are a great example of how a godly marriage should work in spite of great trials. I definitely recommend this book!

Sheryl Albers ~ Church Secretary
Trinity Lutheran Church, Spring, TX

Laura Bichler Hern tells a beautiful story of love and loss that will break your heart while lifting your soul. Transplanted Faith is an amazing true story of how the light of God's love shines through, even in the darkest hour.

Krisi Keley ~ Author of the On The Soul Series and Editor/Owner of The Scrupulous Scribe

One warm and humid Wednesday in April of 2004, as I was sitting at my desk working on the final details of our Board of Parish Education meeting for that evening, the intercom of my office phone broke the pattern of clicking my fingers were making on the keyboard. Our church receptionist was telling me that my hubby was on Line 2. I glanced at the computer's clock. It read 12:30 p.m.

Right on time, I thought.

For that past 22 years, David, if he was in the country, called me at precisely 12:30 p.m.

I punched Line 2, tucked the receiver between my shoulder and my chin and, without losing my train of thought for the meeting agenda that was glaring at me on the computer screen, said, "Hello, my love."

"What's going on?" was always his response, to which I would say "Nothing much. Just work." It was then that he would either ask if we needed anything from the grocery store, which he could pick up on his way home, or would let me know that he was being sent out of the country for whatever project he was presently in charge of. Sometimes he would talk about being transferred to another city. This was one of those days.

"A headhunter called me today. Want to move to Wisconsin?" he asked.

"Sure! What city and when?" was always my answer and this was my response again today.

David was a mechanical engineer who had worked in the oil industry his entire professional career. He was one of those math nerds who could take an Einsteinian math problem and solve it in a couple of minutes. He loved math and working with numbers. Being the quintessential engineer that he was, he would invariably have a pen and pad in his front shirt pocket. How he mourned when pocket protectors went out of style! Still, a look at his dress shirts hanging in the closet would show heavily-starched, cuff-linked shirts with one front pocket with blue/black ink marks forming a dotted line across the bottom of it. David always said he felt naked if he didn't have a pen in his pocket.

Over the years, through his work, he was blessed to

travel to places like Indonesia, Malaysia, Singapore, Egypt, Jakarta, Saudi Arabia, Argentina, England, Scotland, Canada, and remote places whose names are almost impossible to pronounce. But he had never been sent to Wisconsin. Wisconsin might not have been quite as exotic, but making a home there sounded inviting, especially since David grew up in South Dakota, had relatives in Madison, and it would be a welcome change going back to a rural area.

At the time of this proposed move, we had been living in Tomball, TX., and for the last eight years were members of Trinity Lutheran Church and School in Spring, TX. I had been working within the church and school for most of those years as band teacher and Children's Ministry Director. We had made many friends, played many hands of '42' and sat through many Bible studies.

This would be our first move since becoming empty-nesters in the fall of 2002 when our daughter went off to college, and we were looking forward to being transplanted from the humid, traffic-delayed, big city of Houston to a small, rural community similar to the ones we had both grown up in.

Because we were empty-nesters, we didn't need to research school districts or find homes that were close to school so that we could avoid driving the hours away back and forth from activities. This made us excited, and we were looking forward to another new adventure. Making memories is what we called it.

The decision made, David was to be in Wausau in May and I would stay in Tomball until the house sold.

David and I were blessed to grow up in Christian homes, both of us being Missouri Synod Lutheran and very involved in the church and its activities. In fact, David and I met during choir practice at Trinity Lutheran Church in Borger, TX. He was fresh from college, attractive, and an engineer from Deadwood, South Dakota who came to work in Borger for Phillips Petroleum Company in late 1981.

Trinity was the only Lutheran church in Borger at that time, and I happened to be accompanying the choir. He had appeared at a couple of rehearsals, and we would slyly sneak glances at one another when we thought the other was not looking. The church's organ was very tall, in order to support the three keyboards and the numerous stops or pulls that made the sounds, so when I sat on the bench to play, only my forehead down to my eyes showed above the organ top. David always told me that he fell in love with my eyes because that's all he could see! We dated only a few months and were married in November of 1982 in the same little church.

For these reasons, finding a church home was a priority anytime we moved. Since we had never lived close to any of our relatives, our church home became our family and most, if not all, of our social activities revolved around the church and its school activities. David had served on many boards and committees as president of a congregation, chairman of the education board, church council member, elder, and more. My job was to get involved with the school (as we had decided to have our children attend Lutheran schools) and the kids' activities.

Over the years and moves, we had developed a great system that eased the transition for everyone. The move to Wausau was no different. As David went to his first day of work in May, I was in Tomball busily researching realtors, getting to know more about Wausau, and finding churches that we might attend. The plan was working well.

During the months we waited for our home in Tomball to sell, David was acclimating to our new city: visiting different churches, seeing which one would be our new family, and beginning yet another workout routine of walking. He was one of those lucky people who was never sick a day in his life. Perhaps a cold or headache here or there, but he never missed a day of work. He was 5'11" and weighed between 220-230 lbs. most of the time. Over the years he had battled a 'bulge' around his middle, a tummy that just would not tuck. We blamed it on gravity, of course! He would grumble as he lifted his foot up on a chair – one at a time in order to tie his shoes – that he was going to have to get those 'zip' shoes like the ones children who hadn't learned to tie laces wear so he wouldn't be short of breath after bending over. He had tried dieting and exercise routines to rid himself of this pesky bulge. It would seem to disappear, only to reappear within a few months. His love for chocolate did not help matters. So his current strategy, in 2004, was to walk each day around the apartment complex where he was temporarily living.

He would often call me while on one of his marathon walks, and I began to notice that he had a bit of a cough. Not a bad cough, but he always seemed to be out of breath. I kidded him that he must be walking at super speeds to not be able to walk and talk at the same time without panting. He would just laugh.

The closing on our Tomball home was the week of Thanksgiving 2004. The movers were coming two days before the holiday to pack our belongings and load the truck. David flew back to Houston the Sunday before Thanksgiving. I had not seen him since the company had flown me to Wausau on a house hunting trip in September and, when he entered the airport, I was pleasantly surprised to see that not only was his tummy bulge gone, but he was quite a bit thinner. My thoughts were, *Wow! He looks terrific!*

After I gave him a big hug and kiss, we started walking down the long corridor to the elevators that would take us to the parking garage level where our car was parked. Usually, David walked quickly and his long legs gave him a large stride. Normally, I had to work to keep up with him. This time, however, I noticed he was not walking at his usual pace. In fact, I had to slow down a couple of times in order to stay even with him. I asked him if everything was okay and he gave his usual response, "I'm just tired, that's all."

There are wonderful things about being married to someone for many years. The feelings of security, of routine, of trust and of being so comfortable with another person that you could almost read his or her thoughts. So, I heard my husband say he was just tired, but my heart knew there something else. Something he wasn't sharing with me.

Bright and early the next morning, we began the process of readying things for the movers to pack. After experiencing the chaos of several corporate moves, David, being the terrific engineer he was, had devised a system to make the process as efficient as possible.

Okay, good.

Lined up neatly across the kitchen counter were four large, black permanent markers, four neon-colored sticky note pads, four rolls of scotch tape, two big rolls of duct tape, and one chocolate bar. We were to take a marker (the other two were extras in case we needed them) and one neon-colored sticky note pad, along with one roll of scotch tape. The duct tape was to be used in the garage, David's territory.

He had drawn a simple floor plan of the new home in Wausau, giving each room a number. He had measured our furniture and figured out what furniture would fit in which room. Our first task was to clearly mark each piece of furniture with the corresponding room number in the new home. He would then make a copy of the finished floor plan to give to the movers in Wausau so they knew what furniture went in which room. I shook my head and laughed. Life with an engineer was never dull. Oh, and when I asked about the one chocolate bar... he said it was brain food for later.

Throughout the day, I was aware that David, who usually outworked everyone, wasn't moving very quickly. In fact, he was stopping every so often, sitting down to mark notes or to get a drink of water. Sometimes he would just look around the room, almost as though he was daydreaming. When I asked him if he needed anything or if he was feeling ill, he would always smile and answer, "I'm fine."

By the day's end, we had gotten through most of the chores on David's spreadsheet. I was starving since he had eaten the 'brain food' bar earlier in the afternoon, so I ordered a pizza. We devoured it in no time.

Since becoming empty–nesters, we had gotten into the habit of sitting in the recliners after supper, talking about the day's happenings or watching a movie. Tonight, he turned to me as he sat down, and I saw something in his eyes I had not seen before. Uncertainty. David was a wonderful listener and a deep thinker. He calculated all the pros and cons of any situation before deciding. He was never uncertain.

"I'm not sure what is going on with me," he said, "but for the past couple of weeks I haven't felt right." He went on to say that he hadn't been sleeping well lately and had attributed his tiredness to that. But, even though he had lost over twenty pounds, he still, at times, felt out of breath. "It's not like me," he said.

I suggested that we call our doctor the next morning as a precaution, before heading out of state.

"No, no, I'm fine," he muttered. "Just a little tired and stressed. That's all."

I could tell by his tone of voice that he didn't want to discuss this any further.

We talked a bit more about the movers coming the next morning and decided to call it a night. We tried to always say our bedtime prayers together, holding hands as we would drop off to sleep. This night my prayers were for him.

CHAPTER 2

The moving company 'packers' came, followed the next day by the 'loaders' and, before we knew it, we were heading north on I45, smiling and laughing about leaving behind the mass of cars and snarly traffic. It was Thanksgiving Day and our conversation turned to the subject of our trips. More particularly, it turned to the schedule.

Now the schedule, although not set in stone, mind you, had been reviewed many times, allowing for variances including pit stops, meals, fuel, and lodging, if necessary. Fueling and pit stops played an important factor in our travel time as the schedule declared we needed to be at the destination before or at the predicted time.

Before getting into the car, David had taken out his mileage pocketbook, carefully noting the starting mileage and the number of gallons it took to fill up the tank. I smiled to myself and thought about the times before when he'd left on an overseas company trip, and how he'd written down the mileage just to make sure he knew how many miles I drove and the fuel consumption rate.

Once, while he was in Singapore and before the days of caller ID, the phone had rung very early in the morning.

"What's going on?" he'd said as always.

The only thing I said was, "Not much. Just getting ready for work." That's all I said.

The next words out of his mouth were, "You got a speeding ticket, didn't you?"

I stood there with my mouth wide open, grinning from ear to ear in disbelief. Holy moly!! Just the day before I had gotten a speeding ticket!

"How did you know that?" I laughed into the receiver. I thought he was psychic because he could tell if I had been speeding. He claimed it was something in my voice, but I still swear somebody had to have told him! Then again, maybe he was psychic.

The next two days of our trip to Wisconsin were spent driving and talking about the many things that had to be taken care of once we arrived in our new town. A few times while speaking, he would cough as though he needed to clear his throat, but not for very long and not very often.

The closer we got to Wisconsin, the colder the temperature got. We began to put on more layers of clothing, marveling at the snow-covered areas that we saw through the windows.

We pulled into the hotel in Wausau on Saturday, as scheduled, and were ready to head to church on Sunday morning. David had been visiting churches during his months here and had settled on a small congregation named Christ Lutheran that seemed very warm and friendly.

Great! One day here and already we had a church home. Mark that off our list.

December came and so did the beastly cold Wisconsin weather we had been warned about. It only took a day or two of shoveling the snow in our oversized driveway to see that we needed mechanical help.

One day, shortly before Christmas, I heard David come through the door earlier than usual.

"Laura, Laura," he was saying with great excitement. "I got a great deal on a snow blower!"

Whew! I thought. *No more shoveling for me!* I went out to the garage to see his new purchase, looked around, and saw nothing. He was standing beside me, grinning.

"Where is it?" I asked. "You did get a little snow blower, didn't you?"

"Sure did. Wait about five minutes," he assured me.

I said, "It's freezing out here, and I'm standing here watching you grin over a simple little snow blower that appears to be invisible."

He said nothing, just kept on smiling.

In the distance, I could hear the grinding gears of a diesel engine on one of those big rigs. The sound grew louder and louder until I saw this bright purple big rig turn onto our street. I'm watching it go past our house, thinking, where in the world is that big 'ole truck going on our street when it backed into our driveway. I glanced at David as he started walking toward the back end of the diesel truck, still not quite sure what was going on.

The driver jumped onto the trailer, opened the big latch on the back door and dropped down a ramp. David walked into the trailer and was talking to the driver, when I heard this loud, grumbling roar from way in the back of the truck, and then I saw the biggest, reddest, tractor-looking machine to ever shine its bright headlights into the air moving down the ramp with David as the driver!

Snow blower? That thing was a monster truck, a piece of farm equipment, a combine, or some kind of bulldozer! We could snowplow the entire city with that thing.

As the truck driver pulled out of our driveway and drove off to his next delivery, David was already happily plowing the sidewalk in front of the house and the neighbor's sidewalk and their neighbor's sidewalk and the neighbor's neighbor's sidewalk. He must have driven that snow blower for a few hours before returning triumphantly home. He was very proud of his purchase, saying that, dollar for dollar, he had gotten a terrific deal and couldn't wait to hear the forecast to see when more snow would be falling. I was so happy for him. His first snow-toy!

We never dreamed that day would turn out to be one of the few times he would be able use it.

Through the dreary, cold days of January and February, David continued to lose weight, though only a pound or two here and there. We both also noticed that his coughing was becoming more frequent and more violent, lasting several minutes. Sometimes these cough spells left him short of breath and teary-eyed from straining so hard. Up until then, he had been the type of person who rarely, if ever, complained about how he was feeling. He had been blessed to be extremely healthy, hardly ever even taking an aspirin for a headache. But, on the last Friday of February 2005, I knew something was terribly wrong when he came home from work at noon, saying that he was too exhausted to complete the day.

I looked at him as he stood before me and, instead of seeing that familiar glimmer shining through his deep brown eyes, I saw worry, confusion, uncertainty, and... fear.

We held each other's hands and prayed that God

would grant him sleep and lead us to the right doctor who could find out what was wrong. I called my Trinity Church family in Houston to add David to their prayer list, and then began looking in the phone book for heart doctors.

David slept through the entire weekend, waking only to sit up when the coughing spells occurred and to munch on a few crackers or sip some soup.

We scheduled an appointment with a heart specialist in Wausau on Monday afternoon, February 28th. David had gone to work and we were to meet at the doctor's office at 3 p.m. By this time, he was already somewhat perturbed about sitting in front of a doctor, taking time off from work, going through chest X-rays, blood work, etc. I remember him saying, "I am not sick, probably need blood pressure medicine. Let's not make a fuss about this. I've got work to do."

We were waiting in one of the examination rooms for the doctor to look at the X-rays and give us a prescription, when the doctor entered the room.

Sometimes doctors have the task of writing prescriptions, telling patients to exercise more, eat right, or to come back in a few weeks for a recheck. Sometimes doctors have the difficult task of giving bad news to patients. As the doctor shut the door and turned to face David, there was a seriousness about him that made the air in that tiny room seem too heavy to breathe.

"Mr. Bichler," he said, "when was the last time you had a chest X-ray?"

David replied that he couldn't remember the last time.

"Mr. Bichler, you have a serious issue that is beyond my realm of expertise and I am sending you next door to a pulmonary specialist that I know. You will need to go there right now."

David looked at me and I looked back at him. "What did you say?" he asked.

The doctor stated again that a nurse would be escorting us next door to the specialist, and then he left the room.

Wait a minute. I was the one who had been asthmatic for years and seen pulmonologists. I was the one with the inhalers and nebulizers. Was he telling us David was asthmatic, too? How could that be? We were not smokers. We were not in the habit of frequenting smoke-filled places.

It seemed to be only a few seconds after the doctor left the room that a nurse opened the door, saying, "We are ready for you, Mr. Bichler."

Just beyond the door stood an empty, slightly worn wheelchair with a beat-up, green, portable oxygen tank with what looked like several feet of tubing that one would use for a fish tank air filter system attached to it. You could hear the oxygen oozing out with a loud hissing sound.

"I don't need that!" David said in a gentle, but firm voice as he waved it away with his hand.

With the same firmness in her voice, the nurse stated that all pulmonary disease patients were required to be transported in a wheelchair.

David and I looked at each other in disbelief.

What? What are they talking about? Wait, there is a mistake being made here. He's not on oxygen. He's not a pulmonary disease patient! I thought frantically.

David reluctantly sat down in the wheelchair while I grabbed our coats and things from the exam room. The nurse handed him the oxygen cannula to wear in his nose, and he looked at her and said, "Really?"

The nurse must have seen the confusion, bewilderment and frustration on his face and gently said to him, "No, I suppose it is not necessary for you to wear it. We are only going across the hallway."

As the nurse pushed the wheelchair, the movement caused a rhythmic clinging and clanging sound as the heavy steel tank banged against the handle of the wheelchair. I walked beside it, our coats and my purse over my arm, trying to hold onto David's hand and avoid colliding with the oversized wheel spinning next to my left leg. The specialist's office was located only two doors down on the left side of the hallway, but it seemed to take us hours to navigate the narrow hallway, through the door, and into the pulmonologist's waiting room. I piled our coats onto an empty chair and sat down while the nurse checked David in. The look on David's face was one of growing concern, embarrassment, and frustration.

"Laura, please find out what's going on. I have to go back to work and I do not need to be in a wheelchair!"

As I got up to approach the receptionist, the specialist's physician's assistant was walking toward us.

"Hello, Mr. Bichler," he stated as he positioned himself behind the wheelchair and began rolling it toward the entry to the exam rooms. "We have been waiting for you. First, we are going to do a few tests before the pulmonologist will see you. Your wife can fill out the paperwork."

David was wheeled away to the breathing lab to go through pulmonary function tests. I was handed a stack of paperwork on a clipboard with a pen attached to it by a string. As I was filling out form after form after form, I would glance into the function testing room. There sat David, in a small, glass-enclosed, egg-shaped cubicle trying to blow into a tube that was recording his lung volumes.

My eyes filled with tears as I heard the assistant say, "Blow into the tube, Mr. Bichler, without coughing." The minute David would try to blow, he would cough and choke and struggle to relax. Over and over again I heard, "Mr. Bichler, please try to breathe into the tube without coughing." Each time David experienced harder, longer, more violent coughing spells. His face was scarlet and he was sweating profusely.

Why don't they let him catch his breath? I thought. *Give him a couple of minutes, and then he will be fine.*

Finally, thankfully, the assistant gave up, released David from the cubicle, and wheeled him into the exam room where I was waiting. David's face was flushed and tears had been streaming down his cheeks from the strain of the vicious coughing he endured while trying to breathe into the machine. He was visibly shaken and exhausted. I had to fight back tears when I kissed his cheek, telling him the worst was over.

"Sweetie, we are going to get the bottom of this I promise you," I said to him. "Rest up till the doctor comes in, and then we will have answers as to why you are being subjected to this."

Our wait was not long. The specialist came into the room carrying X-rays, a clipboard, and a file folder.

"Hello, Mr. Bichler," he stated as he put the X-rays onto the white-lighted board on the wall. "How long have you had lung problems? Do you have records from your previous doctors?"

David's eyes grew wide as he opened his mouth and said, "I'm sorry, sir. There has been a misunderstanding. I do not have lung problems and I don't have previous doctors. I simply have a problem with blood pressure and I'm confused as to why I was sent to you in the first place. I would appreciate an answer as to what is going on here."

It was apparent the specialist was taken aback by David's comments. He stopped looking at the X-rays, turned to look at David, and said in what seemed to be a sarcastic way, "You're kidding, right?" It took him only a moment to see that David was completely serious.

"You have a problem with your lungs." The specialist walked back over to the lighted X-ray on the wall and took a pencil from the pocket of his long, white coat. "Look at this X-ray taken today. Do you see the outline of the lungs?"

"Yes, of course I do," David replied.

"Good," the doctor answered. "Do you see the white, smoky looking areas within the lungs?"

I strained to get a look myself.

"Yes, I see it," David responded.

"The entire lung area is filled with that white, smoky-looking stuff, isn't it?"

"Yes," David said slowly. He was making a huge effort to remain civil. I could tell he was getting a bit put off by the condescending way the doctor was talking to him.

"Well, Mr. Bichler, those areas on an X-ray are supposed to be black...no white, smoky-looking stuff at all."

David and I looked at each other. I dared to speak.

"Does he have an infection then? Pneumonia? What antibiotic will he need and when can we pick it up?" I found myself stammering. I knew that David wanted to get out of that office as quickly as possible. So did I.

The doctor chuckled, or smirked, I couldn't tell which, and said, "This is no infection. You'll have to be admitted to the hospital as soon as possible, where we will do a lung biopsy. I'll make the arrangements now. Wait here."

Biopsy? I could tell that David was thinking the same thing I was: *biopsy means a chance of cancer, doesn't it?*

The silence in the room as we waited for the doctor to return was as deafening as the roar of a tornado swirling overhead. Shocked, confused, scared. We were feeling all those things, all at the same time. My heart was pounding so hard I felt like the floor was moving. *Cancer? Please, Lord, don't let it be cancer!*

When the door opened this time, an older, slightly plump, silver-haired woman, wearing scrubs that were the deepest shade of purple I had ever seen, came bouncing into the room. Her smile was the kind that would calm an angry bull ready to charge. There was warmth flowing around her.

"Hello. I have information and hospital orders for you, Mr. Bichler." She handed David a couple of pieces of paper and patted him on the shoulder. "The biopsy is considered day surgery, but most lung patients are asked to spend the night, so please be prepared to do that. You are to report to the hospital around 6:30 a.m. on Friday, March 4th. If you have any questions, please call the number listed on the first page."

David was busily reading through the paperwork. I smiled and said, "You are very gracious. Thank you."

She nodded and asked, "Wouldn't you like to get out of that old wheelchair, hon?"

David eagerly rose from the chair, shook her hand, and we started for the door. "Blessings to you," I called back to her.

"Same to you," she replied.

CHAPTER 3

The rest of that week was a blur. The procedure cast a dark, black, eerie shadow over us as we tried to go about our regular routines. Both of us were avoiding the topic of the upcoming biopsy, except to talk a little bit about the logistics of getting David there, packing if we had to stay overnight, and so on.

David was a quiet person, preferring to keep our daily life's happenings private. He was always listening, always thinking, always trying to be prepared for any circumstance. This biopsy was no different. He worked long hours that week to cover for missing Friday. We prayed each night for God's healing power to bring the biopsy back benign, as we were still worried about cancer. God was soon going to answer our prayers, but not in the way we hoped He would.

David and I were up very early Friday morning, as we had not slept well the night before. I was the cheerleader, trying to pump him up, lessen his worries, and take away his concerns by placing little notes around the bathroom and bedroom for him to find. On those notes were Bible verses of strength, courage, perseverance, and love. Our family's Bible verse had been Joshua 1:9, paraphrased as: "Be strong and courageous for the Lord your God will never leave you." Today we recited that verse silently over and over again. I knew in my heart that David was a good man. He was a good servant. God would heal him!

We checked David into the hospital and he was in a gown by 6:00 a.m. Even though he was a quiet man, at times he could have quite a sense of humor. That was evident when I walked into the 8x10 holding area where David was waiting to see the doctors. The curtains were drawn, of course, when he had been asked to change into a gown. I waited outside the curtains, chatting with the nurses whose shifts were ending.

David called out, "It's okay to come in, Laura."

I flipped open the curtain only to see him standing there facing me, gown on backwards, proudly showing off the front side of his birthday suit and grinning like a Cheshire cat!

I burst out laughing. And to his embarrassment, so

did the two nurses who followed me inside the curtains!

"Whoops!" he said sheepishly as he struggled to pull the sides of the gown together to hide his 'birthday suit.' "I thought Laura would be by herself!" he grinned.

We were all giggling. One of the nurses quickly quipped: "It's okay, Dave, it happens to us all the time and, believe me, we have seen many a birthday suit. Don't worry, you won't get that lucky this morning!"

Our laughter would have continued for several minutes, but it was abruptly interrupted as David began to cough and choke, struggling to catch his breath.

While the nurses completed their checklist, David quickly turned his gown around just as the surgeon and anesthesiologist came in. Both were very professional, very kind, and very informative.

"David, this is a routine procedure that will cause you very little pain. The lungs cannot feel pain, so any discomfort you may experience will come from the small incision on your left side," the surgeon told him. "This procedure will take about 30 minutes from start to finish. We should have preliminary results this evening. I'll come by your room between 6:00 and 8:00 p.m. to let you know what we find."

I was holding David's hand, squeezing it tightly at the mention of knowing results as early as that evening.

The orderlies came to push David's bed into the operating room, and I kissed him as he was leaving, telling him I was praying for him, that everything would be fine. He winked at me, gave my hand a big squeeze and said, "I love you."

I sat down in the designated waiting area and prayed. *Dear God, I praise your holy name! You are the Great Healer! Please guide the surgeon's hands, give him the wisdom to see what is wrong and, Lord, please help David to heal quickly. In Jesus' name I pray. Amen.*

Our family was also praying for him at that moment. My friends in Houston at Trinity were praying for him at that moment, too.

Please Lord, hear our prayers!

I heard my name over the intercom, telling me to come to the recovery room, and I looked down at my watch. It had been 21 minutes since I left David.

Great! Everything must have gone smoothly.

When I got to the recovery area, David was still a bit groggy, still sleepy. I sat down quietly and watched him breathing. He was resting better than he had in weeks.

Once he awoke, we were moved to a private room on the second floor.

David looked fantastic. Bright eyes, smiling, very little pain from the four-inch incision on his left side. By noon, he was using my cell phone to call his office and he led a meeting via conference call from the hospital room at 1:00 p.m.!

Thank you, Lord! All is going to be fine.

By late afternoon, he was getting restless and we went for a stroll around the 2nd floor corridor. He was dragging the IV pole along with his left hand, and I was pushing the oxygen tank along on his right. We made several laps around the floor, David commenting on how great he was feeling. By the time we got back to the room, his supper tray was waiting.

As he sat down to eat, both of us were struck with the same thought. Amazingly, he had not coughed one time since returning from surgery! He had laughed, he had talked, he had walked, and he had eaten. But he had not coughed!

We prayed a prayer of thanksgiving to the Lord. We thought the biopsy had gotten rid of whatever was making him cough and were excited to hear what the surgeon had to say. As Christians, we are taught to pray for God's will to be done in our lives. But sometimes human nature has us hoping that our will might be done, forgetting for a moment that our will may not be His will.

It was getting late, around 7:00 p.m., when the surgeon stopped by David's room. They shook hands, the surgeon commenting on what a strong handshake David had. As he pulled a chair closer the hospital bed,

I said happily, "We are so excited! David hasn't coughed once since the procedure this morning! Did the biopsy remove whatever was causing him to cough?"

David was smiling as the surgeon smiled back at him and then looked down at his hands. He looked up again and said, "Well, I wish I could tell you that the biopsy corrected your problem, but that is not the case."

David's smile disappeared as he sat back against the bed pillows, and my heartbeat was pounding in my ears.

The surgeon continued, "In order to avoid puncturing the lung, we inflate the side with oxygen before taking the biopsy. The reason you are not coughing, David, is because there is still oxygen trapped inside from when we inflated the lung this morning. Within 24-48 hours, that oxygen will have worked its way out and you will begin coughing on exertion as before."

Silence. Dead silence. For several minutes, I stood beside David's bed, trying not to cry, trying to decipher what the surgeon had said.

Sensing our disappointment and confusion, the surgeon finally began speaking again. "David, we took many pictures of your lungs during the procedure, and my radiologist and I have been studying them closely. We are going to send you home tonight, but I want you to come to my office first thing in the morning. I have asked a couple of other doctors to confer with me on your case. I will be able to tell you more tomorrow."

David had a pasty white pallor to his face as he watched the surgeon speak, listening to every word.

"You get some rest tonight, and don't do any heavy lifting for a couple of weeks till we take the stitches out. I will see you folks in the morning."

Somehow I managed to say "thank you" as he left the room, but my thoughts were garbled.

David and I quietly got his things together and went home to think, to pray, and to sleep.

Why haven't they told us what is wrong? What did the biopsy show? Was it cancer? Can it be cured? These were our last thoughts that night as we lay next to each other in bed, holding hands and praying just like we always did.

The next morning, we found ourselves once again waiting in an exam room for a doctor to come in. Neither of us had slept well and we were unable to eat much breakfast. It had been an odd morning with both of us trying to talk about everything from the weather to what we needed from the grocery store. Anything but the biopsy results. Now, the topic could no longer be avoided and the anxiety of waiting for the surgeon was mounting minute by minute.

It was a relief of some sort when the door opened

and the surgeon came in. Not wearing his scrubs, he was in jeans and a sweatshirt, looking like an ordinary guy ready for the weekend's activities. I remember what happened next as vividly as if it were yesterday. David was sitting upon the examination table, I was in one chair, the surgeon was facing us in the other.

Slowly, the surgeon began speaking. "David, I do not like having to give patients results that are different from what they expect, but I respect you enough to be honest with you. After we have discussed these results, I will be happy to visit with you and answer all the questions you may have."

I felt the blood rush from my head down to my toes. My fingers were tingling and I thought I was going to black out. I climbed upon the examination table with David and took his hand in mine. His hand was cold and he had no expression on his face.

"I have conferred with several experts," the surgeon said, "and we believe you have interstitial pneumonitis with emphysema as a result of interstitial pulmonary fibrosis or what we call IPF."

Both of our mouths dropped open and we starred at each other in shock. *IPF? No way! Did he say IPF? Isn't that what Linda had last year? Didn't she have a double lung transplant? This guy has made a huge mistake! We need another doctor! I don't believe it! Dear God, he didn't say IPF, did he?*

The surgeon saw the astonished look on our faces and said, "You know about IPF? It is a relatively unknown disease."

Before I could think, I blurted out part of the story of David's younger sister, Linda.

David was the middle child with an older sister, Mary, and a younger sister, Linda. Growing up in Deadwood, South Dakota, their dad worked at the Homestake Gold mine in Lead and their mom worked for Thorpes Black Hills Gold Company.

David and Mary were a little more than three years apart in age. Linda was a little more than seven years younger than David. Naturally, he and Mary were closer to each other growing up than they were to Linda.

Over the years, all three had married and, while never living in the same area together, kept in touch through weekly phone calls. In the summer of 1999, Linda called us to say she had been having trouble breathing and had been going to doctors who first diagnosed her with asthma, then pneumonia. But none of the treatments seemed to be working. In fact, she was getting steadily worse.

In August of 1999, Linda, who was living in California, was referred to a pulmonary specialist at the University of California in San Francisco (UCSF). She had been through many days of CAT scans, pulmonary function tests, a bronchoscopy, blood draws, and X-rays before they came up with a diagnosis, one that we had never heard of. It was called IPF or interstitial pulmonary fibrosis.

Linda told us that IPF was not a common lung disease and the cause of it was unknown. We researched it online and found that IPF is a disease that produces scarring of the lung tissue. What causes the scarring to begin is unknown and, in some people, once the scarring begins, it cannot be stopped or cured. It appears on X-rays and CAT scans as honeycombing within the lung. Each time a scar appears, the area or tissue that it covers in the lung is no longer able to stretch or expand, eventually causing the lung to become hard and shrink in size, no longer able to move oxygen through the bloodstream. At that point, the only option for patients is death or lung transplantation.

The surgeon seemed very interested to hear about Linda and that we were familiar with IPF. He went on to say, "Since you live in Wausau, I have called and made an appointment for you at the Mayo Clinic in Rochester which is about a four hour drive from here. You are to be there on Monday, March 21st and it will take about a week to complete the testing." He continued, "Before you leave the clinic, they will have developed a plan for your treatment that could include pulmonary rehab, regular testing, dieting, and exercise."

David and I were still stunned. David asked, "How far along is this disease?"

The surgeon tilted his head and shrugged his shoulders slightly. "Mayo will have a much better idea of that after your tests next week. It's hard for me to say." He added, "I am putting you on a large dose of prednisone until you can get to the clinic. It will help you breathe and lessen the inflammation in your lungs. Take it once every day."

We left the office still shell-shocked by what we had been told. David said, "We need to get in touch with Linda as soon as possible."

"I'll call the minute we get home, okay?" I replied.

It doesn't take long to drive anywhere in a smaller town like Wausau, and we were home in less than ten minutes. David pulled a legal-sized yellow tablet out of his work briefcase, along with his mechanical pencil, while I headed for the phone to call his younger sister, Linda. We were determined to find as much information as possible, search out other specialists, and get rid of this IPF diagnosis. After all, David had been working at his new job for less than one year. The good Lord would not have moved us across the country only to have David be diagnosed with something like pulmonary disease! No way. There had been a serious mistake here and we were going to figure it out.

Linda was working and we left a message for her to return our call as soon as possible. She had been a store manager for Kmart for many years, working long hours, including shift work. She knew the transplant teams at UCSF.

In early 2003, Linda began experiencing more severe symptoms. It became harder and harder to breathe. Her oxygen levels were dropping and she had been steadily losing weight. By late summer, she had to be put on oxygen around the clock. She continued to go to work, although her staff would joke that between her constant coughing and the loud banging of the wheels on the oxygen tank she had to pull behind her, they could tell where she was at all times, anywhere in the store.

It was evident that she was quickly approaching the end stage of IPF and, in September of 2003, Mary and David decided to fly out to California for a short weekend to see her, visit with her, and tell her they loved her.

Linda's condition deteriorated rapidly, and on February 5, 2004 she had to be transported from her home in Redding to the University of California, San Francisco, known as UCSF, via ambulance. She had been listed on the transplant list for several months, but no lungs had been a match for her. As she arrived at the ICU, she and her doctors knew her only chance was the hope that lungs would be found quickly; otherwise, she would not survive.

Praise God that He did provide a pair of lungs for her and, on February 7, 2004, Linda became a double lung transplant recipient. Her recovery was nothing short of miraculous, with her doctors calling her the poster child for lung transplants.

Within a few days of the surgery, Linda was walking the hallways. The doctors were so pleased that they let her walk outside the hospital. She and Mary (who had flown in from South Dakota to help with her recovery) were walking up and down Parnassus, the hilly street in front of the hospital. In fact, Mary had a hard time keeping up with her sister!

In what was considered an extraordinarily short span of time –nine days after surgery – Linda was dismissed from the hospital. She had experienced few, if any, complications and was ready to start living again. God was good! She was given new life from a family who cared enough for their loved one to have them become an organ donor. She was active, happy, and enjoying life once more.

It was not long before Linda returned our phone call, and we told her about David's diagnosis. She, too, was speechless for several moments, not believing what she was hearing.

"How can that be, Dave?" Linda asked. "Neither one of us smoked!"

David was busy writing down questions to ask her, details of the testing he might be required to go through while at the Mayo clinic. Then they began speculating as to what they could have in common that would have caused this.

"Dad was a smoker, as were most of his friends. Think that might be a reason?" Linda asked.

David replied, "I don't know. We did live in a mining area and I did work in the Homestake mine one summer."

Linda said, "But Mary and I didn't work there."

David nodded his head in agreement. Both Linda and David had lived in Singapore for several months, she managing a Kmart store and he doing engineering work at that time for Baker Hughes. Could they have been exposed to something while living there?

They talked about many possibilities, not coming to a conclusive answer, but agreeing to talk with each other frequently.

"They are sending me to Mayo on March 21st," David said, "and I'll call you when I know more." With that, he hung up the phone and turned to me with a lost look in his eyes that I had never before seen. We hugged each other for several moments, not wanting to let go to face the reality of this situation. We agreed not to mention this at church or get on their prayer list until after we returned from Mayo.

Exhausted, we both tried to sleep, holding hands and praying. My prayers continued long after David had drifted off to sleep. "Heavenly Father, we need you. What is happening? This man means so much to me. Please, please, please, take him in Your healing arms and bring him back to health. I love you, Lord. Help us. Amen."

CHAPTER 4

David and I had received our 'orders' from the Mayo Clinic a few days before we were to leave. We were to report there by 9 a.m., Monday, March 23rd, not the 21st as we were first told. We had decided to leave the day before and get settled into the hotel so as to find our way around. The hotel/family rooms were connected to the clinic by enclosed walkways, making travel back and forth quite easy.

We checked into the room and decided to walk over to the adjacent clinic, finding the office we were to report to the next morning. To our amazement, the end of the walkway had doors that opened into a massive open area that resembled a mall more than it did a lobby. There were tons of people milling about, each one concerned with their specific mission.

We walked past a bookstore, a gift shop, a coffee shop, and into the vast expanse known as the lobby. Sitting areas were spread about and a black baby grand piano graced the middle of the floor. A thin, older man wearing a beautiful black tux played the piano with such passion that he was oblivious to whether people were watching him or ignoring him.

Escalators were strategically located throughout the lobby, and large signs pointed the way to different buildings inside this huge complex: this way to the Gonda Building, turn left to the Hilton Building, Plummer Building South, Landow Atrium to the North. We were a bit overwhelmed.

Mayo had mailed us an appointment schedule for the week, complete with instructions on what procedure was to be done, what to eat or drink, and what not to eat or drink. David, always the organized engineer, was impressed with the detailed schedule. The first day's schedule read:

8:00am   March 21 – Hilton Building, Court Level (Subway), Desk West 3

Specimen collection, sputum testing.

9:00am   March 21 – Mayo Building, Third Floor, Desk West 3

Esophageal X-ray (included instructions about the procedure)

10:00am   March 21 – Gonda Building, Sixth Floor, Desk 6 South

Echocardiogram

10:20am   March 21 – Hilton Building, Court Level (Subway), Desk C

Blood testing

2:00pm   March 21 – Plummer Building, Third Floor, Desk 3 South

Pulmonary Function testing – Home overnight test required

2:50pm   March 21 – Plummer Building, Third Floor, Desk 3 South

Pulmonary Function testing – (we thought it ironic that one of the requirements was to stop smoking one hour prior to the test)

Each day had a similar schedule, back and forth across one end of Mayo to the other. David found it difficult to walk quickly between these appointments and had begun coughing frequently. We had to reschedule a couple of these tests simply because we were late getting to the testing room or because he was coughing so violently that he couldn't catch his breath to perform the test.

Soon, what was to be one week at Mayo turned into two. By Wednesday, March 30th, all we had left to complete were two consultations and another pulmonary function test called 'the walk.'

David and I were sitting in the waiting area playing Gin. He was a fabulous Cribbage player, one of those people who knew exactly what cards you were holding before you played your first card. I would laugh and call it 'cheating.' His eyes would kind of squint, the left corner of his mouth would turn up slightly in the cutest way, and he would say, "Laura, it's all math and logic." He could beat me anytime he wanted, but most of the time he would let me win! Lately, we had begun playing Gin as a way to pass the time between appointments and take our minds off IPF.

He was beating me as usual when we were called back to see the doctor. We walked through the maze of cubicles where people were sitting while scheduling their next appointments and through a doorway that led down a tiled hallway with exam room doors on either side. I thought to myself: *Which room will we be in this time? Will it have a window we can look out? How long will this wait be?*

David had been a real trooper. He had seen more exam rooms, explained his symptoms to so many doctors, nurses, and physicians' assistants and had been poked, prodded, X-rayed, and scanned over the last two weeks. He was tired. Very tired.

We were surprised that the nurse led us into a larger room with a huge window but no exam table. Instead, there were dark brown leather chairs that had golden buttons tracing the outline of the arms and across the top, and an oversized mahogany desk with ornate carvings that graced the legs and front. It was beautiful. And sitting in a high-backed leather captain's chair was the doctor! He stood to shake our hands and motioned for us to sit down.

This man looked very young, very well-dressed, and was very well-spoken. He began, "Well, Mr. Bichler, may I call you David?"

"Of course," David replied.

The doctor continued, "You have had quite an adventure these last weeks, haven't you?"

Adventure was not the word we would have used.

He leaned back in his big captain's chair and said, "How long were you going to wait before coming in to see us?"

David and I looked at each other. *What was that? Was he being sarcastic?*

I said politely, "Excuse me?"

The doctor had a strange look on his face, and I didn't know if it was confusion, amazement, or surprise. He said, "You must have had symptoms for several years, correct?"

David, who had been leaning back in the chair, sat up straight and leaned forward. "I have not been sick a day in my life, sir," he replied.

The doctor was obviously startled. He paused for a moment, looking through the paperwork on his desk. His look had turned to concern when he said, "I apologize David. Usually when patients have the symptoms you are experiencing, they have already been in treatment with us."

Now both David and I were sitting on the edge of our chairs. We didn't know what to say. There was an awkward silence hanging heavily in the air, and I was finding it hard to breathe. It seemed like hours passed before the doctor spoke again.

"Mr. Bichler, you have idiopathic pulmonary fibrosis. It's a disease that causes scarring in the lungs and, over time, the lungs become hardened and not able to carry oxygen into the blood stream."

David had a blank expression on his face. He was focusing intently on every word the doctor was saying. I took his hand and looked back at the doctor.

"We are setting up appointments for April 6, 7, and 8 to do further studies. Part of the testing requires you to stop taking your acid reflux meds and the steroid prednisone until then, as we need to have an accurate measurement of your PH levels."

For several years, David had been taking something for his heartburn. When he began taking the tiny yellow pill, he had marveled that technology had made it possible for something that small to stop the burning he experienced.

David said, "Okay. I understand that."

After the doctor had explained what procedures would be done during the next visit, he paused and asked, "David, do you have any questions before you leave?"

David opened his mouth to speak then paused as if thinking how to word his question. Then he asked, "IPF is not curable, correct?"

The doctor replied, "No, it is not curable."

David continued, "What is the normal progression of this disease?"

The doctor sat back in his chair, rocking back and forth for a moment before saying, "Patients we see with the degree of scarring that you have..." he hesitated, "... most will have up to two years before transplantation is the only option."

David sank back in his chair.

I couldn't breathe. I couldn't speak. It was like everything was moving in slow motion. *Two years? David was only 46. Two years?* I found myself silently praying, *Dear God, please let that not be so.*

The doctor, seeing the disbelief in our eyes said, "Do not worry about that now. You are a long way from transplant and we will set up a program for you that will include exercise and regular testing. We will monitor you over the next year and re-evaluate then." He got out of his chair and put his hand on David's shoulder. "Go home, get some rest. I will see you in about 7 days or so. If you have any problems between now and then, call us. The number will be on the paperwork for you next appointment."

I remember standing up, shaking the doctor's hand and somehow stumbling out the door and down the hallway. *What was happening? I don't believe this. Only two years? Two years?*

As we sat down in one of the many cubicles to get our appointment schedule, I watched David and tried to choke back my tears. He was expressionless, going through the motions as if he were a robot. When I glanced into his big brown eyes and saw them moist, red, and swollen, I could not hold back any longer. Tears began streaming down my face as I sat silently watching him sign papers.

The receptionist kindly handed us both tissues and said something like, "It's okay. Everything is going to be okay."

We left the cubicle and weaved our way back through the mob of people milling about the large lobby, down the hallway to our room. Once inside, we hugged each other and cried. We prayed to God for strength, for courage, for healing, and for guidance. As we gathered our things, ready to head back to Wausau, our tears had dried and we began talking about a plan of action. I would drive, David would try to sleep, knowing that the good Lord would keep watch over us, sending His angels to protect us as He had always done.

CHAPTER 5

We were glad to be home and David was glad to be back at work. It was serving as his release right now, his escape from IPF, his outlet. He had several projects to manage that kept him very busy and now he had to plan to be gone again for a few days.

It was April 1st, April Fool's Day. We were trying to get back to our normal routine, but the diagnosis and David's frequent coughing bouts were constant reminders. I had called our family to keep them informed and had spoken with my friends in Houston at Trinity.

Jean Smith had worked with me at Trinity and was going to be the liaison for us, forwarding the information I'd sent her about David to the entire church. One of the many strengths of Trinity Lutheran is the prayer chain. Several times each week, a prayer list is updated and e-mailed or mailed to members who had volunteered to pray for each person listed. I asked that David be put on the prayer list and knew that hundreds of prayers would be said for him.

That day, I watched David when he came home from work. He was still losing weight and had dark circles underneath his eyes. The length of time at Mayo the week before had taken its toll on him and left him feeling tired with almost no energy.

I called the type of house we had purchased in Wausau an "up/down" house. When you entered the front door, you either had to go up seven steps to the main floor or down seven steps to the basement. In reality, it was a split-level home with two bedrooms, two baths upstairs and one bedroom, one bath downstairs.

My heart began pounding as I watched David enter through the garage door. He didn't see that I was watching and had slowly taken off his hat and coat to put it in the entryway closet. Standing there for a couple of minutes more, he glanced at the seven steps that would take him upstairs. Then, carefully, he stepped onto the first step and stopped. I could see that he was holding his hand on his chest over his heart. He tried to take a couple of shallow breaths, waited, and then stepped onto the second step. Again he stopped. Again he tried to take a couple of shallow breaths. He waited a bit longer and then stepped onto the third step and stopped. He had to stop to recover his breath with every step.

My heart was aching as I watched him labor to take each step, still holding onto his chest. I ran to help him, but he raised his hand and motioned for me to stop. He wanted to do this by himself. He was so brave. It was heartbreaking, but I was so proud of him. It took twenty minutes for him to climb those seven steps, and I knew something had gone terrible wrong. Only yesterday he was walking through Mayo and today he was struggling to climb steps.

When he reached the top, I hugged him and kissed his cheek. He paused for a moment and then very slowly walked toward the bedroom. He had not spoken and I wasn't sure he had the air to speak and walk at the same time. I walked ahead of him and pulled back the bedspread.

Mayo had told us to prop his head up to at least a 30-degree angle in order to lessen the chance of acid reflux backing up into his throat. I had purchased a wedge pillow that afternoon and I hurriedly plopped it onto the bed.

David didn't even take his shoes off before collapsing onto the bed. He made a motion of drinking water to let me know he wanted a drink. I went to the kitchen and poured a glass of water, grabbed a piece of candy from his chocolate stash, and headed back to the bedroom. His cheeks were flushed and he seemed to be breathing a little easier now.

After sipping on the water, he said, "I don't know what's going on. Suddenly this afternoon my heart started racing when I walked. It pounded so hard I thought I was having a heart attack."

I could see frustration in his eyes and sat on the edge of the bed to talk with him. I said to him, "Sweetie, I don't know what is wrong. Maybe we'd better call the Mayo number."

Shaking his head and frowning, he muttered, "I don't need to call Mayo every day. Let me rest. I am sure this will go away."

I took a warm washcloth and ran it over his face and neck, which seemed to ease him a bit. His eyes were already closed and he was beginning to snore by the time I finished. Quietly, I walked out of the bedroom and into the living room and began to cry.

I was never one to cry. That would show weakness! But lately, for some reason, all I could do was cry. I debated calling the Mayo clinic but decided not to go against his wishes. Instead, I prayed. It was the prayer of a confused and worried woman who was afraid. "Thank you, God, for listening to me," I cried. "Please help him to breathe. Please help him to be able to breathe."

Thank goodness the next day was Saturday. David could certainly use the time to rest up and I could catch up on the daily chores of laundry and cleaning. There was still a chill about the air this April morning, but most of the snow was gone. 'Mud season' is what the locals called it. The time between the frozen snow beginning to melt and the return of spring when one could see grass again. This day, the weatherman predicted, would be overcast, making it easy to become drowsy and sleepy during the day.

I found myself stretching and yawning to get up around 6:30 a.m. David was lying on his left side with his back facing me. I laid my hand on his shoulder and watched as he was breathing. He appeared to be able to breathe in deeply, his entire rib cage rising up to inhale. But when he tried to exhale, the rib cage would drop down suddenly, causing a small shudder to run through his upper torso. No wonder he wasn't able to sleep soundly! I prayed quickly and asked the Lord to give him strength for this day.

I got up carefully, trying not to disturb him and went into the kitchen to eat a bowl of cereal. As I reached into the cabinet for a bowl and a box of Wheaties, I had to smile.

I was considered a tomboy while growing up, preferring to spend time being my dad's shadow rather than learning how to cook and sew with my mom. I remember Dad eating a bowl of Wheaties with me every morning. Boy, did I think I was special!

During my 7th grade year, Poppo, as I called him,

had taken on a 2nd, part-time evening job with a local janitorial service to generate a little extra spending money. The van he used to carry all the cleaning equipment had windows on the two front doors only and was the worst color of yellow known to man. He had nowhere to park it except right in front of the house. My mom would cringe, saying that a space satellite could easily find our house by zeroing in on that ugly van.

Poppo had allowed me to work with him on Tuesdays, Thursdays and Saturday mornings. My job was to empty trash, clean the bathrooms and dust. He graciously paid me $2.00 per hour, and I am sure there were times when he had to follow behind me and redo my cleaning.

I stopped daydreaming when I realized I was spilling milk on the cabinet instead of pouring it on the cereal. I thought to myself, *I need to talk with Dad. Think I will call him today.*

After I finished my cereal and put my bowl in the dishwasher, I walked back to the bedroom to check on David. I bent down to give him a kiss when he awoke. I looked at the dark, gray circles that were now both under and over his eyes and said, "Morning, sweetie. What can I get for you?"

He raised his arms to stretch then began coughing. This cough was relentless, and I was startled when he began coughing up dark green-looking mucus. He

strained and choked, still being forced to continue
coughing by this horrible disease. I was helpless. All I
could do was watch him fighting for air. His face had
turned red and his lips were beginning to turn purple. I
was scared and moved toward the telephone on the
nightstand to dial 911.

Almost as suddenly as it began, his throat relaxed
and the coughing spell passed. Beads of perspiration
had formed on his forehead and he leaned back against
the wedge pillow, completely exhausted. I re-wet the
washcloth by his bedside and gently washed his face
and forehead. Thoughts were swirling around in my
head faster than a spinning centrifuge.

*He is getting worse, Lord, I can see it. This is not
supposed to happen. Help him! Please help him! What can I
do to help him?*

He slept for another hour before a second coughing
spell forced him to wake up. These spells seemed to be
lasting longer, and the amount of dark green-looking
mucus he brought up was also increasing. When he
stopped coughing and had a moment to recover, I
confronted him and said, "David, something has
happened. I think we need to contact the doctors at
Mayo."

He looked at me for a long moment before calmly
saying, "Laura, I have an appointment with them in six
days. God will keep me safe till then. You worry too
much."

I took a deep breath and sighed. He knew I didn't agree with that and wanted to get him there today if possible.

"Would you please bring my work laptop, an extension cord, my briefcase, and the plastic zipper pocket with my pens in it to me? I think we can set up a little desk on the bed here so I can do my work. I have a lot to finish before we go to Mayo on the 6th."

I said, "Sure," and got up to retrieve the things he requested. He stopped me before I reached the bedroom door and said, "Oh, bring my Bible, too. And maybe a glass of orange juice."

Within half an hour, he had turned a four-foot area around him into an engineering office workspace. I had to laugh when I saw the finished product. He was wearing his maroon pj's, his hair was mussed and his glasses were perched slightly crooked on his nose. He had put three regular pillows between his back and the wedge pillow which forced him to sit up even straighter. He had placed his computer on a small, scratched, medal TV tray we had purchased from a garage sale. The tray fit perfectly over his extended legs. An empty shoebox was turned into a pencil holder on his left and his briefcase was open on his right.

I giggled. "Wow! Look at you! Maybe you should go into interior design!"

He smiled but tried not to laugh as that would start

another coughing attack. He said, "Mind if we read today's Portal of Prayer lesson together?"

The Portals of Prayer is a small quarterly publication from the Lutheran Church Missouri Synod and contains a short, daily reflection based on a Bible passage for each day. As with all great reading material, we kept the tiny paperback book in the bathroom, usually reading it before getting ready for work. David would always carry one in his suitcase when he traveled.

"I would like that, sweetie. I'll go get it."

David stayed in bed working on his computer all day, getting up only to use the restroom. I kept filling a glass of 7-UP for him throughout the day. He sipped on it but did not eat anything. He seemed content, ruling over his impromptu office in the bedroom. And as long as he stayed still, he didn't cough much. By 8:00 p.m., he was trying hard to keep his eyes open. We closed his 'office' for the night. I prayed that the coughing would not keep him up and that tomorrow would be a better day for him.

I was thankful that he slept fairly well through the night, and the next morning it seemed to me that the dark circles around his eyes were lightening a bit.

Thank you, Lord, I thought. *Thank you.*

David woke up and walked slowly into the bathroom. His heart was still racing when he walked.

We did not realize that he was suffering from pulmonary hypertension at the time.

As he was returning to bed, I asked, "How are you feeling this morning, sweetie?"

He got back into bed and leaned against the wedge pillow. "Well, I thought I felt better until I went to the bathroom. Think I'd better stay in bed today, too."

I hoped he couldn't see the disappointment on my face. I had so hoped he would be better today.

"That would probably be a good thing. Let's get your office back up and running. I think I'll stay home from church today to help you."

David always had a way of looking at you that caused you to feel extremely guilty about something and now he was giving me that look. "Don't you think you should go to church? I think you should. Agree?"

I sighed. "Yes, you are right. I'll go to church this morning. Will you be alright till I get back?"

"Sure," was his predictable response.

Reluctantly, I dressed for church. Usually when he would travel out of the country, it never bothered me to sit alone in church. No big deal. But today was different. I felt a strange emptiness all around me, even though there were many people sitting nearby. I tried to concentrate, tried to join in singing the hymns. But tears kept burning my eyes and I kept worrying about how David was doing at home. The service seemed to drag along and as soon as I could, I hurried home.

This Sunday the sun was shining and that made me feel better. David and I spent the day working for a while, playing cribbage for a while, and napping. He and I talked about things we remembered from when we met or from our childhood.

There was only one thing that was causing him pain. He said he was feeling so much acid burning down his throat and chest that he was having a hard time swallowing. Since he had been told to stop his meds, the acid was churning inside him, making him very uncomfortable.

In the back of our minds, we both felt confident that in a few days we would be on our way back to Mayo. The extensive testing would certainly give us more information and we needed that. David was planning on going to work tomorrow morning, even if he had to stay seated at his desk most of the day. He wanted to finalize the details for the rest of the week, and I was to get things washed and packed for the trip. We kissed each other good night and said our prayers.

Monday, April 4th: I woke up just before the alarm went off at 5:00 a.m. I scooted over to snuggle with David for a minute. At times he had rested. At times he had struggled with the cough. I think he was glad Monday morning had arrived and that he could escape to work, keeping his mind occupied. I got out of bed first, sleepily tripping over the house shoes I put at the end of the bed.

"Laura, will you get me a cup of 7-UP?" David said while sitting up in bed. I am going to shave and shower."

No problem. I left the house shoes where they were and trotted off to the kitchen. I poured a glass of that sparkling beverage and was walking back to the bedroom when I heard this horrible, low, growling sound and then a loud bump as though someone had slammed a door extremely hard. I ran into the bedroom as David collapsed onto the bathroom floor. I dropped the 7-UP glass and ran to him.

"Dave, Dave, oh my God, Dave!" I screamed.

He had grabbed the medicine cabinet door as he fell, tearing it off and shattering the glass front.

"Oh dear Lord, Dave!" I repeated as I leaned over him.

He had fallen face up and while his eyes were open, they were glassy. He could hear me, but he could not speak.

"Hang on, David, I'm calling 911. Dear God, where is the phone? David, stay with me, stay with me!"

I frantically found the phone and dialed 911. The second someone answered I yelled, "Help him! Help him! My husband has a lung disease and he has passed out. Get an ambulance here now and bring oxygen... he needs oxygen!" My hands were shaking so hard I could barely hold onto the receiver.

"They are on their way, sweetheart. Don't leave me.

David. David. Can you hear me?" His lips were blue and he could no longer blink.

Dear God, please get the paramedics here now. I am not ready to lose him. Please God, don't take him away from me now!

I heard the doorbell ring and I ran to answer it. "He needs oxygen," I screamed as I opened the door. "He needs air. Help him."

The paramedics followed me upstairs to where David was lying.

"Sir, sir, do you understand me?" the young paramedic said while he was putting a gadget on my husband's finger to measure his oxygen level. "What's his name, ma'am?"

"David, David Bichler. He's my life, please help him!" I begged.

The second paramedic had gone back out to the ambulance for an oxygen tank and blankets. I kept repeating over and over again, "David, I am right here. Stay with me. They are bringing air for you." *Where was the oxygen tank? Why haven't they got it running?*

"Please, he needs oxygen. He has IPF. Get him oxygen," I pleaded.

"Ma'am." The second paramedic took my hand and led me across the room so the first paramedic could get the oxygen mask on his face. "Ma'am," he repeated, "where is your oxygen tank?"

I couldn't take my eyes off David. Was he breathing?

"We don't have one. He was just diagnosed a few days ago at Mayo."

The man let go of my hand and said, "Ma'am, his oxygen level is 47 and we need to get him to the emergency room as soon as possible. We will bring in the stretcher and get him loaded in the ambulance. We need you to keep the oxygen mask on his face till we put him on the stretcher. Can you do that?"

"Yes, yes," I told him. "Just help him. I can't lose him."

Looking down at him, I noticed that he was beginning to blink again. *Thank you, God! Thank you, God!*

"David, are you able to hear me?" He blinked. The oxygen tank was releasing oxygen with so much force I could feel it in my face. "Don't worry, sweetie. God is here with us. You are going to the emergency room in the ambulance. I'll be there with you. You are going to be fine. You are going to be alright."

By that time the men were in the room, loading David onto the stretcher. They told me to grab a coat and follow the ambulance in my car. They carried David down the steps, out the door and into the back of the ambulance that was parked a few steps from the door.

I grabbed my coat and car keys and ran out the door. I don't even think I shut the door. The driver waited for me to back out of the garage. The sirens were blaring, the lights were flashing, and my heart was beating outside my chest. I kept repeating the Lord's Prayer over and over again while following the ambulance to the hospital.

Dear God, please don't take him yet. I love him! I need him! Please, dear Lord, save him!

CHAPTER 6

It was still dark when the ambulance pulled into the emergency entrance of the hospital, where a huge garage door had opened up to allow them to drive directly in. I parked in front of the garage door and hastily got out, only to be greeted by another paramedic telling me I couldn't park there.

"My husband was just brought in and I need to get to him. Here's my keys, put my car anywhere. I've got to go inside!"

The paramedic gently held onto my elbow and said, "Miss, we will take good care of your husband, and you can see him as soon as you move your car. Go back out the entrance you came in, turn left, and you will see a sign that says, 'Emergency Room Visitor's Parking.' Then go in those automatic doors and turn right. You'll see the nurses' station there."

My heart was pounding and tears were running down my face. Thoughts were racing in my head. *Park the car?! What? Forget the car, I need to see my husband!*

Somehow I managed to back the car up, turn around and speed toward the entrance driveway.

Did he say turn left or right? Oh, dear God, help me find the right entrance.

Even I could hear my tires screeching as I floored the gas pedal, whipping into the Emergency Room Visitor's parking lot and slamming on the brakes to park at the first curb I could find. I ran in through the sliding glass doors and searched frantically for a nurse.

"Please, please, my husband was just brought in. David Bichler. Where is he? Which way do I go?" I blurted out at the first person I saw.

A startled gentlemen, whom I later found out was a security guard, led me back to the nurses' station.

"Mrs. Bichler?" a nurse questioned.

"Yes, yes. Where's my husband?" I answered.

"He is all right and we are stabilizing him. We need some information from you before you can go back."

"You don't understand," I replied. "He needs me. Please let me see him. I'll fill out whatever forms you want but let me see him." As I stood there, wearing the old football jersey I'd slept in, a pair of sweatpants I had used to paint in, and house shoes, my voice was cracking and I couldn't stop shaking.

"Honey, he will be fine. Right now we are giving

him the best care possible. Why don't you sit in the chair behind my desk and I'll go check on his progress. Okay?"

I sat down as she went through a large double door into the emergency area. *Laura, you have to get a grip*, I told myself. *David doesn't need to see you panicking. That will only scare him. Lord, please help me.* I was repeating our verse, Joshua 1:9, when the nurse came back through the doors.

"Mrs. Bichler, he is stable and we have notified the pulmonologist on call. He should be here shortly," she said. "Are you able to answer a few questions now?"

"Yes. Thank you for being sounderstanding," I answered.

She handed me a clipboard with several pages to fill out. Birthdate, Social Security number, insurance carrier, blood type, smoker or non-smoker, what medications he was taking. The questions seemed to go on forever. After finishing the last page, I handed her the clipboard and said, "I really need to see him. Please!"

She thought for a moment, then nodded and said, "Go through those double doors and he is in the third room on the right."

I said a hasty "thank you" as I turned and ran through the doors. *Third room on the right, third room on the right.* The door was closed, but through the window I could see him sitting up on the gurney, surrounded by piles of tubing. The IV monitor was beeping, and I could see that he was not wearing the oxygen mask over his mouth, but now had a nose cannula.

There were four people with him, all talking at the same time, giving orders or following orders, I wasn't sure which. I knocked on the door and went inside. The room was as cold as a meat locker and the noise level was frightening. The IV monitor, the heart monitor, and the oxygen tank made deafening sounds that echoed throughout the large exam room.

I walked over to the right side of the bed and said, "Oh, my love! Are you all right? Are you okay?"

He squeezed my hand and said, "I feel much better now." He gave me that wonderful little crooked smile of his, and I leaned forward to hug him, when another monitor suddenly started beeping.

"Mrs. Bichler, you must be careful not to move him. We are monitoring his heart, and he has sensors across his chest and abdomen."

"Oh," I stammered. "Sorry!"

The paramedics had left the room and the remaining two nurses, one male and one female, were filling out charts on him. The male nurse asked, "How long has he had lung disease, Mrs. Bichler?"

I said, "We just found out last week at the Mayo clinic. We have appointments scheduled for later this week to evaluate his condition."

The male nurse continued, "We want Mr. Bichler to

remain still and rest till the pulmonologist on call arrives. I need to ask you a few more questions."

I looked at David, and he nodded his head. "Okay," I replied.

"Is he a smoker?" the nurse began.

"No, not a day in his life and neither am I," was my answer.

"Why wasn't he wearing his oxygen at home?" he continued.

I said, "As I told the paramedics, we do not have oxygen at home. Mayo didn't give us any orders other than to stop taking his acid reflux medication and the steroid he was on, which he did. That's all. He was to go there at the end of this week for testing and evaluation and they would develop a plan for him."

At that moment, the doctor on call came into the room. It happened to be the pulmonologist who had referred David to Mayo.

I looked at David and said, "It's a God-thing, sweetie! Look who is on call!"

David smiled as the doctor went over to review his chart. "Well, David," he said, after taking some time to look through the records, "I thought you went to Mayo. What is going on?"

I began telling him the details of our trip the previous week to Mayo and the appointments that were scheduled for later this week.

"I'm ordering chest x-rays and a CT scan," the

doctor informed us. "I don't understand why your oxygen levels are so low. When I saw you two weeks ago, your saturation was around 92%. Let's see what we can find out."

David and I were quickly becoming familiar with the medical jargon concerning 'saturation levels'. Oxygen saturation refers to the extent to which hemoglobin is saturated with oxygen. Hemoglobin is an element in the blood that binds with oxygen to carry it through the bloodstream to the organs, tissues, and cells of the body.

Oxygen saturation levels, usually measured through pulse oximetry placed on the tip of the index finger, are normally 95-100%. In patients with lung disease, however, oxygen saturation levels tend to drop below normal, especially when the patient is exerting himself. This is due to chronically low levels of oxygen in the blood, otherwise known as hypoxemia. A drop in oxygen saturation levels is called desaturation. When oxygen saturation levels drop below a certain level there is a need for supplemental oxygen. When the paramedics arrived at the house that morning, David's saturation level was 47.

I was standing by the gurney, holding David's hand and watching him breathe as he dozed off to sleep. My heart was no longer racing and I was putting on a brave front. The female nurse noticed I was shivering and offered me a warming blanket. "Thank you so much," I said, "that feels good."

She replied, "He is doing well right now."

I heard the rattling sound of a gurney being pushed down the hallway and looked toward the door to see that an intern was coming to take David for the X-ray and CAT scan. The intern said, "Mr. Bichler, are you ready to go for a ride?"

David opened his eyes and responded, "Sure."

The intern looked at me and asked, "Are you Mrs. Bichler?"

I replied, "Yes, I am."

The intern continued, "It will take about an hour to hour and a half for these tests. He is going to be admitted to Room 205 on the second floor. You can wait for him there."

"Okay."

I told David I loved him and let go of his hand so they could transfer him to the new gurney. It took several minutes to move him, the tubing, the IV pole, the oxygen, and the heart monitor from one gurney to the other.

"We are keeping your head at a 45-degree angle, Mr. Bichler, to help with your breathing. Does that feel comfortable for you?" the intern asked.

David nodded.

Finally, they handed him the charts and whisked him away.

As I handed the blanket back to the female nurse and started to get my things together, she put her hand on my shoulder and suggested, "Why don't you go home, clean up and put on something warm? The rooms upstairs are as cold as this one. Your husband will be fine."

I gave her a hug and said, 'Thank you for taking care of him. He means the world to me."

She smiled and nodded.

As I walked out of the emergency room toward the doors leading outside, I stopped suddenly and said to myself out loud, "Oh, my gosh. I have no idea where I left the car."

A man standing to the left of the door said, "You were the little lady who came in here looking for her husband, right?"

I smiled and answered, "Yes. He is doing fine now."

He grinned and said, "Well, that's good. I'm the security guard who helped you find the nurses' station." He chuckled. "I saw you try to park your car. I'll be happy to walk you to it."

I shrugged my shoulders and said, "I'm so sorry. I was in a hurry and all I could think of was getting to my husband. Thank you for helping me, sir."

Again he smiled and said, "Oh, that's all right. If that had been my wife, she would have driven our truck right through these double doors. What a darn mess that would have been!"

When I got home, I quickly showered and dressed, wanting to make sure I was back in Room 205 long before David returned from the tests. As I was leaving, I picked up a few pieces of his chocolate stash, my cell phone, his Bible, his robe and slippers, and headed back to the hospital. While parking, I was very careful to park the car in the correct visitor's lot, in between the white lines this time instead of horizontally across three lines and a curb.

David's room was a small, private room in the intensive care unit and one nurse was assigned to him. I had been waiting about thirty minutes when he was brought back from X-ray. The head of his bed was still elevated and he had much more color in his face. Still wearing oxygen, he was smiling and waving as he came in.

"Hello, sweetie. How are you feeling?" I asked.

"Really good," he said. "I don't know what happened this morning. Did you bring the cell phone and my Bible?" he asked.

"I thought you might want those," I answered. "And maybe this will cheer you up a bit." I put my hand in my jeans pocket and brought out a piece of his favorite chocolate.

"Mmm," he said as he reached for the candy.

"He cannot have anything to eat," the nurse chimed in as she walked into the room. She took the candy from my hand and said, "His sugar level is elevated and we have given him insulin to help bring it down. I'll hang on to it until I get approval from the doc."

David stuck out his bottom lip and looked like a small child who was pouting about not getting his way. The nurse and I laughed, and she said, "I'm going to like you two, I can tell." David and I grinned at each other.

David's oxygen level was staying around 85% with the nose cannula. The oxygen was being forced into his nostrils at the rate of 8 liters per minute (normal room air is considered to be at 2 liters per minute). He called his office to update them about what had happened and then read his Bible for a bit. Long ago he had purchased tabs with the names of the books of the Bible on them and placed them neatly in order on the first page of each new chapter. I must admit, those tabs did make finding chapters such as in the book of Habakkuk easier.

It was about noon and, to our surprise, his nurse brought in two lunch trays. One for him and one for me. "The doctor said you both needed to eat. The food's not great, but try to eat what you can," she said.

David looked the beef broth, orange Jell-O cup, and hot tea that sat on top of his tray. Then he looked at the pork chop, mashed potatoes, cup of soup, milk, and carrot cake that sat on my tray. He looked up at the nurse and asked, "Don't I get dessert?" He grinned for a moment, until the nurse replied, "You are on a restricted diet in case we have to do surgery tomorrow."

I turned to David, both of us stunned. "What surgery?" he asked.

The nurse began, "The doctor will be coming by to update your orders. Your diet is a precaution. You will need to ask him that question." As she was leaving the room she added, "Both of you should try to eat your lunch."

I ate a few bites and David tried to drink his beef broth. He was frowning when he said, "I want to know what is happening, Laura. The doctor needs to tell us something soon."

I agreed. Then, to change the subject and help get his mind off things, I said, "Let's play cards. I might even let you win!"

He smiled and we decided to play Gin. I think we played a dozen hands before the doctor finally came into the room.

"David," he said as he walked over to his bedside, "after reviewing the CAT scans, I believe they indicate an acute worsening of the IPF."

I tried to swallow and choke back my tears. David was watching the doctor and listening intently.

"A month ago, the biopsy showed the IPF as rather patchy. Today's scan shows a marked progression throughout both lungs. There appeared to be no pulmonary emboli, but there is a marked worsening of the interstitial infiltrates." The doctor added, "I am starting you on Tobramycin, 80 mg every 8 hours, Cefepine, 2 gm IV every 12 hours. You are also getting a large dose of prednisone to help with the inflammation. This could be the cause of your elevated insulin levels."

I was hearing everything the doctor was saying, but not understanding a thing.

I reached over to take David's hand and it was very hot. His face was flushed and he had opened his mouth to take short, shallow breaths.

The doctor said, "David, are you having a problem breathing?"

David nodded yes.

The doctor called for the nurse to bring another oxygen mask to replace the nose cannula. Once the mask was on his face, the doctor turned the oxygen up to 15 liters. "Take a few deep breaths, Dave. Breathe slowly," the doctor told him.

David closed his eyes and tried to breathe deeply. He began coughing and choking, unable to catch his breath between coughs. He began coughing up bloody sputum and I could tell he was in distress.

"What is happening?" I said in a panicked voice.

"He can't breathe." The doctor had called for the nurse and now told me to leave the room. I didn't budge.

The nurse said, "Mrs. Bichler, you must leave the room so we can help your husband."

I slowly backed out of the room and the nurse closed the door. Tears rolled down my face and again I prayed: *Lord, stop his coughing. Please let him breathe.*

I could hear the doctor telling the nurse to clear the sputum out of David's nose and mouth. Two other residents had gone into the room and all were talking at once. The tension in their voices was frightening. For a few moments I could still hear David coughing and choking. Then it seemed to calm and become less frequent. Terrified for my husband, I couldn't stand waiting any longer and opened the door to enter the room.

David was soaking wet from perspiration caused by the huge amount of energy the coughing took from him. He was sitting back against the bed with his eyes closed, breathing through the mask. His breaths were fast and shallow. But he was breathing. The doctor motioned for me to follow him outside the room where he said, "David's condition is rapidly declining. I am afraid to treat him with anything else because it might ruin his chance for a transplant from the Mayo Clinic. I'm not familiar with the protocols for lung transplantation, but I do feel that if he was subjected to certain drugs such as the large doses of prednisone I would have to give him, it could lessen the chance that Mayo would accept him into their program."

I was dumbfounded. I was confused. I said, "But we were just at the Mayo clinic. They said he had two years before he would need a transplant. What has happened? What can we do?"

The doctor put his left arm across his chest and put his hand under his chin. He didn't hesitate before he said, "I am going to get in touch with the doctor he saw at Mayo and get their advice on the next step."

The rest of the evening David slept. I sat in the chair next to his bed, holding tightly to his hand and praying. I called our family and friends to update them and asked them to pray for him.

It was late and the night shift had come on duty. Our nurse was a pleasant older gentleman who had been a nurse during his years in the military. He would come in to get David's vital signs or put medicine in the IV and we would talk quietly. The doctor did not come by again that night.

I slept off and on, but I had loosely wrapped a bit of unused IV tubing that had been left on his blanket around David's left hand and my right I wanted to feel it if he moved. I was not going to let go of him.

By morning, David looked a bit better, more rested. He had not been allowed to get out of bed and was complaining about the hard mattress on the bed. Our night male nurse heard him and laughed. "You should have been sleeping on the old army cot I had. I swear it had nails in it."

David chuckled. "Were you an Army man?" David asked.

"Yes, sir. Did two tours of duty and came home after Desert Storm."

David told his nurse that he had been in the Reserves, and then the Army Engineering Corp, making the rank of Captain before getting out. They seemed to have much in common and I was glad David felt well enough to talk.

Breakfast trays came and again there were two trays. On David's tray was chicken broth, green Jell-o and a cup of sherbet. I looked on mine and saw the same thing! No more pork chops and mashed potatoes to make my husband envy my meal, apparently.

Our male nurse looked in once more before leaving from his shift and my suspicion was confirmed when he said, "Just wanted the Captain not to feel too special. He's still one of the guys."

David smiled and I laughed. I choked down the chicken broth and my Jell-o while he ate his sherbet. David said, "I hope God blesses that man. He's a good man." Less than gourmet meal aside, I agreed.

It was Tuesday, April 5th, well past 10:30 a.m., and still no doctor. David was still on 15 liters of oxygen, and still taking the breathing treatments. I could tell he was getting restless waiting. I was, too. The only visitor we'd had was our pastor from Christ Lutheran. He played a hand of Gin with David, prayed with us and then left about noon.

When the doctor finally came into our room, I looked at my watch and it read 1:30 p.m. He pulled up a chair beside the bed and began talking. "David, I have spoken with the pulmonary team at the Mayo clinic and it is their opinion that we should get you back there as soon as possible."

He paused to see what our reaction was before continuing, "You will be transported to Mayo by ambulance in order to monitor your oxygen levels. You wife can follow the ambulance. I can't do anything more for you here."

David asked, "What time?" I could tell his mind was churning.

"You will leave in approximately thirty minutes. I'll send the paperwork with the driver."

David turned to me and said, "Laura, go home and pack a bag. Get my work computer, my briefcase, and extra clothes."

I was surprised at how calm he was. "I will call the office to let them know what is happening," he said.

I grabbed my purse, kissed him on the top of his head and started to leave when the doctor reminded me, "Mrs. Bichler, the ambulance will leave in thirty minutes. If you are going to follow them, be back at the Emergency parking area before then."

My heart began pumping hard again. I rushed

home, threw some things in a suitcase, and grabbed David's work computer and briefcase. My mind was racing and I couldn't seem to think of anything. I pulled into the parking lot just in time to see the driver close the door on the back of the ambulance and walk toward the front of the vehicle. I could see David through the back window. He was sitting on the gurney, facing the back of the ambulance, still wearing the oxygen mask. He blew a kiss to me as they drove off. I panicked. I hadn't been given a map, the route the ambulance would be taking, or a phone number to reach them if I lost sight of them.

There was a paramedic riding in the back monitoring David and they were heading out Hwy 29 west. I had to drive 85-90 mph just to keep up. I prayed that we would be safe.

In my car's CD player was a new tape by Josh Groban that had *Jesu, Joy of Man's Desiring* as one of the songs. That CD played over and over again through the entire four hour drive. I just kept praying and keeping my eyes on David in the back of the ambulance.

CHAPTER 7

My mind was racing and I was so frightened. I frantically called Jean Smith at Trinity, begging them for prayers of healing for David. Tears were streaming down my cheeks as I cried out in panic and fear. Jean said she would gather our friends together to pray as soon as I hung up. "Thank you, Jean," I sniffled, "I know God will heal him. I believe in the power of prayer!"

I called David's sisters, Mary and Linda, and our daughter.

"Do I need to come to Mayo? I can get a flight out of Rapid City," Mary asked.

"I'm not sure," I replied. "Let me see what the doctors say then I will call you back. Please pray for him."

It was dark when we pulled into St. Mary's hospital

emergency area in Rochester. Once again I found myself trying to find parking in the correct designated area. I got out of the car, leaving the small suitcase in the backseat, and ran to the entrance where the ambulance was still parked.

David gave me an insecure look as the gurney he was strapped to was wheeled into the emergency room. I hurried to follow the medics pushing him. As they were checking him in, giving paperwork to the nurse on duty, I grabbed his hand and kissed him on the cheek. Those ever-noisy machines surrounded him – the oxygen mask with green elastic straps and the oxygen tank pumping 15 liters of oxygen into his nostrils.

His eyes had dark circles around them and his face was completely without color, except for the faint outline of his 5 o'clock shadow. The pulse oximeter was now bandaged around the first finger of his right hand and a loud, high-pitched siren would sound each time his levels dropped below 90% saturation. I tried to be brave and strong for him, but I was just as frightened and unsure as he was.

"I don't know why this is necessary," he said, taking off his oxygen mask in order to talk. "I'm fin…" Before he could finish his sentence, the siren went off, signaling a drop in his oxygen saturation.

"Sir…" A young intern came rushing over to silence the loud, screaming siren. "Sir, you must keep this mask on at all times," he instructed as he quickly placed the elastic green straps around David's head and the mask back over his mouth. "You are being taken to the Medical ICU unit so we can better monitor your condition." The intern looked over at me and continued, "You, ma'am, can follow us. A representative from emergency admissions will come to the room shortly and have papers you will need to fill out."

The paramedics wished David good luck and returned to the ambulance to head back to Wausau. I followed the intern pushing my husband's gurney into what looked to be an over-sized service elevator. He pushed the 6th floor button. There was an eerie silence as the elevator doors closed and it began slowly rising. When it came to a stop, the doors opened and the intern skillfully maneuvered the gurney and the machines that accompanied it into a large open area.

This ICU floor seemed to be square in shape with glass-door patient rooms lining the outside perimeters. Filling the center of the floor were stations with desks, chairs, computers, monitors, doctors, and nurses. These stations were also in the shape of a square, leaving a six foot wide 'walkway' between the nurses' station and the patient rooms. These stations had more technical equipment, blinking lights, and people milling about than the old control room at NASA.

David was taken into a corner room, still on the

gurney that had brought him in the ambulance. Several nurses were waiting for him and they quickly transferred him and his electrical devices onto a hospital bed. It only resembled a bed in the fact that it had a mattress, sheets, and blankets.

This state of the art ICU bed had long, thick side rails with four different control panels on each side. These controls could move the bed into a chair position, allowing the patient to feel as though he or she were sitting in a puffy chair. Or they could move it into a reclining position with the feet, the head, or both, raised. The techno-bed was programmed to calculate the weight of the patient, allowing for the variances in the weight of the sheets, blankets, pillows, and tubing. Trying to lift David's spirits a bit I chuckled, "Captain James T. Kirk would be proud to sleep in this bed."

He grinned. "Yes, and Bones would wave his electronic wand and give me new lungs, too," he sighed.

Two more nurses came in to check David's vital signs, introducing themselves as the night shift who would be looking after him. As the intern had said, they handed me a large clipboard with a pen attached to it (not on string this time, but on a tiny, elastic, crinkled cord). There must have been twenty pages I needed to fill out. I pulled up the only other chair in the room and sat it next to the techno-bed so I could be as close to David as possible. Once more I filled in the blanks: birthdate, social security number, insurance number, symptoms, medications, and on and on.

David, whose bed was in the 'sitting' position, was having a hard time keeping his eyes open and he asked the nurse if she could lower the bed so he could sleep. I looked at the clock. 11:43p.m. He must have been exhausted. But, the nurse replied, "I am sorry, David. I can't lower the bed until the doctor has seen you. We will be taking blood and monitoring your vitals every thirty minutes. Try to relax."

Tears filled my eyes again and I tried desperately not to let David see them.

It was not long before the head of the ICU came into David's room. "David, you are a very sick man," the doctor began. "I have checked your medical records from last week when you were here and the notes from the Wausau doctor."

David and I looked at each other, too tired to say anything.

"Your O^2 (oxygen) levels are stating at 86% with the oxygen mask. I feel it is necessary to put you on BiPAP as soon as possible."

BiPAP? I asked the doctor, "What is a BiPAP?"

The doctor, taking moment to ask the nurse for another chair, explained that a BIPAP is a Bi-level Positive Airway Pressure machine that reduces the pressure in the lungs when the patient is exhaling and increases the pressures when he is inhaling. "The BiPAP has a dual pressure adjustment that helps the patient get more air in and out of the lungs without exerting much effort. This is especially useful for patients like yourself with congestive heart failure and lung disorders," the doctor told David. "You are experiencing above normal levels of carbon dioxide, due to your decreased lung capacity. If we use this machine, it could keep you from intubation and prevent complete respiratory failure," he finished.

My heart was pounding so quickly and with such force that my head hurt. *Heart failure? Respiratory failure? Intubation? Dear Lord, what is happening?*

"I thought he had IPF, a lung disease," I stammered at the doctor. "Is his heart failing?" I asked, dreading the answer.

The doctor patted my hand and said, "He appears to be in acute pulmonary distress from IPF. That alone puts a high level of stress upon his heart. The BiPAP is a means to avoid having to put David on a respirator at this time."

David had fallen asleep, slumping down in the chair-bed and, thankfully, he did not hear what the doctor had just explained.

"Please, do what you can for him. I love him. He means so much to me," I quietly said to the doctor.

"We have to keep his head elevated at a 45 degree angle at all times. I will have a nurse adjust the bed for him," the doctor added. He walked out of our room to advise the nurse.

Within thirty minutes, nurses had drawn blood, checked David's vitals, brought in the BiPAP machine and had it connected to the apparatus he was to wear on his head. It reminded me of the mask a baseball catcher wears. Instead of the wire face guard to protect the catcher though, the BiPAP had a massive, hard, plastic mask that covered most of David's face and chin, resting tightly underneath his eyes. His mouth and cheeks would puff in and out uncontrollably each time the BiPAP would force air down his throat and into his lungs. This mask was so tight that white marks were appearing on David's face. It looked so uncomfortable and he was so brave!

Again I checked the clock. 1:16 a.m. Exhaustion suddenly hit me. I scooted my chair as close to David as I could, positioned my hand between the railings of the bed and the control panels and held his hand gently in mine. I prayed the Lord's Prayer and asked God to continue to watch over us as I drifted to sleep.

The nurses checked David's vital signs every 30 minutes throughout what was left of the night, sometimes giving him a medicine through his IV or replacing the large bag of potassium solution that was rapidly pumping through him. I awoke each time they came into his room and it was a blessing that he did not.

The lights in the hallway came on at 6:00 a.m. and the noise level escalated as the nurses changed shifts, readying the patients for the rounds that each doctor would be making. Our day nurse came in to introduce herself and to check on David's BiPAP. As she began to release David's head from the grips of the mask, he blinked several times, yawned, and quietly said, "I am so dry. That air blowing into my throat all night has given me a severe sore throat. May I have a drink of water?"

While his face had a little color to it, his eyes were still carrying those dark circles. Before I could stand up from my chair and walk to the edge of the bed, however, the pulse oximeter began screaming. David's saturation level was dropping. He had stayed around 90% with the BiPAP the entire night. Yet, the mask had been off his face less than two minutes and his saturation level dropped to 73%.

The nurse quickly tried to refit the mask to David's face and restart the machine. I could see the frustration in his expression.

The nurse looked at the pulse oximeter reading after the machine re-started. Still showing 78%. She turned to me and said, "I know he is thirsty, but keep this mask on him. I'm going to send in a call to see which floor the doctor is on."

I nodded my head to indicate that I understood. David's big brown eyes were troubled and I could see worry lines across his forehead. The rhythmic stretching of his mouth and cheeks to the pulsing of the forced air made him look like he was standing in a powerful wind tunnel. He lifted his hand and motioned to me for a drink of water. I poured a small amount from the little, pink pitcher on his portable tray table and put a straw in the cup. He raised the lower portion of the mask to try to sip from the straw, only to have the screeching oxygen siren blast immediately. He gulped down the small amount of water and quickly put back the mask.

A nurse came in as soon as the siren sounded and caught a glimpse of him sipping the water. As if she were disciplining a toddler, she shook her finger at David and said, "Now, David, the mask has to have a tight seal in order to help you. No more drinks till the doctor makes his rounds."

He nodded his head in agreement and I had to glance away in order for him not to see the smile that was forcing its way onto my face.

As the nurse left, I asked her what day it was and when the doctor usually made his rounds. "Today is Wednesday, April 6, and the doctor and his team will be here between 6:30 a.m. and 8:00 a.m.," she answered.

She was correct. Around 7:30 a.m. a doctor, followed by six interns, came into David's room. "Mr. Bichler, I am one of the pulmonary specialists. This is a teaching hospital and we want to provide quality hands-on training to our promising interns. Would it be alright if they examined you and asked you a few questions?" the older doctor requested.

David nodded his head yes, and the first young man stepped forward. With clipboard in hand, he began to flip through the records of David's vitals from last night while the others quickly followed. The doctor left the room and the questions began. "Are you a smoker?" one intern asked. "Did you ever smoke?"

David could only shake his head up and down for 'yes' or side-to-side for 'no.'

"Do you own a bird?" "Do you sleep on feather pillows or wear a down coat?" One would ask the question and all the others would write down David's answer. "Did you work in a factory?" "Have you lived overseas?" "Have you had a heart attack?" "Have you been depressed lately or have you been diagnosed with clinical depression?"

I thought to myself: *What do any of these questions have to do with his situation at this moment?*

Finally the questions stopped and the entire group of six stood at the foot of David's hospital bed, mumbling amongst themselves. Then they abruptly left.

David mouthed the words, "What was that all about? Where is the doctor?" His blood pressure cuff was inflating for the automatic vital check, and I could see that his pressure was going up. I tried to calm him and said, "I'm not sure, but I will go to the nurses' station and ask."

I stopped in front of the nurses' desk and waited for our nurse to finish some paperwork. When she looked up I said, "We are confused. Those six interns are not going to be treating David, are they?"

She replied, "They are required to make the rounds with different doctors, form an assessment of the patient, and then report their findings to the doctor/trainer. No, they will not be treating your husband."

Whew! I thought to myself. "What is being done for David? When will the doctor return to speak with us?"

She looked back down at the paperwork on her desk and said, "He will be back in shortly."

I could see the relief on David's face when I conveyed the message that the interns would not be treating him. I sat back down, thinking that the few clothes I had were still in the back seat of my car, which was in the emergency parking area, and I realized I had no idea of how to locate that parking area again.

An hour later, the doctor came back in, this time accompanied by a fellow pulmonologist. He shook my hand and David's and began speaking in a very calm, calculated voice. "David, you were scheduled to go through testing for an evaluation by the lung transplant team later this week."

He paused as I said, "Yes, I have the schedule of the tests with us."

The second pulmonologist took a brief look at the test schedule while the first doctor continued, "It seems you are not able to keep your oxygen saturation around 90% unless on the Bi-PAP. I have looked through your past records and see that you were diagnosed with IPF about a month ago. You were given instructions to stop the acid reflux medication in order to have a PF test done when you returned to Mayo. Is this correct?"

David nodded yes, and then the younger, second doctor began to speak. "I am with the lung transplant team and am here to see if you are well enough to be evaluated for lung transplantation. There are several requirements before a patient can be put on the waiting list for a transplant, one of which is a heart cath."

I could tell he wanted to say more, but the older doctor interjected: "David, I am going to put you back on prednisone, a very hefty dose. I am hoping it will reduce the inflammation, allowing your lungs to function better. I want to continue the antibiotic intravenously and may be adding others, depending on your next blood work." He continued as if going through a mental list of tests to run, and said, "I am ordering a CAT scan, PET scan, and VQ scan as soon as possible. And I want to wean you off the BiPAP and use it only at night." He moved close to David's bed. "It will take a lot of work on your part, but in order to be considered for a transplant, you must be able to perform daily, routine functions, including bathing, bathroom, dressing, etc."

I found myself starting to raise my hand to ask a question, but quickly lowered it, like a shy student in school would do.

The younger doctor smiled at me and said, "You have a question?"

God must have put the words in mouth, for I asked, "If his saturation rate drops significantly when he takes off the BiPAP mask and you want to wean him off it and onto a regular oxygen mask during the day, what saturation percent is acceptable to you? You know it will drop into the 70's."

He reflected a moment before answering. "Yes, he will need to be on oxygen at all times. He needs to walk in order to maintain his muscle strength. We will be monitoring him at all times."

Not a definite answer and not the one that told me what percentage to look for as a warning sign, I decided.

The doctor retrieved David's chart from the foot of the bed, flipped through a couple of pages, then went into the hallway to talk with the nurse. Almost immediately, both he and the nurse re-entered David's room and the doctor said, "Mr. Bichler, we need to weigh you."

I looked around for a scale but saw nothing. That's when the techno-bed sprang into action. The nurse cleared away everything that was not a pillow, sheet or blanket on his bed. She pressed a button and a buzzing sound came from the footboard, followed by three short beeps. The doctor who had told David he needed to be weighed looked at the weight shown on the bed.

"Your current weight is 82.9 kilograms or about 181 pounds. On March 5, the date of your lung biopsy, you weighed approximately 100 kilograms or about 220 pounds. Have you been trying to diet?"

My mind was swimming. *Kilograms? What was the rate of pounds to kilograms? I knew David had lost weight, but 40 pounds?*

David shook his head "no" and pointed towards me.

"I know he has been losing weight, but he hasn't been dieting. He's just been trying to breathe. Did you say he has lost 40 pounds in less than a month?"

"Yes," confirmed the younger doctor.

The older doctor sat on the foot of David's bed and his lips formed a gentle, pleasant smile. Then he said, "We need to make sure the nodules in your lungs are not cancer. The PET scan will tell us that. The lung ventilation/perfusion scan, or VQ scan, is a test that measures air and blood flow in your lungs. This test most often is used to help diagnose or rule out pulmonary embolism or PE. A PE is a blood clot that travels to the lungs and blocks blood flow. The scan also can detect poor blood flow in the lungs' blood vessels and provide pictures that could be used if surgery is required."

I was glad he paused for a minute to let that information sink in. The older doctor got up, said he would check in with us later that evening and left the room. The younger doctor, who had been taking notes, said to David, "These tests are part of the evaluation necessary for consideration in our lung transplantation program. The test I need for you and your wife to work on is called the 'six-minute walk test'. I will leave orders for you to start getting up and walking around the floor after your scans. For now, relax. It may take a few hours to get the scans scheduled. I'll see you later." He smiled and went into the hallway.

David relaxed a bit in the bed and tried to sleep. The BiPAP was a constant nuisance, but he was so tired he slept in spite of it. The rest of the day was spent waiting. Waiting for scan appointment times to be set. Waiting to see if the higher dosages of prednisone would be effective. Waiting for the next vitals readings. Waiting for God to provide healing. Waiting.

CHAPTER 8

I used the time that David slept to make update phone calls to everyone, including our Trinity Lutheran family. Mary, his older sister, was flying in from Rapid City, SD the next day (Thursday, April 7) and Linda, his younger sister, and Briana, our daughter, were going to wait till the actual transplant date was determined before making flight arrangements.

Linda, having had a double lung transplant a year earlier, was one of our most helpful resources of information. When something happened to David, I would check with Linda to see if she had experienced something similar. Even though each transplant center has a different protocol when dealing with pre-transplant and post-transplant patients, she did have to complete many of the same pre-transplant tests that were planned for David, including the six-minute walk.

Around 2:30 p.m. David was transported to the radiology department for the scans. There was a designated public computer for family and patients to use at the nurses station and, while he was being scanned, I did research on the process of how a patient was listed on the transplant waiting list. Fortunately, while sitting at this public computer, I could see directly into David's ICU room, which made me feel a little more at ease.

Mayo has an online lung transplantation manual that outlined what was involved with the six-minute walk test, as well as providing descriptions of other tests. I was familiar with the scans but wanted to learn more about this walking test that the doctor had said was an important factor in their evaluation of patients.

For idiopathic pulmonary fibrosis (IPF) patients, this walking test is used to predict mortality rates. Patients who can cover less than 680 feet during the six-minute test are four times more likely to die within six months than those who can walk greater distances. According to the research, there is a small window of opportunity with regard to optimal timing for lung transplantation. Surgery performed too early may rob the patient of months of survival, whereas waiting too long greatly increases the risk of death before and after transplant.

After reading all this information, I sat back in the chair stunned. Were they were going to use the walking test to determine if David was too sick to be listed for a transplant? Would they allow him to die based on these findings? I said a silent prayer that the Lord would allow David to somehow walk 700 feet when it came time for the test. I knew the Lord always answered prayers, but I also knew that sometimes His answer could be 'no.'

I went down to the car to retrieve my small bag, and I realized that I had not changed clothes in three days. I used the restroom in David's room to splash water on my face and put on a fresh change of clothing. As I had only been given 30 minutes to pack when he was being transported by ambulance from Wausau to Mayo, I had grabbed the first things I saw in the closet and a handful of underwear and socks for him and me. Clothing didn't matter. Breathing did.

Several hours passed before David was returned to his room. He looked tired but did have a bit of color still in his face. He was no longer wearing the BiPAP mask but had once again been given a nose cannula. That was a good sign!

He smiled at me and told the nurse, "I'm hungry. Do you think I could have an ice cream cup?"

He had not been hungry for the past three days. Another good sign! *Thank you, Jesus!*

The nurse assured him she would call down to the cafeteria and order him something.

He held up his right hand, opening and closing it quickly, motioning me to come sit by him. As I walked over to the bed, he said, "Think it will be okay if you lay next to me for a minute?" One more good sign!

"Of course I will, my love," I happily replied as I climbed upon the bed. Since the head of the bed had to be raised to at least a 45 degree angle at all times, sitting next to him reminded me of being home, sitting in the loveseat in the living room, watching television. It felt so good to touch him! I felt a peace come over me. A sense of security. I smiled as I took his hand in mine and said, "I love you, my dear. God is going to answer our prayers."

He nodded his head and asked, "Do you have my Bible with you?"

"Yep!" I replied.

"Will you get it so we can read it together? It will help to put my mind at ease."

I got up, took his Bible out of the small suitcase, and quickly climbed back onto the bed with him. I chuckled when he said, "I wish these darn gowns had a pocket in the front. I feel naked without my pens!" He was feeling a little better and that made my heart fill with joy. He grinned, squeezed my hand, and added, "Say, after dinner, how about a little sponge bath?"

I laughed and said, "Sure, which male nurse do you want to bathe you?"

We both laughed. I knew the Lord was healing him. *Thank you, dear Heavenly Father, thank you.*

Another shift of nurses came on around 7 p.m. and we had a different night nurse. She was very kind and patient, but she had an agenda that David was going to follow. She would be monitoring the six-minute walk test and wanted to give him a few chances before reporting the results.

I took a deep breath and said to her, "Can I walk with him? It might be easier for him if I pull the oxygen tank and IV pole."

"Yes, you can for the practice runs. But during the actual testing, I will be pulling the tank and monitoring his vital signs," she answered. "He can use the pole to steady himself if he needs to," she added.

I did not share with David the information I had found while researching the walking test, but it weighed heavily on my mind. He had eaten a small portion of the dinner though and felt stronger, so that was something.

"I am feeling somewhat better," he said to the nurse as she wheeled in the three-foot tall, portable oxygen tank that would keep oxygen blowing into his mouth and nose.

"It could be the steroids. They would be kicking in about now," she answered. "I think you will do better wearing the oxygen mask during the walk. When you return to your bed, we can put the nose cannula back on."

It took several minutes to hook and unhook the tubing and IV's and to trade out the oxygen tank. Finally, the nurse said to David, "Are you ready for a little stroll around the floor?"

"Sure," he answered.

The nurse stood on one side of David and I was on the other side, steadying him and giving his legs a chance to regain their balance. It had been almost a week since he had walked anywhere and it was good for him to take things slowly. It's amazing, but for each day that one lays in a hospital bed, it takes one week to recover the muscle tone and strength lost during that one day.

The nurse had placed another pulse oximeter on the first finger of his left hand, which was connected to a yellow, handheld monitor that the nurse would carry while he was walking. It would give her immediate results on his saturation rate during the walk.

"Try to take a couple of breaths for me, David," she began. "Let's get your saturation rate up to 90%, if possible, before starting your walk."

He could only manage to take shallow, quick breaths, and the nurse had the oxygen tank turned to its highest level of output.

"Let's take this nice and easy, David," she said as he

started walking through the door and into the hallway. He always had a long stride and could out-walk most people, so, for the first few steps, he tried to walk at his usual pace. He had only taken ten steps when the nurse stopped and said, "David, stop. We must get you back into the bed." Her voice was stern and had an edge to it. She motioned for another nurse to get a wheelchair.

"David, please sit down in the wheelchair. Your oxygen level has dropped into the low 60's."

The color that had been in David's cheeks vanished, and I saw the disappointment in his eyes. He sat down and our nurse quickly pushed him back to the room. "I am going to put you on BiPAP, David, till we can get your saturation levels back up. Stay seated in the wheelchair for now."

She was moving very quickly and the BiPAP mask was back on his face, once again forcing air down his mouth and throat. Still monitoring the pulse oximeter on his left hand, she watched the yellow unit's numbers steadily climb until it read 90%. At that point the tension in the nurse's face disappeared and we all relaxed a bit. "I am going to get a couple of male nurses to help me get you back in bed. Do not stand up by yourself."

He raised his right hand and formed the 'OK' sign with his thumb and first finger.

While the male nurses were helping David back into bed, I turned to face the wall so he could not see the tears that were forming in my eyes. My heart was aching because I knew that 10 steps did not equal 680 feet. I regained my composure and prayed he would not see the redness of my eyes. David was obviously shaken by the whole incident.

The BiPAP was on his face for several hours before the nurse felt confident enough to replace it with the nose cannula. "Well, you certainly gave us a bit of excitement around here, David," she jokingly said to him.

This time he was not laughing. "When can I try again?" he asked.

"Not tonight. I will have to check with the doctor before allowing you to get up for any reason," she said. Then she added, "You have had a long few days, why not get some sleep."

He nodded his head in agreement.

"We are still monitoring you every 30 minutes and will try not to wake you too many times," she said as she was leaving the room. "If you or your wife need anything, just push the call button."

I thanked her as she left and turned to talk with David. Once again, he had a blank expression on his face when he said, "I didn't feel short of breath. This is not good, Laura. This is not good."

I sat in the chair next to his bed and tried to reassure him. "Remember, it has been several days since you walked. It takes time to get your strength back," I said as I took his hand in mine. "Let's get some sleep and tomorrow the steroids and medicines will be working in your system, and then you will be able to get this walk out of the way."

I said it with a forced smile on my face. In my heart I knew he was right. This was not a good sign. I prayed out loud for both of us, for healing, for his lungs to hold oxygen, and for rest. I leaned over the side rail to kiss him goodnight, but he had fallen asleep while I was praying. At that moment I remembered what a pastor at the church we attended while living in Utah once said about praying. He said there is not a more wonderful way to begin a peaceful sleep than during a conversation with the Lord.

I sat in the chair watching the love of my life breathing and remembered the many nights we had gone to sleep holding each other's hands. I asked God to forgive me for the times I had taken him for granted and again pleaded for his body to be healed.

I awoke the next morning to the light coming on in the hallway. *Must be around 6:00 a.m.,* I thought. I looked over to see David watching me and smiling.

"Good morning," he said as I reached over to kiss him.

"Morning," I replied. I stood up to stretch and yawn. "You had a pretty good night, didn't you?" I asked him.

"I feel more rested this morning and I am hungry," he said as a nurse came in to check his vitals.

"Well, David, you have a little more color in your face today. I'm glad to see it," she said as she went about checking his IV bags, blood pressure, and temperature. "You are still running a low grade fever. Would you like for me to bring you and your wife fresh water?" she asked.

"That would be wonderful," I replied. My mouth was drier than the Sahara Desert. The nurse left to retrieve the water, and I said to David, "Mary is flying in this afternoon. I believe she is taking a shuttle from the airport to St. Mary's." I was relieved that I didn't have to pick her up.

A fear had come over my entire being and I did not want to leave David's side. Not even to walk to the cafeteria. I could not leave. What if something happened? What if he needed me and I was not there? I would never be able to forgive myself for not being by his side if the worst should happen.

The nurse came back in with fresh water and, to our surprise, the young doctor from the transplant team followed her into the room. "Good morning, David," he began. "I see that you had a fairly good night."

David said, "I do feel better this morning."

The doctor continued, "The transplant team has been reviewing your test results from yesterday. The PET scan showed no 'hot' spots and we do not think there is cancer in your lungs."

I smiled and said, "That's a relief. Thank goodness."

"As we expected, the CT scan showed evidence of diffuse pulmonary infiltrates, causing hypoxemia, which required the use of BiPAP support."

David cut his eyes over at me, then back to the doctor.

"The VQ scan results didn't confirm the presence of a pulmonary embolism, but your pressures are very high, causing the pulmonary hypertension you are experiencing."

I had grabbed the menu from yesterday and was trying to write down what the doctor was saying on the back of it.

"Hypertension involves the heart, right?" David asked.

"Yes," the young doctor said. "Because the lungs are no longer carrying a significant amount of air to the blood stream and not moving blood efficiently, the heart has been working much harder than normal. We do not believe the heart has been damaged, but without a heart catheterization, EKG, and Echocardiogram, we cannot be sure."

David glanced down at his hands for a moment, then looked up at the doctor.

There was little expression on the young doctor's face as he said, "You have improved with the large dosage of steroids and antibiotics, and we will be moving you to an intermediate care floor this morning."

My heart perked up. Intermediate care is better than ICU, I thought to myself.

"However, upon exertion, your saturation level drops dramatically," the doctor continued. "Therefore, we want you to stay in bed. Do not get up to walk or go to the bathroom. It is very important that you understand and abide by our decision," he stated firmly. "The head of our lung transplant team will be visiting you to discuss your options once you have settled into your room." He shook David's hand, said "take care," and then left the room.

David and I looked at each other as I sat down beside his bed.

"What option is he referring to?" David asked me.

I was wondering the same thing. "I'm not sure, but at least the head man is reviewing your case. That has to be a plus," I mumbled. I was trying to stay positive, trying to cheer him and give him something to hope for. It was terribly hard. He could read my mind like a book.

"I'm going to need a transplant now, aren't I?" he said aloud.

"We don't know that," I said. "But, look at Linda and how well she has done with her double-lung transplant. She recovered in no time and is happier and healthier."

Linda's recovery was truly remarkable. She had returned to work within five months, when most patients needed six to nine months. I remember saying to David, "God will provide a pair of lungs for you, too, and then you will be able to have your life back." Even now I shudder when I think of how naïve and bold I was to assume that his life, our life, would return to normal.

It was Thursday, April 7th, and by 9:00 a.m., we had been moved to the intermediate care floor, meaning that one nurse was assigned to many patients, not a one-on-one situation as was the case in the ICU, because it was determined that the patient and relative could provide the basic needs without a nurse's assistance. It also meant that David's vitals were not monitored every 30 minutes. Because of this, I feared it was even more important that I not leave him. Who would call the nurse if he couldn't breathe? This room had two chairs, one a recliner. That would make a nice bed for me.

The tension in the room was evident by the quiet, solemn expressions on both David's and my own face. We were scared of the unknown. When would a doctor be coming by to tell us the plan of action? We tried to play cards or watch television. But our minds were preoccupied as we both realized that transplant was the option this doctor would offer.

There was one unique thing about being on the

intermediate care floor. Interns. Every hour (and sometimes more frequently) an intern would come into the room pushing a spiffy, portable computer table-cart apparatus and introduce him or herself.

This portable table-cart thingy had only three wheels and resembled a three-foot-tall floor lamp with a television tray attached to the top. The intern would always say the same thing: "Mr. Bichler, I am researching IPF patients and would like to ask you a few questions. Is that alright?"

They would then proceed to ask David the same twenty-five questions each time and record his answers on their laptop computer. Their routine became predictable. How old are you? Do you smoke? Have you ever smoked? Do you own a bird? Do you sleep on down pillows or wear a down-filled coat? Have you worked overseas? Have you worked in a factory or poultry processing plant? Are you depressed? Have you had a heart attack? And on and on and on. After the third intern left the room, David looked at me at said, "Find a piece of paper so we can write the answers down."

I went to the nurses' station and asked for several pieces of paper and a pen. The fourth intern came into the room and began the questions, when David said, "Wait a moment." He numbered the paper from 1 thru 25. "Proceed," he said to the intern. David wrote down his answers, one by one on the paper. The intern never looked up to see what David was doing. After the intern finished and had left the room, David turned to me and grinned. "Now, see if you can get a piece of tape or something." All I could find were two sterile Band-Aids in the drawer of his small nightstand. He grinned and said, "Tape this paper to the foot of the bed and the next time an intern comes in, we'll be ready."

The constant bombardment of questions was funny at first and gave us something to do while waiting for the head of pulmonary. It was not long before two interns came in at the same time. After they introduced themselves and stated their purpose for being there, David smiled and pointed to the foot of the bed. "No need to waste your time asking questions. The answers are posted on the foot of the bed." They had a startled look on their faces. I tried hard not to laugh as the interns, looking a bit confused, pushed their little carts to the foot of the bed.

David was smiling. We thought they would pick up the paper, copy the answers down in their computer and be on their way. Nope! Each of them would look at the question on their screen, look at the paper bandaged to the foot of the bed, look back at the computer screen and then fill in the answer. It took twice as long! David and I chuckled when they finally finished and had left the room. "Maybe you should hand them the paper to read each time," I suggested, giggling. "It might save time." He shook his head and grinned.

Shortly before noon, a middle-aged man, wearing a very professional business suit, came into David's room. "Mr. Bichler," he began, "I am the head of the lung transplant team. How are you doing?"

David said, "Fine, sir. I understand you have a plan of action for me."

My hands began to tremble and I clasped them together across my lap so David wouldn't see them shaking. I prayed silently that this doctor would give David hope and new lungs.

The doctor continued to talk, standing by the bedside. "I understand you are familiar with lung transplantation because you have a sister who also had IPF and received a bilateral transplant, correct?"

"Yes," David replied. "She had a transplant at UCSF in San Francisco in February 2004."

"You are in what we believe is the beginning of the end stage of the disease and, therefore, our options are extremely limited."

I felt the blood rush from my face. I looked at David and my eyes began tearing up. "David, you need a lung transplant in order to survive. The problem here in the Midwest is the long waiting list for donors."

The pit of my stomach turned sour and I felt a sense of dread engulf me. I thought I was going to be sick.

The doctor continued, "Right now, the waiting time for a lung transplant is two to three years."

My mouth fell open. David's eyes were swollen and red.

"Our donor pool is much smaller than that of a larger city such as San Francisco because we have a smaller population to draw from."

Tears were running down David's face, but he never stopped looking directly at the doctor. It was breaking my heart. The next question that the doctor asked confirmed our worst fears.

"Have you and your wife discussed your last wishes? Have you signed a Living Will?"

I could hold back no more and tears of despair covered my cheeks. "What?" I found myself saying. "This can't be our only option. Isn't there another transplant center that would take him?" I was standing up, holding David's hand tightly in mine. David's eyes were glassy and he sat there, emotionless.

The doctor answered, "Well, there is a Mayo lung transplant center in Jacksonville, Florida. Let me check on their waiting list statistics. I will return shortly."

As he left, I got on the bed, hugging David and saying, "This is not an option. God is not ready for you, I believe it. We will find lungs for you. Dear God, help us!"

After a couple of moments, I got off the bed to find tissues, when the doctor returned. "If you want me to arrange a transfer to Jacksonville, I certainly can. But there are several things you need to consider. Do you have any relatives in that area who could help you? Patients are required to stay close to the hospital for at least the first month after transplant. You will be required to return for any necessary tests or procedures once a month, and after that for at least a year."

My head was spinning. *Move to Florida? How?* I suddenly, impulsively interrupted the doctor and said, "Wait! We can go to UCSF. Linda knows the doctors there and lives a few hours away. Can we go to UCSF?"

The doctor looked puzzled and said, "I am not familiar with any of the lung physicians at the University in San Francisco."

Again I found myself saying, "We have the phone numbers! Linda has all the numbers! We have the surgeon's number! I'll call her right now and get it!" It was a God-moment. One He provided for us in a desperate time of need.

The doctor said, "Talk your options over between yourselves and make a decision. I'll check back with you. In the meantime, I will ask one of our social workers to bring a Living Will form for you to fill out, David." He left the room.

David had blotted his eyes and was looking directly into my heart when he asked, "Do you think they will take me at UCSF?"

"Yes!" I said in a determined voice. "Yes, I know they will take you."

I called Linda and explained the situation.

"I have all the numbers at UCSF. Let me find them and call you back," she said through her tears.

I looked at David, took his hand, and prayed, "Dear God, please open the hearts of the doctors at UCSF. Please let them see what a treasure this man's life is. Please, please let them give David new lungs."

Within ten minutes, Linda had called back with several phone numbers, including the direct line to the surgeon who had performed Linda's transplant. "Laura, he is one of the preeminent heart and lung transplant surgeons in the nation," Linda said, "and his name is Dr. Charles Hoopes."

After I copied down the list of phone numbers and hung up the phone, I looked at David and said, "See! God has provided for you! His name is Dr. Hoopes!" I hugged him and hit the call button for the nurse. When she answered, I knew I was yelling when I said, "Please find the doctor! I have phone numbers for him!"

CHAPTER 9

After what seemed to be an hour, our day nurse came into David's room and said, "What phone numbers are you trying to give the doctor?"

As I handed her the paper of phone numbers and names, I said excitedly, "He is going to call the UCSF to see if David can get on their transplant list!"

She took the paper, looked at it for a brief moment, and then with a confused expression she asked, "UCSF?"

I quickly replied, "Oh, it's the University of California at San Francisco. These are the phone numbers for the doctors and surgeon in their lung transplant program."

Frown lines began to appear between the nurse's eyebrows and she repeated again, "UCSF?"

It was an awkward moment, and I looked at David, seeing he was as confused as I was.

"Is there a problem?" I asked. "I'm sure the doctor included our conversation in David's charts, didn't he?"

After several more moments of silence, the nurse said in a very matter-of-fact way, "You are in the best lung transplantation program in the country. Why in the world would he want to call another transplant center?"

It was David's and my turn to look bewildered. David's expression had changed into a worried grimace and he said to the nurse, "Please give that information to the doctor and ask him to call San Francisco as soon as possible."

The nurse, hearing the intensity of David's voice, shrugged her shoulders ever so slightly, and as she left the room she muttered, "Okay."

I looked at David and said, "Don't get upset, sweetie. She probably hasn't read the chart. The doctor knows your situation and how important it is to get lungs for you. I'm sure he will call UCSF as soon as he has the numbers."

David nodded his head in agreement, but his dark brown eyes gave his thoughts away. He wasn't certain about anything at the moment.

"Mary should be in late this afternoon," I said, trying to change the subject. "And I am sure she will be ready to play lots of Gin." I was trying to be positive, happy and upbeat, but even I didn't buy it. I silently prayed that the doctor was already making a phone call. "How about playing a hand with me?" I asked him.

He looked at me, the left corner of his mouth turning up slightly in the crooked smile I loved so much, and he said, "Do I have to let you win again?"

I stuck my tongue out at him and tried to pout a little before grinning and saying, "I realize that I am a bit competitive, but I can beat you without you letting me win!"

He raised one eyebrow and gave me that "oh, really" kind of look.

"All right! At times I can be a bit of a sore loser, but only after losing to you repeatedly!" I laughed as I leaned over to tweak his nose and give him a peck on the cheek.

Whether we played Cribbage, Gin, or Old Maid, David seemed to be able to beat me anytime he wanted too. "Hmpf," I said, "I still think you cheat!" He just smiled and responded, "You deal."

We were glad to see Mary when she came bouncing into the room later that afternoon.

"Hi ya, bro," she said as she walked over to the bed to give David a hug. "What the hell is going here?"

Although we had been keeping in touch by cell phone, David and I began filling her in on the latest developments, informing her that the doctor had the

UCSF phone numbers. I said, "We are just waiting to hear back from the doctor."

"Great," she said. "We'll get you up and around again in no time, Dave."

Mary, who was the oldest by two and a half years, and David had been quite close growing up, and that there was a mutual respect and love between them was plain to see. If anyone could bring a little laughter to David, Mary would be the one. She is the type of person who is constantly smiling, very kindhearted, very outgoing and loves to live life to the fullest. She and David laughed about some of the funny things they did as kids growing up in Deadwood, South Dakota. It was good to think about something other than the transplant for a short while.

Since the hospital's policy was to allow only one person to spend the night with a patient, I had gotten information on a small hotel room across the street from the hospital, so one of us would be able to be with David twenty-four/seven. Mary could see the exhaustion in my face and she agreed to spend that night in David's hospital room.

I waited till the hall monitor said visiting hours were over before hesitantly preparing to head over to the hotel. David saw my hesitation and said, "Go get some sleep, Laura. I will need you tomorrow when we hear what UCSF says."

Tears welled up in my eyes and I blinked to try to

keep them from flowing down my cheeks. "When the outside doors open at 6 a.m., I will be back. If you need anything or hear anything or..."

Mary stopped me. "I promise you will be the first person we call."

I kissed David, gave Mary a big hug, and walked out the door into the hallway.

I had barely walked the short distance to the nurses' station when panic and fear overwhelmed me, and I burst into tears. My legs lost all their strength, and I leaned against the wall, shaking and sobbing. *Why can't they help him? He is my world. Why is God letting this happen?*

A nurse came over, gave me a hug and said, "Honey, he will be okay. I promise you I will check on him and call you if his condition changes." She guided me over to a chair by the elevators and brought me a small sip of water while I tried to regain my composure.

The tears subsided, and I rode the elevator to the first floor and walked over to the small hotel and into a cold, silent room. This was the first night I'd slept in a bed in a week, and I felt the quietness all around me. David had traveled overseas and been away from home for months at a time, so sleeping by myself was nothing new. But this night was different. The room had a sadness about it, almost as if it knew someone was missing.

I glanced at the side of the bed that he normally

slept on and began crying once more. I couldn't turn the bed down or turn the lights off. I lay across the bedspread and prayed. Tears were pouring out of me with my prayers. I cried, "Dear God, please heal him. Please provide lungs for him. Don't take him from me! I'm not ready to lose him! You are the Great Healer. Have we not prayed enough? Are the doctors not seeing how desperately he needs air? I beg you, Father, please, please heal him."

I was standing in front of the hospital sliding glass doors when a security guard unlocked them at 6 a.m. It was Friday, April 8, and I just knew that the doctor would come by when he made his morning rounds and tell us what UCSF had said. I walked quickly, wanting to be in David's room when he awoke. The door to his room was still closed when I arrived, and it made a squeaking sound as I tried to slowly open it. Mary had been sleeping in the recliner and David's nurse was changing out the bag on his IV pole.

I walked over to the bed and said, "Good morning, my love. Did you get any sleep?"

He rolled his eyes and answered, "As much as you can get in a hospital, I guess." He grinned at the nurse.

She smiled and said, "I know. I have a tough time sleeping during the night here, too." We all laughed.

"Thank you for watching him last night for me," I said to the nurse, as she was the one who had comforted me the night before.

"No problem. He is a pretty good patient." She finished checking his vitals and said, "I'm working again this evening and, if you are still here, I will be your nurse. Take care, and I hope you get some good news this morning."

"That sounds encouraging," Mary said after the nurse had left the room. But that turned out to be the only encouragement of the entire day.

There was one small, square clock on the off-white wall facing David's hospital bed, and I was constantly looking at it while waiting for the doctor's return. This Friday, the time for doctor rounds had passed; lunchtime had passed; 1:00 p.m. passed; then 2:30 p.m. passed. The small, square clock seemed to be ticking too slowly, almost stopping at times. I even checked the battery once or twice, thinking that could be causing the time to drag by. Mary, David and I played cards, read or talked while waiting for news about the phone call to UCSF. But no doctors came by, no interns came by, no news of any kind. There was only one social services representative who came by to give David the Living Will form to sign.

He filled it out quickly and decisively. "Laura, I do not want to be kept alive if I am brain dead or a vegetable. Promise me you will not agree to that."

I nodded my head 'yes' and said, "We are not going to worry about that because God is our Physician. He is here with us now and holding you up. You are going to be fine!"

He soberly handed me the paper to initial and continued, "Ask them to make a copy, and keep one in your backpack at all times."

The day nurse did make a copy for me and I put in it my dingy, old maroon and white backpack, along with his power of attorney. David had always taken his role as head of the household and spiritual leader of the family seriously. He'd made a great effort to plan for our security in case something unexpected happened to him and he was slowly but surely socking away savings for our retirement.

"We need to talk with our transplant coordinator, Joanie, and make sure that UCSF is an in-network provider before any decisions are made," David said. I had purchased a little pen and pad set from the hospital gift shop for him and he was busy compiling a list of questions.

I called Joanie and set my phone to speaker so we could all hear. Thankfully, our insurance, Blue Cross, did list UCSF as a preferred transplant facility. To be a preferred center, the hospital and insurance company agree upon greatly reduced rates or charges for the first 90 days after transplantation (as most complications arise during that time.)

This 90 day period or 'umbrella,' as Joanie referred to it, covered any and all expenses related to the transplant. Once the 90 day period was over, our regular plan deductibles would kick in up to the lifetime maximum of one million dollars. If the lifetime maximum was reached, all coverage would be terminated and the insurance would be cancelled. I could see David was somewhat relieved by the news that UCSF was an accepted transplant facility, though.

"However, there are many stipulations, many reviews, many medical records to review before David would be approved for a lung transplant," Joanie said.

"You have to be approved?" I asked out loud.

We had no idea of what might be entailed in the process, and our gracious transplant coordinator explained. "Your doctor or doctors and anyone who has treated you for pulmonary fibrosis need to send us all your medical records, including any procedures ordered, blood work, scans, and so on. The more groundwork establishing a need for a transplant that you can provide with these records, the more it will benefit you." Joanie continued, "There is a review board consisting of doctors and nurses who specialize in the transplant field. For instance, the panel would include experts in pulmonary, heart, and lung diseases."

David, who was writing everything down, looked up and asked, "How long does the review process take?"

Joanie paused and said, "It can take anywhere from two to four weeks, depending on how quickly the medical records are received." There was an obvious silence on our end of the conversation. Sensing our concern, Joanie continued, "Don't worry, Mr. Bichler, they can rush decisions on a critical need basis. Can you give me the names of the doctors that are currently treating you and the doctors at UCSF that will be treating you? I will contact them and see if we can't get the records faxed as soon as possible."

David let out a huge sigh and said, "Thank you very much, Joanie. That takes a load off my mind."

We gave her the names and phone numbers we had and told her once again how much we appreciated her kindness. "Blessings to you and your family, Joanie," David said as he ended the call.

It was getting dark outside and still we had not seen a doctor. The nurses kept telling us there were no orders for David, no tests, no planned rounds. David's level of anxiety was increasing and so was his blood pressure. Still receiving 15 liters of oxygen through his nose cannula continually, he was restless and growing more concerned with each hour that passed.

Tonight, it was Mary's turn to sleep in the small hotel room, and after she left for the evening, I positioned the recliner chair next to David's right side. Holding his hand was comforting and it made me feel so secure. We talked a little more about the insurance and transplant review committee's decision and then we prayed. David prayed out loud this time and, when his voice cracked, tears began running down my face. He didn't ask for lungs. He didn't ask for air. He said, "Dear Lord, I know that I do not deserve one moment of life on this earth. I ask for Your forgiveness and for You not to forsake me or my family. All I ask is that Your will be done in my life always. In Jesus' name. Amen."

What a faithful man! I cried as I climbed on the bed to lie next to him for a couple of minutes. *Thank you, God, for putting this man in my life! Please let him be healed!*

Thankfully, we had an uneventful night but, when the lights came on in the hallway to signal the start of another day shift, our anxiety raced into high gear. It was Saturday, April 9th, and we had to know something today. Did the doctor call UCSF? Did UCSF agree to accept David? David was continuing to lose weight and when the day shift nurse checked his vitals, his blood pressure was higher and his saturation level was lower. His normally bright eyes were cloudy and he was clearly getting worse, not better.

"His temperature is going up," the nurse said.

"We have been waiting since Thursday for the doctor to come in and give us news about UCSF. Can you please page him or find out something for us? Please," I pleaded.

I looked over at David, who was trying to sit straight up in the hospital bed. He was definitely weaker than a few days ago, and my heart felt so heavy in my chest.

After struggling a moment to catch his breath, David said, "Every minute is important at this time, and I need to know something in order to make arrangements."

The nurse, who had been observing David while he battled to pull himself up in the bed, said, "Yes, I will put in an urgent page for him." She walked over to the bed to feel David's forehead before saying, "I'll see if there are orders for medicine to bring down your fever. You stay still for now."

David nodded while I adjusted his pillows, and he leaned back against the raised head of the bed.

He took my hand and said, "Laura, I think you better go home tonight and pack a few more things, just in case we do go to UCSF. It will take you about five hours to drive to Wausau, so spend the night at home and come back tomorrow. I have phone calls you need to make for me." His face was emotionless while he talked. It scared me so.

"I'm fine," I said. "I can make the calls from here. I am not going to leave you for one minute." I didn't want to leave him *and* I wanted to talk with the doctor. Though my voice was strong as I answered him, my entire body was shaking.

David agreed for the moment, but I could tell he was not going to accept my answer for long.

Breakfast trays came, but David didn't have much of an appetite. Neither did I. My mind kept repeating the same questions: *God, where is that doctor? What is wrong? Why haven't we heard? God, are you listening?*

The nurse came back into the room and told us that the doctor was on the floor and she would make sure he came in to talk with us. We both perked up!

Finally! Thank you God!

I was using a cool washcloth to wipe David's forehead, trying to bring his temperature down and ease the headache he was experiencing, when the doctor appeared. Even at 7:30 a.m. he was wearing a very nice business suit. Not what I expected to see him wearing. I wasn't expecting to hear what his next words were either.

The doctor shook David's hand and said, "Well, have you decided what you want to do?"

Huh? What was he talking about?

David and I looked at each other and then back at the doctor.

"What?" I said. "Didn't you call the doctors at UCSF?"

It was his turn to look startled. "No, you never gave me any numbers and I assumed you were calling the family in since there is nothing we can do for David."

I felt the blood rush from my face, and tears began streaming down my cheeks. *Call the family in? Nothing they can do?* I squeezed David's hand and looked into his vacant eyes. He was in shock. He was just staring at the doctor.

I cried out to the doctor, "I gave the numbers to the nurse on Thursday night! You cannot give up on David! We were sitting here all day yesterday, waiting to hear from you. What happened? Why haven't you called?" The pitch of my voice was escalating with every word. I couldn't help crying. My heart was aching. *Give up? They have given up! I'm not giving up! What now? Oh my God! What can we do now?*

The doctor looked puzzled and said, "No one gave me phone numbers. I thought you had decided to let the disease take its course since David won't survive long enough to be put on the waiting list for a transplant. Let me check the nurses' station. I'll be right back." He left the room quickly and he knew we were upset.

I looked at my dear David. He was as white as the sheets on his bed. He had tears in his eyes and he was looking down at the foot of the bed.

"I'm going to call UCSF myself, sweetie. We are not giving up. You can't give up! I love you! I need you! We are going to get answers."

He nodded but couldn't say anything.

I felt as if an elephant was sitting on my chest. I cried and kept holding his hand. *They are not going to write him off!* I cried inside. *Lord, where are You? We need You now!*

Time stood, and I'm not sure how long it was before the doctor came back into the room. "I don't know what happened to any phone numbers and I'm sorry for the confusion. You will have to give me the numbers again. Since it is Saturday, I don't know if I can reach anyone at UCSF, so we may have to wait till Monday. Is that what you want me to do?"

David looked at me and I said, "Yes, it is! I'll need to make a few phone calls to get the numbers for you again. I want to hand them to you directly. How do I reach you when I get the numbers?"

He replied, "Just have the nurse page me. I may not be in the building, but I will return as soon as I can." With that said, he walked out of the room.

My mind was whirling. "Linda is in California, and they are two hours behind us. I'll wait till 7:00 a.m. California time to call her for the numbers again," I said to David.

He was slowly regaining his composure and replied, "Okay. I really think you need to run home and get a few things. Mary is here and we won't make any decisions till you get back."

But I did not want to leave and so responded, "David, I do not want to leave you. Are you sure I need to make the trip?"

He nodded his head 'yes.' "Mary and I will call Linda to get the numbers. You head home now. I've made a list of things to bring."

Over the past few days tears had filled my eyes at the drop of a hat. This moment was no different.

David reached over to wipe away the tears from my cheek and said, "I'll be fine. Try not to get a speeding ticket, Lead Foot." He grinned and I chuckled. Yes, I tended to drive a wee bit above the speed limit. Places to go, people to see, you know.

"Okay, but you call me if you hear something. Promise?" I asked.

"Yes, yes… just get on the road. Be careful," he said as he motioned for me to leave.

"I love you with all my heart, dear. God cares for us and He will protect you."

David nodded and said, "Love you too."

As I walked down the hospital hallway to the elevators, I suddenly realized that I had no clue how to get back to Wausau. I had followed the ambulance to the Mayo. I hadn't read street signs or taken note of the route we took. I panicked. Where could I get directions back to Wausau? I had no computer so couldn't use MapQuest, and we didn't own a GPS. My heart was racing. Then it hit me. Maybe the information desk would have a map.

I walked up to the man at the information desk and said, "My husband is in the lung transplant wing and I live in Wausau. I followed the ambulance here and have no idea how to drive back there. Do you have a map or any directions that might help me?"

He smiled and replied, "Little lady, this is your lucky day. I grew up in Wausau."

Yes! Thank you, God!

"God bless you, sir!" I exclaimed.

He found a piece of paper and began to write down directions for me. When he had finished, he looked up and said, "Be careful driving through Rochester. Police are always giving speeding tickets."

I laughed and thought about what David had said. "You are so kind. Thank you, thank you." I turned to leave. *Now... where was the car parked?*

CHAPTER 10

I found the car and headed toward the freeway. Four and half hours to go. I had the list of things David had asked for and began thinking of what I needed too. After all, we shouldn't need more than a week's worth of things, right? We could always wash clothes. I turned off the radio and called Jean Smith at Trinity to fill her in on what was happening and to ask her to update the prayer chain. Trinity Lutheran was our extended family and they are prayer warriors.

"Jean, David needs prayers." I said. "Lots of prayers." Jean was such a sweetheart, always listening when I was crying, always comforting me with scriptures and prayers.

"If you need anything, Laura, just call me day or night," Jean said. "Just be safe driving, and I'll let everyone know what's going on."

I had not been on the road more than one hour when the cell phone rang. Mary was on the other end and she was shouting through her tears. "We gave the phone numbers to the doctor. Dr. Hoopes answered! He's taking David! Dr. Hoopes answered the phone!"

My heart was pounding and I had to pull off the road. "What? What? Dr. Hoopes said yes? Oh my God! They will help him? Thank you, Jesus!" I screamed into the phone.

Mary gave the phone to David and he explained that they had gotten the phone numbers from Linda again and had given them to the doctor. The doctor had called UCSF and, to his great surprise, Dr. Hoopes answered the phone.

David said, "The doctor went out into the hallway to call, and then poked his head back into the room and said, 'This is a Dr. Hoopes. Who did you say was your sister?' Mary said, 'Linda Willis. Her name is Linda Willis. He transplanted her last year!' The doctor went back out into the hallway and talked for a few more moments. When he came back in, he said with a somewhat surprised look on his face, 'This Dr. Hoopes said he would take you as a patient. We will make arrangements to get you there as soon as possible.' Then he left the room."

"That is great, my love!" I said through my tears. "Maybe I better turn around and come back to Mayo."

"No, no," David said. "I need those things. As soon

as we know any plans, we will call you. Just be safe," he added.

I sat for a few more minutes crying and praising God before I could get back on the road. I felt a tremendous sense of relief. Everything was going to be fine. God had provided for David as I knew he would. Now I needed to get home, pack a few things and get back to him. I was excited! He was going to get new lungs!

The drive went smoothly and I arrived home around 1:30 p.m. on Saturday. I had barely walked into the house when the phone rang again. It was Mary. This time she was a bit more excited when she said, "They are making arrangements to airlift David to UCSF. You better get back here as fast as you can! They might take him this evening!"

I was excited, scared, tired, and confused all at the same time. "Okay, okay," I repeated. "Don't let them leave without me! Whatever you do, don't let them take him without me!" I hung up the phone and ran through the house, trying to gather the things from the list. This was a good sign.

Suddenly I stopped dead in my tracks. Wait. *Airlift? How could he fly in a plane?*

I quickly called David's room. "My love, did they say they were going to airlift you? How?"

David replied, "You are thinking the same thing I

was. Get back as quickly as you can. We should know something by then."

Great!

I wasn't home an hour when I had repacked the car and was back on the road heading for Rochester. I walked back into David's hospital room around 9:00 p.m. that night. He looked a bit happier, had a bit more color. He and Mary had been playing Gin most of the day, excitedly talking about the great news. I only wanted to hug him. We slept a little better that night, still holding tightly to each other's hand. *God is so good. He is going to heal David.*

Sunday we heard nothing. The nurses said since it was a weekend, we probably wouldn't hear anything till Monday. We spent the day playing cards, calling friends, taking naps and talking. We had decided that Mary would drive our car back to Rapid City, South Dakota since I would be riding in the plane with David. She and her husband Larry would bring the car out to San Francisco if we decided we needed it. Our plan seemed to be set.

Linda lived in Redding, only a four-hour drive from San Francisco. She would be there if we needed anything. David would get a new pair of lungs and be able to live his life again in no time. We all thought we knew how David's transplant journey would end. We were wrong. Dead wrong.

Monday morning brought some confusion and

problems with our ready-made plan. There was a mix up with David's orders. A coordinator who was responsible for finalizing the details for airlifted patients came to the room and was confused. She said, "We have patients transferred *to* Mayo from all over the country. We are prepared for that. We have never transferred a seriously ill patient *from* Mayo to another center before and we are having a bit of trouble finding a transport plane that is covered by your insurance carrier."

David looked at her and said, "I have a transplant coordinator. Have you contacted her? UCSF is in our preferred network of transplant centers."

She nodded. "Give me her number and I will call her. The plane we use is our own transplant carrier. It is contracted to travel between Mayo centers only."

David gave her the number, and she left saying she would return when she found out something. We were obviously worried.

"Surely there are medical transport services that Blue Cross covers," I said to David.

He replied, "Let's call Joanie and see what she says."

I dialed the number and put her on speakerphone once again. Joanie explained that the medical transport had to have specialized equipment on board in order to monitor David's condition and would be forced to fly at a very low altitude in order for David to be able to breathe. She mentioned that she was working with the coordinator at Mayo and would call us with the details when they were settled.

Tension was mounting with each passing hour and by nightfall, we had heard nothing from either the Mayo coordinator or Joanie. We tried to sleep but were unsuccessful. We needed information. Time was against David and we needed to get to UCSF as soon as possible.

I was awake the next morning when the hallway lights turned on at 6:00 a.m. It was Tuesday, April 12th. We had been at the Mayo hospital one week. David's condition was deteriorating each day, and I was in a constant state of worry, running on adrenaline, waiting and watching my love struggle to breathe.

Our cell phone rang at about 9:30 a.m. that morning and it was Joanie, letting us know that she had found a medical transport company that would be covered by our insurance. The only problem was that they were carrying another patient to Florida and would not be available to pick David up till late Tuesday afternoon.

She reminded us to get all the medical records, CD's, and other information from Mayo and carry it all with us on the plane as the review committee would be meeting later this week and would need everything. I told her I would make sure I had it all and thanked her for helping us. As it turned out, we would soon need her more than we ever could have imagined.

Around 2:00 p.m., things suddenly began to move into high gear. Nurses buzzed in and out, checking and recording vital signs. The transport coordinator was bringing me folder after folder filled with medical records and CD's. David was being asked to sign one release form after another. I had a small overnight bag with me and my backpack was filled to the brim. We would be leaving around 4:00 p.m. Central Time, stopping in Colorado to refuel, and arriving in San Francisco around 8:30 p.m. Pacific Time. Shortly before 3:00 p.m., five people came in to introduce themselves. They were the Medical Airlines transportation team, consisting of a pilot, co-pilot, and three triage nurses.

"Hello, David." said a short, redheaded young man. "We are the transport team that will be insuring you have a safe trip to San Francisco."

I looked at the group of five: four men and one woman, dressed in what looked like NASA-type flight suits, each wearing a cluttered tool belt of sorts around his or her waist.

"My name is Adam and I am the pilot. My team will be taking your vitals every five to ten minutes during the flight to insure that you are comfortable," continued the redheaded young man.

I was handed a release form to sign and, to my surprise, the woman team member took a small calculator from her tool belt. "We will need a credit card before we can board the medical air transport," she explained.

Huh? A credit card? Now?

I glanced over to David who was frowning as he said, "I thought this was covered by our transplant umbrella. Why do you need a credit card?"

She smiled politely and answered, "We require pre-payment before any services, sir."

"Did I even bring a credit card?" I wondered out loud while digging through my heavy backpack.

The team was bustling around David's hospital bed, securing four sets of straps around his feet, thighs, waist and chest. David's dark brown eyes looked as if a hurricane were swirling around inside them.

Finally, I dug out my credit card and handed it to the woman.

"What is your card limit, ma'am?" she asked. "If we max this one, we may need to put the balance on another card."

My jaw dropped to the floor. "How much does this cost?" I stammered as I watched the woman slide my credit card through her tool belt calculator. "Approximately $13,000, but that is just an estimate. After the flight, we will add any additional charges that may have occurred while we were in the air," she stated quickly.

Oh my gosh! Additional charges?

David looked stunned and scared. I began patting

his forearm with my left hand and stroking his hair with my right hand. "Don't worry, sweetie," I found myself saying to try to comfort him. "Things will be okay. God is in charge here." My stomach was churning and my mind was racing. *Dear Lord, what is happening here?*

In less than ten minutes, the transport had David ready to board the airplane. As they pushed his bed into the hallway and down the wide corridor, my mind was blank as I tried to keep up. I kept saying the Lord's Prayer over and over again, asking Him to get us safely to the hospital in San Francisco. An ambulance was waiting to take David to the small airstrip where the medical transport was fueled and waiting. I watched as they lifted David into the back and then stepped forward to climb inside myself.

"I'm sorry, Mrs. Bichler. There is not enough room for you to ride back here," the redheaded young man said as he pulled me aside. I strained to catch a glimpse of David before they closed the ambulance doors. I turned to Mary, who had followed us, and said, "Will you drive me to the airport? We must follow this ambulance!"

It wasn't very far to the small airport, and I could see a tiny plane sitting on the side of a runway with its side door open. The ambulance parked very close to the open door and within moments had David out and secured inside the plane. I said goodbye to Mary and stood in front of the tiny door, waiting impatiently to get inside. The plane had two propellers, one on each wing. As I climbed inside, I was startled by the interior. No seats, no finished sides with windows and shades, no bathrooms. It looked like a cargo plane. The inside was a drab grey color and so small that even the short, redheaded young pilot could not stand up straight.

David was on a small, thin gurney with the head raised to 30 degrees and he was trying to smile at me as I looked for a place to sit down among the bulky medical equipment. His head was about six inches from the ceiling of the plane and he was still strapped onto the gurney. I sat down on a wooden crate that read "Plastic gloves, antiseptics," my knees bent as if I were going to do a somersault.

Medical equipment was everywhere – on the floor, on the walls, hanging from the ceiling and equipped with flashing lights and high-pitched alarms that echoed loudly as the sound bounced off the bare, metal walls. Three of the five team members were busy reading and recording David's vitals, as they sat in a straight line, one behind the other, and talked back and forth on walkie-talkies. There seemed to be miles and miles of plastic tubing threaded throughout the walls of the plane, connecting each heart monitor, oxygen generator, IV pole, and machine to each other piece of equipment and pumping pure oxygen into David's lungs through his nose cannula.

The pilot and co-pilot were sitting only a few feet away from me in the cockpit as they readied for takeoff. There was no door into the cockpit, and I could see the vast number of gauges, levers, switches and monitors they used to fly the plane.

"We will be flying at a very low altitude to allow your husband to breathe easily, but we will have to stop in Colorado to refuel," the redheaded pilot yelled back to me.

I turned my head to look at David, trying to find a way to hold onto his hand, but the oxygen tanks and EKG machines were in the way. I smiled at him, blowing him a kiss, as the tiny plane took off.

The noise level in the plane was tremendous. No wonder walkie-talkies were necessary! For the next three hours, I felt completely isolated from David even though he was only a few feet away.

Emotionally, I felt as though I was struggling to keep my balance on a thin tight rope that was many stories above the ground. Extreme panic was on one side and calmness on the other. I pleaded with God to help me hold my emotions together, to not lose my presence of mind.

I needed to touch David. Hold his hand. Make sure he was not in pain. Make sure he was breathing. I tried to talk to him, but the noise was too loud. He was staring at the top of the plane, not able to move his arms or legs. Thankfully, his eyes closed and he slept for a few minutes.

Over the next three hours, the medics took turns monitoring David, checking his vitals, talking with him, and adjusting the various machines according to what they observed. When the readings went down, I could feel the sense of urgency in the medics' actions, always trying to stabilize his oxygen levels. I felt completely helpless and I kept praying that we would land in San Francisco quickly and David would receive new lungs soon.

Even though the noise in the plane was making my ears hurt, I felt the dip when the pilot finally pointed the nose downward. We would be landing soon. *Thank you, dear Jesus!!* I smiled at David and he winked back in reply, not having the energy to speak.

The landing lights were bright as the landing strip came up to meet the plane. I could see through the cockpit window an ambulance with lights flashing parked in the distance. The medics once again began their preparation in order to move David from the plane to the ambulance. It seemed everyone in the plane was moving at one time. Everyone but David, who was still strapped down on the gurney.

No sooner had the tiny plane come to a stop, when the door abruptly opened and more emergency medics were yelling at me to get out of the plane. I grabbed my backpack and jumped through the door onto the ground. I stepped back in order to let the medics get David's gurney out of the door with all the equipment still attached.

Within minutes, David was moved from the plane into the ambulance that was only a few yards away. Before I could step inside the back of the ambulance, the doors shut and the two medics inside began monitoring David. The ambulance driver pushed me toward the passenger door saying, "Please sit in the front seat, ma'am. I have forms for you to fill out."

It could have been 8:00 p.m. or 9:00 p.m., I wasn't sure, but it was very dark outside. The ambulance, with its lights flashing and sirens blasting, took off before I got the passenger door completely closed. The driver was talking to the hospital, the University of California, San Francisco, on the radio, speaking with two-digit codes that made it sound like I was a part of a police-chase movie. The driver put down the radio and handed me a clipboard with six pages and a pen attached.

"We need these filled out before we unload your husband at the hospital."

I looked down at the forms and began filling out David's name, birthdate, social security number, and other requested information. Once again they needed a credit card number that would guarantee payment of their services. I glanced up to see that the ambulance was traveling at a speed of about 87 miles per hour.

My heart was racing. *Dear God, help us get to UCSF safely!*

I kept looking through a tiny window into the back of the ambulance, but the only things I could see were many IV poles, blinking machines, two medics, and the top of David's dark brown hair.

The walls of the ambulance were rocking back and forth with the movement of the road. It wasn't long before the ambulance headed up a steep hill lined with tall, dark buildings on each side of the narrow street. In the distance, I saw a huge group of buildings that were many stories higher than the other buildings on the street. And it seemed every light in those buildings was turned on. I caught a glimpse of a street sign and read, 'Parnassus,' as we speed by. The driver, still gripping the radio, said, "Mrs. Bichler, we are arriving at the hospital and you will be escorted to a holding area until we are able to stabilize your husband. Someone from the hospital will direct you to his room."

Before I could ask any questions, we had driven into the emergency entrance and a team of medics had gathered around the ambulance. One young man opened the passenger side door and said, "Are you the wife?"

I answered, "Yes. I want to stay with David."

He took my arm gently and said, "You'll have to wait inside until your husband has been safely transported to the room. Inside the door is a nurse whose name is Sarah. She will help you."

I was more or less pulled between two big glass doors that had been propped open. I stood there, clutching my little backpack, watching while an army of people went in and out of those glass doors. They all seemed to be talking at the same time and very loudly. Weren't they listening to each other? I heard the words, "We need that oxygen stat!" and tears began to burn in my eyes.

Dear Lord, please don't let me cry! David doesn't need me to cry! Help me be strong! I prayed over and over again.

The lights on the ambulance were still flashing when I saw David on the gurney being pushed inside the hospital doors. Medical people and machines surrounded him, and I couldn't get close enough to even see his face as he was wheeled past me.

Somehow, all these people, machines, and David's gurney disappeared down a hallway, and suddenly I was completely alone. It became deathly quiet and I realized I was still standing inside the doorway, clutching my little backpack.

Where was that nurse who was supposed to help me? What was her name? Where is David? Is he okay?

It was like I was frozen and couldn't move a muscle. I don't know how, but I began running toward the hallway where David had been, only to be met by two nurses who stood in my way.

"Are you supposed to help me?" I said, my voice cracking with fear. "They took my husband and I need to be there with him!"

One of the men said, "Yes, your husband is doing okay and you will see him, but first you will need to come with us."

I saw that his nametag said "Mike" and the lady with him was "Sarah."

"What's your name, sweetie?" Sarah asked me.

"Laura, my name is Laura," I replied as they escorted me down a different hallway to an elevator.

"Well, Laura, we are going to take good care of David, but we need to ask you a few questions first. Okay?"

I nodded yes and I stepped into the elevator that read, "Moffitt." Mike pushed the button for the 10th floor. When the doors opened, the hallway was quiet and they led me to what looked like a waiting area or lobby. It had several padded blue chairs, a coffee pot, a television, and lots of windows. And again, there were more forms waiting to be completed.

CHAPTER 11

Once again, I sat down to fill out forms with what seemed to be the same information as the other forms. They asked me David's age, his height, his weight, what type of work he did, and was he a smoker.

"Smoker?" I said again, stunned. "We never smoked, ever."

I kept asking when I could see David and they kept replying 'soon.'

Finally, the forms were complete, and Mike and Sarah were leading me toward the elevators once more. This time when the doors opened, four male nurses were pushing David on the gurney out into the hallway.

"David!" I said loudly. "Dave, are you okay? I'm here with you, right here with you."

He gave me a tiny, crooked smile as they started pushing him around a corner. I followed quickly, noticing that the sign above a set of double doors I passed through read: '10 ICU'. As I turned the corner, following the nurses and the gurney, I saw Linda, David's younger sister, standing in the hallway waiting for us. She had driven from Redding to meet David at the hospital. Only one short year ago she had been the one on the gurney waiting for a lung transplant at USCF.

I hugged her as they pushed David into a room across the hall from the nurse's station. "Linda, I'm glad you came."

She was crying. "How is Dave doing? The people here are great and they will take good care of him."

As I walked through the door to his hospital room, I saw at least ten people dressed in either white or colored scrubs, and each one was hooking up a different machine or monitoring device. There was more activity in that room than in an angry beehive shaken with a stick. In the middle of all the hubbub, lay David on the hospital bed with his dark brown eyes looking sadly at me as if to say, "Why is this happening to me? Help me!"

Under my breath, I was thanking God that these wonderful doctors and nurses were taking care of the love of my life; but their obvious urgency and the seriousness of the situation scared the daylights out of me. Only two weeks ago David and I were at home in Wausau planning a little weekend getaway to enjoy being empty-nesters. Now, my head was swimming with questions, thoughts, worries and confusion. David was my rock, my life. This hospital room filled with hi-tech monster machines was not in our plans. *What was happening and why? Why, dear Lord, why?*

I tried to get someone's attention and asked, "What is happening? Where is Dr. Hoopes?"

"Hoopes is in surgery and one of the pulmonary docs will be in to see you as soon as possible. Just sit tight," replied one male nurse.

Sit tight? Sit tight! David needed new lungs and he needed them right this minute.

"I hope the doctors come soon," I said as I stood there helplessly watching as the heart monitor began beeping, showing David's heartbeat, rate, pulse, and more.

Suddenly, as quickly as the mob ran into David's room, they were gone and the only sound left was a symphony of high-pitched beeps, blurps, blips, and the clicking on and off sound of the blood pressure cuff that was securely fastened to David's left arm. His oxygen cannula was fit snuggly under his nose, and the wall unit was pumping oxygen to him at a rate of 15 liters, the highest level on its glass scale. Linda and I stood next to his bed. I leaned over to give him a kiss. "How are you doing, sweetie?"

He raised his hand for me to take hold of and answered, "I guess I can cause quite a commotion, huh!" He grinned as I clasped his hand in mine. "I was hoping that cute brunette was going to ask if I needed a sponge bath." He smiled as he tried to lessen the tension in the air.

I giggled. "Don't be silly! I have requested only male nurses to bathe you!" Our eyes met and even though we were smiling, I could sense fear and uncertainty in his dark brown eyes.

Linda began talking with David, and I noticed the dark circles and wrinkles that had appeared under his eyes. His skin had taken on a pasty pallor, as though he was suddenly aging right before my eyes. I glanced around the room and noticed a white board mounted on the wall at the foot of the bed. It was to share information with patients about the nurses on a certain shift. Above that was a very plain round clock with black trim. The hands on it said the time was 1:30 a.m.

At that moment, a young male doctor walked into the room and said, "Mr. Bichler? I am one of the transplant team's pulmonologists. You've had quite a day, haven't you?" As he spoke, he put out his hand to shake David's hand in greeting. The doctor looked over to Linda and said, "Hey, Linda, how're things going?" The handsome doctor had treated Linda for several years prior to her double lung transplant in February

2004. Linda answered fine and thanked him for working with her brother, David.

The doctor looked at me and said, "And you must be his wife, Laura." I said 'yes' as I shook his hand, but before I could get any more words of out my mouth, the doctor spoke again. "David, we will be using tonight to get a better handle on your situation and will be doing tests throughout the night. We have a team of pulmonologists and you will become familiar with each one of us," he said as he reached into his white lab-coat's pocket and pulled out a pager. After turning it off, he said, "Right now, you need to try to rest while you can."

He turned to Linda and me and said, "Ladies, I am afraid you cannot sleep in his room. Try to get some rest, too. Tomorrow will be a busy day." With that, he turned and left the room.

"I'm not leaving you, David," I said as I held his hand once again.

This time he was frowning. "You and Linda need to sleep. I'll be fine here."

I looked at Linda and, after some discussion, we decided to sleep in the lobby for the night. Tomorrow we could make other arrangements.

A nurse came in to take David's vitals and reminded us we needed to leave the room soon. I gave David a kiss and told him I would be back in his room as soon as they'd let me. "I love you! Joshua 1:9, my love. God is watching out for you."

I followed Linda out the door, but not without turning around to catch one more glimpse of David. His eyes were following us and he looked like a frightened little boy who was trying to be brave. It broke my heart to have to leave for even a minute. I blew him a kiss and forced my legs to walk forward. My stomach was at the top of my mouth and the elevator ride down to the lobby seemed to take forever.

I had thought the lobby would be empty at this hour of the morning, but it wasn't. The lights were on and the security guard was giving everyone an armband showing what time they had arrived and what patient they were visiting. It seemed the hospital had been having trouble with homeless people wandering in at night for a warm place to sleep.

Linda and I found two chairs side by side and sat down to try to get some sleep. I prayed under my breath, "Dear Lord, thank you for letting us arrive here, but please bring a set of lungs to David quickly. And please protect Linda from catching any germs or bugs that might be in this lobby. Amen."

I looked at Linda who, at age 37, was a year out from her double lung transplant and still very thin compared to her usual weight. Once a patient receives a transplanted organ, the natural immune system has to be broken down and basically obliterated in order to keep the patient's body from attacking the new organ in what is called 'rejection.'

Rejection is deadly and once it begins, it is extremely hard to stop. Transplanted patients are considered immune suppressed and highly susceptible to all viral, bacterial, or fungal germs that exist in everyday life.

I was very worried that Linda might catch a stray bug or virus from any of the hundred people or so lying or sitting in chairs in the lobby, and I certainly didn't want that to happen.

The dark brown, cushioned chairs in the lobby did not recline and had wooden arm rests that made it impossible to lie down across two of them. We had no pillows, just my little maroon backpack and small suitcase. Linda sat in one chair and propped her feet up on the suitcase, closing her eyes in an effort to sleep. I struggled to get comfortable, alternating between sitting and standing, and pacing back and forth across the narrow entrance hallway. The hours from 2 a.m. until 6 a.m. dragged by so slowly that I felt every tick of my watch's second hand as if it were a hammer slamming against my wrist in slow motion. I walked and prayed; I sat and cried; I walked and prayed more. The security guard never left his station, even though his eyes were watching the movements of every person in the lobby. He never smiled, as if his face were etched into a stony pose.

Finally, at 6 a.m. on the dot, the security guard stood up and motioned that the hospital was now 'open.' I quickly grabbed my stuff, woke Linda, and headed to the elevator. As I walked into David's room, the night nurse was just finishing with a check of his vitals and was replacing an IV bag. David smiled and I couldn't wait to give him a hug. I felt so relieved to see him! I felt secure. He was going to be fine. God would see to that, I just knew it.

He asked what day it was, and I told him it was Wednesday, April 13th. Frown lines appeared across his forehead and he asked, "Have you called my office? I need to talk with my office."

I nodded that I had called them and then looked at the large oxygen-monitoring machine that was above his bed. Even though he was being given oxygen through his nose cannula at 15 liters, his oxygen level was 78, despite that he was only lying in bed. He began speaking in short sentences simply because he would run out of air.

All the while, I could see that he watched every movement of my face and eyes. I had to be strong! I could not cry! He needed me to be strong for him, and I prayed that God would help me keep a smile on my face and give him a sense that everything was going to be all right.

During the next four days, doctors, interns, nurses, and technicians were constantly streaming in and out of David's room. But no Doctor Hoopes. When would he come? David had lost fifteen pounds since being admitted and you could see that he was going downhill quickly. He tried to read his Bible and, when he couldn't hold it anymore, I read to him. He was not able to get out of bed and his oxygen level had steadily dropped.

Linda had gone back home and I was being allowed to sleep in David's hospital room. I sat and slept in a chair next to him, only letting go of his hand when his vitals had to be taken or he was wheeled down to X-ray for another test. The pulmonologists continued to say he was in the end stage of Pulmonary Fibrosis but could not explain why the disease had progressed at such an extremely fast pace. They were as puzzled as we were.

Monday, April 18th, David was visibly struggling to hold his head up. He was so weak. I would prop up his head with pillows to keep it from dropping down onto his chest. My heart hurt, my head was pounding, and tears were burning my eyes. David's mouth dropped open as he wasn't strong enough to close it. His hair and skin had turned completely grey and he was shriveled up in the bed like a man of 100 years old. I still held his hand. My prayers were desperate and harsh. *God, why haven't you given him lungs? Why haven't we seen Dr. Hoopes? Why are you doing this to him?* You could feel the sadness in the room and even the nurses seemed to lose hope. The day passed with me wiping David's forehead and telling him how much I loved him and that everything was going to be okay. He was going to be okay.

Around 2:30 a.m. on the morning of April 19th, I rang the button for the nurse. There was a deep, dark feeling of dread that had somehow pushed into the room. The air was heavy as a cloud of fear engulfed the room. Something was wrong. Something had worsened. David's eyes were now sunken into their sockets and he had lost control of his bowels.

I begged the male nurse to help me change his bed sheets. The nurse lifted David up gently, as one does an infant to put it on the shoulder, and he tried to sit him in a chair; but David couldn't stay sitting up.

I sat down in the chair first, and then the nurse put David on my lap. As I held him, he seemed so helpless, so lifeless. As the nurse hurried to change the bed sheets, I felt as if someone were watching me. I looked toward the door and saw a man standing in the hallway, observing all that was happening. He didn't say anything, he just watched.

We got David back into bed and the nurse left the room. I laid my head on David's chest and prayed for God to please not let him die. *He is too young! I'm not ready to let him go! Please, please God... where are You? Why is he suffering so? Help him!*

Around 5 a.m., a respiratory therapist came into

the room, followed by a couple of other men pushing two more large pieces of equipment. The therapist said, "We need to do a chest x-ray and scan on David. These are our portal units. You'll have to step out of the room for a minute." The two other men were busy hooking up all kinds of wires between David and the machines.

I nodded and squeezed his hand. "I'll just be in the hallway, sweetie. I love you." He nodded slightly, but his eyes were still closed and his jaw seemed to drop his mouth even further open.

Watching from the hallway, I suddenly felt overwhelmed and tears began streaming down my face. I covered my mouth so David wouldn't hear my sobs.

One of the other nurses came over from the nurses' station and gave me a hug. "He is important to you, isn't he?" she said as she hugged me.

"He is my life," I managed to say between sobs.

She stood next to me while I gathered my wits and dried up my tears.

I asked her as I had often asked the nursing staff, "When will Dr. Hoopes come?"

She smiled and said, "Oh, my dear, he was watching your husband just this morning."

I blinked in disbelief. "The man I saw standing outside his room this morning was Dr. Hoopes?" I stammered.

"Yes," the nurse replied. "He's working on lungs for your husband."

Every muscle in my body wanted to scream out, "YES! Thank you, Jesus!" I couldn't wait to get back to David's side and tell him that Dr. Hoopes had seen him. Dr. Hoopes was getting lungs for him!

A nurse was in the room with David and me continually now, taking vitals and adjusting machines. I kept holding my husband's hand, even though he could no longer move it himself.

"Laura, David's condition is rapidly deteriorating. Perhaps you should call in your family to say goodbye," the nurse suggested as she laid her hand upon my shoulder. Her words made me sick to my stomach, and I began to vomit into the trash can next to the bed. *No, no, no. Oh dear God, no!*

The nurse left the room, and I tried to gather my wits about me to make calls to our family. I looked down at my watch and it said 10:46 a.m. That's when I saw a man walking into David's room in quite a hurry. He began to speak very quickly in a soft, low tone as if we had been in a discussion previously and were picking up where we left off.

He was a thin man almost six feet tall and was wearing green scrubs, a surgeon's cap, and had booties on his shoes. He went to David's bedside, checked the machines and then turned to me and said, "He's going to have to be put on life support and if he goes on it, he will never get off."

I stared at him in confusion and fear. "Who are you?" I asked as I swallowed my tears.

"I'm Dr. Hoopes. We have two options and neither one is a good option," he said.

I was happy, scared, and sick all at the same time.

He continued softly, "I have a left lung that isn't a great match for him and it is damaged, but I think it will recover. If we transplant that left lung, it may buy David enough time to get strong enough for a double lung transplant." He was looking at David as he went on, "If we try to wait for a better match or a double lung, he will have to go on life support or ECMO. In my experience, if they go on ECMO, they never get off."

I was still stunned, trying to comprehend what this miracle worker was trying to say to me. "You mean he will only get one lung? Can he live with one lung?" I asked.

"It's not a good idea to transplant one lung and it *is* damaged, but I think it will come back. At this point, it's his only chance," Dr. Hoopes said. He walked over to David's bedside, pulled down the railing, and sat down. He leaned close to David's head, which was propped up by pillows, and he said, "David, I'm Dr. Hoopes. I've found a lung that will work for you, even though it is damaged. We want to transplant it, try to get you stronger, and then transplant a double lung that matches your body. If we don't use this lung, you will be put on life support and I know you don't want that." He asked if David understood what he was saying. David's nod was barely noticeable. Dr. Hoopes continued, "David, do you want us to use this lung and try to get you stronger?" Again, a little nod 'yes' from David.

Dr. Hoopes stood up, put the rail back, walked over to me and said, "Things are going to get crazy around here for the next several hours. I'm moving him to a room where my transplant team can take care of him. I'll try to keep you informed. Just be ready at any time."

I gulped, nodded, and tried to say, "thank you," but he had already turned to go out the door. I sat by David, grabbed his hand and said, "Thank you, dear Lord! Thank you! O dear God, thank you!"

CHAPTER 12

D r. Hoopes was right when he said it would get crazy! Within minutes of his leaving David's room, two male interns were readying David's gurney for the trip to the ICU room where the transplant team could take care of him.

"Mrs. Bichler," one nice young man said, "grab all the things in this room that are yours. We are moving David to an ICU room. Follow us or you'll get lost."

Oh my gosh! I grabbed whatever I could see and fell in line behind the gurney, two IV poles, the oxygen tank, and the heart and oxygen monitors. These interns moved very quickly, and David was whisked down the hallway, through two large double doors, and into a world of individual rooms, machines, nurses, doctors, and surgeons.

It was busier than any Houston freeway I'd ever

driven on. Patients were walking in the hallway, pushing IV poles and oxygen tanks. Nurses were walking back and forth from room to room with medicines or charts. Groups of interns were following doctors to patients' rooms, writing down every word they said. IV drip lines were beeping and hip pagers were going off. And right in the middle of all the bustle was David's gurney and his entourage of people and machines.

We stopped at the nurses' station long enough for the intern to write on a huge white board, filled with columns and room numbers. David's name was written under room number 14. Next to his name was the word "Hoopes".

Room 14 was a large room in which one entire wall was made up of sliding glass doors. This room had different equipment in it than previous rooms, including huge, operating-room type lights on the ceiling, a large sink and storage cabinet, and at least twenty different pieces of medical equipment hanging on the wall behind the head of the bed. One nurse was assigned to each room which held a single patient. I would later find out that Dr. Hoopes had certain criteria for the nurses on his team. They were the best of the best and had to have years of experience before they were allowed to work within the transplant team on 10 ICU.

As the interns were setting up David's machines,

the day shift nurse who would be watching David spoke to me and said, "My dear, are you his wife?"

I nodded 'yes' as I kept my eyes on David.

"Let me help you put your things down, dear, you look so tired," she said as she took my backpack and placed it in the corner of the room by his bed.

"Thank you," I said. "What is going to happen now? Can I sit by David?"

She told me that Dr. Hoopes had gone to get the lung and that David was going to be prepped for surgery. Once again, she handed me a clipboard with questions on it for me to answer. My sigh was so loud and obvious that she looked at me and said, "Tired of all this paperwork, aren't you? I certainly understand that. Well, this paperwork is different. This is telling you what to expect when he comes back with a new lung." She smiled and, with this news, I could smile, too.

A short time later, I stood out in the busy hallway and began making phone calls. First, to my daughter, and then to David's sisters, then his boss. I told the family to come as soon as possible because God was answering our prayers and David would be getting one new lung. When I spoke with Jean Smith from Trinity, I told her to please let our church family and the prayer chain know to begin praying for David right that moment. And they did. God tells us to pray His words back to Him and He provided David and me with hundreds of prayer warriors that did just that.

When I returned to the room, David's oxygen level was in the 60's and dropping. I took his hand in mine and, even though he couldn't speak to me, I talked with him about how wonderful he was going to feel when he could breathe with his new lung. I told him his daughter and sisters were coming to see him and that Trinity had their prayer warriors praying for him. I kissed his hand and told him that God was answering our prayers and he was going to be fine. He would get this new lung and his life would start again right where he left off.

Suddenly, a team of six people dressed in scrubs came in and began to move David. "I'm sorry, but you'll have to stand in the hallway till we get him ready to transport. Dr. Hoopes is waiting in the operating room for him," one man told me. I didn't know what to say.

The man gently pulled me away from David and led me into the hallway where all I could do was stand and watch. This team of six worked in unison like a fine-tuned machine. Each seemed to know what the other was thinking and, within what seemed to be seconds, David's gurney was once again being pushed into the busy hallway.

"You can come as far as the operating room door," someone said to me, and I began following.

Only one member of the team was talking and he was giving orders into a walkie-talkie device. We walked and walked and walked. Suddenly we stopped in front of two green double doors that had no windows in them. "You better tell him goodbye now," I heard someone say.

I stumbled forward and saw that David's head had been tied to the gurney to keep it from moving. "I love you, I love you!" I cried in his ear. "God is here and taking care of you. I'll be right here waiting for you. I'm not going anywhere," I said and kissed him on the forehead.

The doors opened up, he was pushed inside and the doors closed behind David and the team.

I looked at the doors and began to cry. Standing in the empty hallway, I began to sob. I put my hands over my eyes and just cried for a moment. When I looked up, I realized I had no idea what hallway I was in or how to get back to the ICU unit.

My heart began racing and my feet felt as heavy as bricks. I was lost. Completely lost. I couldn't get to David. I couldn't get back to the ICU. Lost. My ears were ringing and I began walking back down the hallway, looking for any open door, anyone who could help get back to the ICU.

I came across an elevator that was moving up. I stood in front of it, praying that it would stop on this floor. When the elevator door opened, a lady delivering food trays was inside. She must have been startled by what she saw. There I stood, not having had a bath or a change of clothes in more than five days, crumpled and wrinkled, and crying and asking her, "Please, can you help me get back to 10 ICU #14? It's my husband's room. Please?"

Thankfully, she took me back to 10 ICU and David's nurse met me at the door. "Oh, honey!" she said. "You look exhausted. Come back to the room and I'll fix you up."

As I walked into Room 14, I was overcome by the feeling of emptiness and quiet. I stood in the middle of the room where David's gurney should have been, unable to move or talk. I felt so completely alone without him. I tried to pray, but my mind couldn't.

The nurse came back in with a small blow-up mattress. She put it on the floor where the gurney usually stayed and said, "David will be in surgery for several hours. Try to take a nap here. I'll make sure you're not disturbed."

I nodded and said that I would try. I laid down, covered by a hospital blanket, and tried to pray. I don't know if I slept or not, but memories of David kept running through my head. Seeing him smile the day we married, how proud he was to hold his new baby girl, how scared I was to tell him I had gotten a speeding ticket, and how he used to call me and say, "What's going on?", how he would stop by the grocery store and bring me a little bunch of flowers just because. Then I would picture how helpless he was now, not able to hold up his own head, and how he struggled to get even one breath.

We had been making plans to go to Switzerland for our 25th anniversary, just two short years away. Surely God would hear our prayers. He wouldn't let David die this young, would He? David had so much more living. He was a good, Christian man. Didn't God want those kinds of men on earth to help bring the Gospel to others? God just wouldn't let him die. He just wouldn't.

David went into surgery at 3:30 p.m. Around 7:00 p.m., I got news from the nurse that the surgery was going well and that David should be back in his room around 10 p.m.

Thank you, thank you, Lord! He is doing well!

I thought I would relax at the news, but I couldn't until I saw him. I just wanted to hold his hand, hear his voice, and see his smile again. I called everyone and let them know that the surgery went well and to thank God for this wonderful gift.

In my mind, after David healed from surgery, he would be his old self, just like Linda had been after her transplant. Back to work, back to our life, back to our plans for the future. He just needed time to heal.

Dr. Hoopes came to talk with me around 9:30 p.m. He explained that when he'd opened David up, it was apparent that the right lung had completely shrunken up and was about the size of a fist resting up against his shoulder blade. It was causing David's back muscles and trachea to be pulled sharply to the right. The doctor had not touched the right side in order to leave it for the second transplant.

The left lung was deeply scarred, too, but they were able to remove it without too many problems. The new lung was not a perfect fit, but it had attached nicely. It was bruised on the bottom lobe, but over time, the doctor thought it would heal itself. Dr. Hoopes said David had to be put on ECMO just before the surgery because he went into cardiac arrest. The ECMO machine line had been inserted through his left thigh and had allowed them the time to put in the new lung. There was no heart damage that the doctor could see, which was a good sign. David would be sore, but if we were lucky, he would be all right.

I asked Dr. Hoopes if David's transplant was similar to other transplants he had done and he answered, "David was a very sick man, and he got sick very quickly. Sometimes people who get sick quickly don't recover very quickly. Best thing we can do is pray that the lung works."

"Thank you, Dr. Hoopes. You are a blessing sent from God, because Mayo clinic had written him off. Thank you for saving my David."

He said something I will never forget. He said, "I'm not God, but I always pray that God uses me to help people." And I believe that is exactly what God used him for.

Shortly before midnight, David was brought back into 10 ICU Room 14. I thought I was prepared to see him after surgery, but I was still shocked when I was allowed into the room.

He was on a respirator, the mouthpiece held in place by tape across his mouth. The respirator machine was the height of the bed itself and stood on a tall pole. The noise it made was disturbing and loud. The head of David's bed was raised at a 45-degree angle, and nothing was covering him from the waist up.

In the bed with a huge band of gauze securely fastened around his chest that covered the hundreds of staples holding his incision together, David lay motionless. Several IV lines invaded his arms, and a very large arterial line in his neck had four or five valves attached to it. He now had two large IV poles, each one containing between ten and twelve bottles or bags that were connected to his arms.

On the left side of his bed was a rectangular box about two feet in diameter. The box had a glass middle section that was filling with a red fluid resembling blood. There were measurements on each side of the glass middle section. They were measuring how much blood was seeping from his incision. At the foot of his bed was a large, circular catheter bag.

As I walked over to his bedside, I found myself trying to be quiet in order not to wake him, but the nurse said, "Don't worry, we are keeping him out for a little while longer. You won't wake him."

I leaned over the bed rail and said, "You look great! I love you, David. You are going to be just fine. Just fine."

I sat down beside him, taking his hand in mine and being careful not to disturb any of the IV tubing. It was so good to feel his warm hand. I smiled and leaned my head back against the high-backed chair I was sitting in.

Things are going to be fine now, I thought. *God has given him a lung and now our life will go back to normal again.*

I fell asleep, holding his hand in mine, looking forward to when he could walk again without coughing.

CHAPTER 13

The next morning, the nurses were hoping to get David off the ventilator so he could start walking short distances. Dr. Hoopes came around before 6 a.m. and said things were looking pretty good. He explained that David would be weaned off the respirator and then the work of rehabilitating the new lung would begin. He said his team would take over from here, then he left the room.

I asked the nurse if that was the usual procedure, and she answered, "If you are seeing Hoopes in your room, then things are going badly. Patients doing well don't need to see Hoopes." She smiled and added, "He's the best, you know."

I said, "Yes he is. We are so blessed."

During the morning, Linda, Mary, and our daughter, Briana, arrived. They were very happy to see

David and just as stunned as I was to see numerous machines surrounding his bed and connected to him. Except for Linda. She was not stunned since knew firsthand what lung transplantation was about.

David was taken off the ventilator around noon on Tuesday, April 20th. He was very sore and still seemed to be short of breath. When I asked the nurse about his struggle to breathe, she said that was normal for some patients.

"When your body gets sick, the brain learns to adapt to the changes. David's brain learned to adjust when his lungs couldn't breathe. That adjustment meant breathing in and out very, very quickly. It will take time for David's brain to re-learn that it has a lung and that it can breathe properly," she explained.

That made sense. Still, seeing him continue to struggle to breathe after having gone through a transplant was very difficult. And David wasn't the happiest camper either.

The first time the nurse got David up to walk, he could only make it from the bed to the door and back. That took some ten minutes, but he made it. He was still in a good deal of pain, but trying to cooperate with the nurses, respiratory therapists, and the interns.

I constantly asked the nurse on duty what David's vitals were and his oxygen level number. I so wanted him to get better, and he was struggling so very hard. I watched other transplant patients walking the hallways and they seemed to be getting along much better than David.

In the afternoon, we met the woman who was to be our social worker. I was taken back just a bit, unaware that we needed a social worker. She was very gracious, telling us if we needed help or wanted to have other transplant patients come by and tell us their story, she could arrange that.

David was alert much of the time now and, after the social worker left, he spoke to me in a weaker version of his voice, saying, "Did you ask for her?" I replied no, that it must be standard practice for UCSF to ask a social worker to contact transplant patients. I really didn't think much more about it.

Two more days went by and David was still struggling to breathe. He would take many short little breaths and would pant as if he had been running a marathon. Each day I asked the pulmonologists if everything was all right. Each day David had a chest x-ray and blood work, and things looked like they were going in the right direction.

I kept telling David that it just takes time to re-train your mind and body. Since the surgery, he had become somewhat moody and blue, but that was to be expected after going through the amount of trauma he experienced. I tried to reassure him, but I wasn't sure he believed me.

Usually, Dr. Hoopes wanted his patients to get out

of ICU as soon as possible, due to the types of germs and fungus that live in the ICU units. His patients were at greater risk of infection since they were immune suppressed. After patients progressed and could walk well without oxygen, they were transferred to another wing on the 10th floor called '10 Long'. That was intermediate care where patients stayed shortly before being dismissed to go home, and every patient worked hard to get to 10 Long.

It was Saturday, April 23rd, and our family had gone back home thinking everything was going well. David had been trying to walk and eat for four days. Still, he labored to catch his breath and begin a normal breathing pattern.

Around 1 p.m., I was surprised when his nurse came into the room and said, "David, you are being moved to 10 Long."

David smiled, but I looked at the nurse and asked, "Are you sure? He is still struggling to breathe."

The nurse looked puzzled too and said, "I'm surprised too, but they want to get him away from the ICU unit as soon as possible."

I asked if the nurse would double check these orders since it was Saturday and usually only one doctor was on call on weekends. I didn't have peace about this move and was frightened that David would get worse if he didn't have constant monitoring. Then what would we do?

The nurse double checked the chart and assured me that David was to go to 10 Long. So, at 3 p.m., I gathered up our belongings, and the nurse came to walk David to the other side of the 10th floor.

David had a look of worry on his face and said, "I don't think I can walk that far. Can I go in a wheelchair?"

The nurse nodded and brought a wheelchair for him. As David was still connected to several IVs, it was no easy task getting him into the chair with all of that paraphernalia. Finally, we walked out of Room 14, and I prayed it would be the last time we ever saw the ICU again.

The rooms in 10 Long were large and more like a regular hospital room. David's room was on one end of the hall and the nurses' station was in the middle of the hallway. In 10 Long, nurses only checked on patients a few times during the day and took vitals at the change of shifts, since the idea was that the patients were improving each day and would be going home shortly.

As David was getting out of the wheelchair and into his new hospital bed, the 10 Long nurse told me to go get the rest of our things from ICU. It would take her a couple of minutes to check his vitals and get him settled.

Okay, I thought. *It shouldn't take me very long to get to ICU and back again.*

I walked quickly back to the ICU, where they were

already cleaning David's room, readying it for another patient. I thanked each of the nurses that had been so kind to us and asked God's blessings upon each of them and their families. I was heading back to 10 Long when suddenly I had this sick feeling in the pit of my stomach. I jogged down the hallway and reached David's room to find the door closed and no nurse inside. David was leaning back against the pillow with a grimace on his face.

"Sweetie, are you okay?" I asked.

He closed his eyes and began sweating profusely. He said, "I have such a horrible pain in the top of my shoulder." He pointed to his left shoulder and the sweat began dripping from his face and arm.

Oh dear God! "David, I'm calling the nurse."

He looked at me with determination and said, "No, wait. It's probably because I've been moving more than usual. I'm not going back to ICU."

I knew he could see that my face had turned white, but he once again looked me in the eye and said, "Give me a chance here. I'm not going back to ICU."

At that moment, a respiratory therapist came into the room to give David a breathing treatment. I looked at him and said, "Please, get the nurse. Something is wrong and I'm not leaving David."

The therapist looked at us oddly and said, "You just got here, right? Didn't the nurse already check him out?" He walked closer to the bed and saw that David was dripping wet and that breathing was difficult for him.

"Please, go get the nurse!" I said again with panic in my voice. "Have them page Dr. Hoopes. He is David's doctor. He'll know what's wrong."

The therapist turned to leave and I looked at David. He had such disappointment in his eyes and the pain in his left shoulder was increasing. His breath was even more shallow than it had been just a few minutes before. I thought he was having a heart attack.

The nurse came back in with a somewhat bewildered look on her face and asked, "What's wrong?"

As she looked at the monitors and then at David, I said, "He says his left shoulder is hurting with sharp, shooting pains, and he is sweating profusely. He can't breathe well. We need to call Dr. Hoopes!"

She said she would page him for an emergency and left the room. I tried to comfort David and said under my breath, "Dear Lord, what is happening here? Bring the doctor now!"

Just as suddenly as it began, the sharp, shooting pains in his shoulder stopped, but his face was beet red, and his heart monitor was beeping loudly because his pressure was so high. It was only a couple of minutes when two of Dr. Hoopes' Fellows (doctors in training) came in the room. They were from the heart team and began examining David. They looked worried and said,

"Dr. Hoopes is in surgery, but we are paging the doctor who is in charge.

I thought to myself: *Surgery? Dear God, why are you putting Dr. Hoopes in surgery when David needs him?*

The two Fellows stepped outside and called someone. Within minutes, David's room was once again hopping and filled with nurses and doctors.

"David, we are going to do a CAT scan and heart scan," one doctor said as they wheeled the equipment into the room. "We don't know if you have had a heart attack or not."

The doctor looked at me and said, "Could you wait outside, please?"

I went outside but stood in the doorway so I could see and hear what was being said. The x-rays were done quickly and the machines and most doctors left. Only one nurse remained behind, monitoring David and taking blood.

"Don't worry, David. They can tell right away what is happening. You're in good hands." I was holding his hand and trying to be encouraging to him, but he looked so disappointed. He was frowning when the nurse's pager went off. She went outside the room to answer it and closed the door. I kept holding his hand, praying that this wasn't anything serious. I'm not sure how many minutes went by, but once again the door swung wide open and a team of four men came in with a different gurney. My heart sank.

"Mr. Bichler, we are here to take you downstairs. Dr. Hoopes wants to take a look at you," the nurse said as they began very quickly connecting tubes and machines and getting David on the gurney.

I picked up my backpack to follow when another team member said, "Mrs. Bichler, you better grab his things and go back to ICU. They are cleaning out a room for him."

I looked at David and he looked into my eyes with frustration and fear. "I love you, David. They are going to see what happened. You're just going back to ICU for a short time. I'll be waiting for you."

Before I could kiss him, the team had him out the door and down the hallway to the elevator. I turned around, looked at the room we had only spent about 20 minutes in, and tears began to flow. I prayed, "Dear God, let Dr. Hoopes find out what has happened."

I was able to grab our things quickly since I hadn't even had a chance to unpack them, and I headed back to the ICU. The words that a nurse had said earlier that morning were spinning in my head: "If you are seeing Dr. Hoopes in the room, things are going badly."

As I passed the nurses' station in 10 ICU, I saw David's name written once more on the white board with Hoopes name next to it. The nurse at the desk gave me a sad look and said, "We're so sorry, Mrs. Bichler. We heard what happened. David is such a good man and we are here for both of you." She gave me a hug and led me to Room 23. It was in the left hallway side of the ICU, past the station, while our first room, 14, had been in the right hallway. But it looked exactly the same.

Once again I walked into that empty room and felt lost. What was happening and why? I walked over to the window and stared down at the people milling around below on the street. We knew no one in the city of San Francisco and knew nothing at all about UCSF except that Linda had been transplanted here and was doing exceptionally well. Why was David having so much difficulty?

Thoughts and worries were swirling around in my mind as I stood there looking blankly out the window. *How long before I could see David?*

I heard footsteps coming down the hallway and turned around in hopes it was the team bringing David back to the room. Instead, I saw one of the pulmonologists on the transplant team coming into the room, and he was not smiling.

The doctor said, "Laura, as soon as Dr. Hoopes can get away from surgery, he will look at David. We've been in contact with him and he has ordered tests and a bronch which we are going to do in a few minutes. That's all we know at this time."

I was becoming very familiar with the word bronch. It was short for bronchoscopy, which is a procedure used to see inside the lungs by inserting a lighted tube down the patient's throat and into each side of the lung to check for bleeding and infection. The lighted tube or scope is a camera that projects pictures onto an attached computer monitor as the procedure is being done, allowing doctors to see exactly what is happening inside the lung. After a lung transplant, bronchs are done on a daily basis, gradually lessening to once a week, then once a month and so on.

"Thank you. When can I see David?"

The doctor answered, "I don't know. Check with the nurse. We'll try to keep her updated." He smiled a bit then turned to leave.

Okay, I thought to myself, *if they are doing a bronch, then something has happened to his new lung?* Did that mean it wasn't working anymore? Was his heart all right?

I called my family and the church to let them know what was happening, and then began pacing back and forth across the room, from the window back to the glass sliding doors. Over and over again. I couldn't sit down. I couldn't stand still. I walked and talked out loud to God. I told Him what was happening, that I was scared, and asked Him to let the doctors see what was wrong so they could correct it. I asked Him why this was happening to such a good man like David. I begged God to let him heal and get back to our life, just as He had done for Linda.

My ramblings jumped back and forth from asking

for healing to pleading for help and courage. I pleaded with God to somehow let me take David's place since I had been the one with a history of asthma. "David doesn't deserve this illness!" I shouted to God. "He leads Bible studies. He's an elder and leader at church. He is a good man!"

Pacing back and forth, I guess I thought God didn't know what was happening or that He wasn't understanding just how terrified I was and how much I needed David. All I could think to do was tell Him.

Hours passed and still no word about David or his condition. Surely his nurse had an abundance of patience, because I asked her about every half hour if she had heard anything. She would shake her head and say, "No." One time, she asked, "Who were you on the phone talking to? Sounded like you were giving them the third degree."

I stammered, "Oh! You heard that?" I apologized and sheepishly looked down at my feet. "I was talking to God."

She replied, "Well, He sure got an ear full."

Suddenly it dawned on me what I had done. I had been loudly demanding that God heal David right this instant! A huge wave of guilt came over me and I silently asked the good Lord to forgive me. Who was I to be telling Him anything?

At 11 p.m., the lights were turned down in the hallways of 10 ICU and the glow of light escaping from

Room 23 was ghostly bright and illuminating the stark emptiness that surrounded me.

Where was David? What was happening?

I stared at the hands on my watch. Midnight passed and no word. 1 a.m. passed and no word. 2 a.m. passed and still no word. Finally, at about 2:15 a.m., the nurse told me David was on his way up. I stood up and waited outside the door. *Thank you, dear Jesus!* My heart was once again racing and I just needed to see his big brown eyes and hear his voice, no matter how weak it sounded. *Just to hold his hand, Lord. I need to hold his hand!*

As the gurney came into view, there were six people surrounding it, each one pushing an IV pole or oxygen monitor or holding IV bags. I could barely see the top of David's head over the railing, but the blue plastic tubing that was arching out of his mouth made my heart break and took my breath away. Intubated. David was on the ventilator once again. Once more he was not breathing on his own. Tears began streaming down my cheeks. What in the world had gone wrong?

It took more than a few minutes for the team to settle David back into the room, connecting and calibrating each machine, adjusting the pressures and taking more vitals. I tugged on the arm of the intern who was on duty and said, "What happened? Why is he back on the ventilator? Where is Dr. Hoopes?"

He walked me back into the hallway and said, "Dr.

Hoopes will be coming up here soon, but we think that David had a massive pulmonary embolism."

I blinked back tears and asked, "You mean he had a blood clot? Was it in the new lung?"

"We're not sure how much damage there is, but the scan shows the top portion of the left lung whited-out," the intern replied.

I asked quickly, "What do you mean it is 'whited-out'?"

"It means that it's dead, no blood circulating," the intern said as he walked over to the nurse.

The word *dead* hit me like a ton of bricks and I felt the blood rush from my head to my feet.

The nurse grabbed my arm and said, "Oh, my dear, sit down here before you faint!" She brought me a cup of water while I sat in her chair, stunned and in shock. Dead. No blood circulating. Dead. How was he going to breathe? Would the lung recover from the damage?

While the team was still working with David in his room, Dr. Hoopes came down the hallway. He briefly stopped by the chair where I was sitting and said, "Let me check on him and then I can talk with you." All I could do was nod.

Dr. Hoopes checked the ventilator settings, the multiple drips connected to David's IV, and his oxygen level, and then sat on the bed next to David. He looked right in his face, listening to and watching his breathing. The doctor was still dressed in his scrubs and still had a few stains that looked like blood on his coat.

I managed to get out of the chair and walk over to Dr. Hoopes. "What has happened? What has gone wrong?"

Dr. Hoopes stood up and in his soft voice began to explain that David had indeed had a massive pulmonary embolism.

"Deep venous thrombosis is the formation of a blood clot in a vein that is deep inside a part of the body, usually the legs. DVT mainly affects the large veins in the lower leg and thigh. The clot can block blood flow and cause swelling and pain. When a clot breaks off and moves through the bloodstream, it's called an embolism. An embolism can get stuck in the brain, lungs, heart, or another area."

I was trying to comprehend what he was saying as he continued. "David had a clot that probably started in his left thigh where the ECMO had been inserted. He threw hundreds of clots and, luckily for him, most of them went into the right lung, which is shriveled and worthless anyway. Most people who have a massive pulmonary embolism do not survive. He was very lucky."

I glanced over at David, and then back to Dr. Hoopes.

"The intern told me the new lung or top of the lung

left was 'whited-out.' Does that mean it's dead? Will it heal?"

Dr. Hoopes hurried to answer. "There is only one embolus that appears to have gone into the top of the left lung, and the spot where it occurred was destroyed. That spot will not recover. Luckily, the bottom lobe was not affected." He continued, "We are just going to have to wait and see how he does. It definitely set him back in his recovery." At that moment his pager went off and he quickly walked out of 10 ICU.

CHAPTER 14

D avid's condition did not change until late the next afternoon. I had tried to sleep in a chair next to the head of the bed so I could hold onto David's left hand. I knew I needed a spit bath. The ICU room was equipped with a restroom and I would wash my face each day and try to dab on deodorant, but it had been more than a week since I had washed my hair, and I certainly looked the worse for wear.

But anytime I had to wait outside Room 23, I felt a fear that something would happen and I wouldn't be there to help David. The nurses were wonderful, however, and would bring a food tray for me even though I had little appetite, and each of the doctors on the transplant team had come by to see David during the day, telling me how sorry they were about the night's turn of events.

Then, the next afternoon, a new alert sound fired out of the heart monitoring device. I had grown accustomed to the humming and beeping of the ten or more monitoring devices attached to David, but this time he began to wake up and struggle with the ventilator tube. Suddenly a loud, shrill alarm honked from the ventilator machine standing next to the bedside.

Immediately the nurse came to see what was happening. She tried to calm David by patting his shoulder and saying, "David, try not to fight the ventilator. Stay calm and let it breathe for you." He was gagging but tried to calm down and breathe with the rhythm of the machine.

The nurse looked at me and said, "One of the doctors is on the floor. I'll see if we can take him off the ventilator."

She looked again at David, trying to calm him. "Don't fight the machine. Relax and the gagging will stop."

David had opened his eyes and now closed them again.

The week before, when David had begun to wake up while on the ventilator, he would raise up his right hand and, with his thumb and first two fingers clamped together, he would wiggle them. It had dawned on me that he wanted to hold his pen! He wanted to write something!

The nurse had brought out a piece of paper and a pen, and I'd put the pen between David's fingers and lowered his hand onto the bed where I had placed the paper. With his eyes still closed and because he was still on the ventilator, his first words had not been legible, just squiggles across the paper. But he held that pen and wrote for hours. Finally, I could begin to make out his scribbles.

His first words were: "Thank you, Dr. Hoopes." I remember everyone in the room was in tears. He was still on the ventilator, still had his eyes closed, and yet still had the presence of mind to thank the doctor!

This afternoon, he once again put his hand in the air to motion that he wanted a pen and paper. I placed the pen in his hand and put the paper on the bed. "Something is cutting my throat," he wrote.

The nurse had come back in with the doctor, and I quickly showed them the note and asked, "Is the ventilator cutting his throat?"

The doctor leaned over the bed and said, "David, hold on a couple more minutes. We are going to take you off the ventilator, but you will have to work to breathe on your own. Do you think you can do that?"

David nodded 'yes' and began to gag once more. The doctor removed the ventilator and immediately David's oxygen level began dropping. The nurse had another nose cannula on him within seconds and his saturation rate leveled at 85.

"We're going to have to watch him carefully," the doctor said. He turned to David and explained, "You had a massive pulmonary embolism yesterday. We intubated you to help the lung recover. You must try to breathe as deeply as possible or you may have to go back on the ventilator."

David nodded that he understood.

For the next two days, David's recovery went well. He began sitting in a chair for a few minutes at a time, even though he still had rapid, shallow breath patterns. We prayed together often, and I felt that the worst was over. It would take longer for David to regain his strength than we'd thought, but he was going to be fine.

Sitting in ICU, the days and nights blurred into each other, and I was surprised the morning our nurse came into the room and said, "Well, happy May Day." *May? What happened to April?* Had it really been a month since David collapsed at home on April 4th?

David had been walking the hallways and his struggle to breathe was still a worry. He was sitting in a chair beside the bed, catching his breath after his 11:30 a.m. walk, when he suddenly reached out his hand for me and said, "Help me stand, something is terribly wrong."

I grabbed his hand as several monitors began

blaring alarms at the same time. He was pale and his hands were shaking. Immediately his room was filled with several nurses who had heard the alarms. His heart rate had escalated to well over 184 beats per minute.

The nurses quickly got him back into the bed and summoned the transplant team. David had gone into 'a-fib' or atrial fibrillation. His heart was beating much too fast, causing very poor blood flow to and from the heart. The doctors added another medication to his IV in hopes it would stop his heart from racing and put it back into a normal or sinus rhythm.

Over the next few days, David went in and out of a-fib. Nothing seemed to stabilize his heartbeat. He tried to remain positive, but many days were spent reading Bible verses and questioning why God had put this upon him. He would read his Bible, underline verses and then put the date beside them.

During these same days, David had begun to receive get well cards from the members of Trinity Lutheran. Each day, not one or two cards would arrive, but six or seven cards would be delivered to his room. We read each one over and over again, thanking God for these prayer warriors who continually lifted our needs to Him.

It was May 17th and the day's Bible verse was Psalm 39, verse 12: "Hear my prayer, O Lord; listen to my cry for help; be not deaf to my weeping."

Today, David was hoping to be released from the ICU for a return to 10 Long. The reality of life as a transplant patient began to hit us when the transplant team pharmacist came into David's room that morning.

She gave us a handbook to read through and learn, complete with a medication list that would be David's lifeline for the rest of his life. We were to learn their names, what they were used for, and when to take them.

She gave us a blue, two-sided paper entitled "UCSF Heart & Lung Transplant Medicines for: David Bichler." There were instructions across the top and then the list of medications: Prednisone, Cellcept, Prograf, Septra, Valcyte, Vfend, Mycelex, Amphotericin B, Tobramycin, Aciphex, Calcium, Actonel, Advair, Ventolin, Magnesium Oxide, Lipitor, Lopressor, Amiodarone, Lovenox, Vicodin, Zolpidem, and a multivitamin. Twenty-two in all and that was just the beginning!

David's eyes grew wide and his complete disbelief was extremely apparent. He asked the pharmacist, "You're kidding, right? I take these everyday?"

She smiled and said, "Some are taken more than once a day. You'll get the hang of when to take them. We've been giving them to you, but now it's time you and your wife take this over. You'll be receiving your toolbox and first order of meds tomorrow. We want you to be able to go home soon."

As it turned out, every transplant patient, shortly before going home, was given a plastic toolbox. Inside would be their medicines, Tylenol, small plastic pill cups and their list of medications.

David studied his own list for a long while and then began to make notes. He made a chart, complete with times of the day to take each one and their generic names. Very systematic.

I smiled and said, "See! Aren't you glad you're an engineer? Everything logically laid out for you!" I laughed.

He smiled and, as he pretended to put his pen in his pocket, he answered, "Yep. But where is my pocket protector when I need it?"

Just the thought of being released from ICU brought our hopes up and that evening David's mood brightened. I still slept in the chair next to the bed and, as I nestled down for the night, I took his hand and we prayed that the Lord grant him healing and to be released soon. We both fell asleep to the beeping of the heart monitor.

During the night, David's temperature spiked and he was once again sweating profusely. He was back in a-fib and the nurses paged Dr. Hoopes. David's breathing was labored and he was visibly in trouble.

Dr. Hoopes examined him around 3:00 a.m. and shook his head in disbelief.

"I'm not sure what's going on, but we need to intubate him again as soon as possible," Dr. Hoopes said as he began giving orders to the nurse and other doctors who were with him.

David was struggling, and I stood by his bed, holding his hand and wiping his forehead with a damp cloth.

A few minutes later, Dr. Hoopes reappeared but, this time, he came with some twenty doctors, nurses, interns, fellows, etc. I was ushered out of the room and every one of the twenty crowded around David's bedside.

Confused and scared, I asked the nurse what was happening.

She said, "Dr. Hoopes is going to do a tracheal intubation right in David's room. Anytime Dr. Hoopes does surgery, every medical student, nurse, and surgeon wants to watch. He's a genius."

As I watched from the hallway, Dr. Hoopes, with his team watching, made a small hole in the base of David's neck for placement of a flexible metal tube into the trachea (windpipe).

The tube would maintain an open airway or serve as a conduit through which to administer oxygen. Tracheal intubation is frequently performed in critically-injured, ill, or anesthetized patients to facilitate ventilation of the lungs and to prevent the possibility of asphyxiation or airway obstruction.

The procedure took less than ten minutes, and David was again hooked up to a ventilator, except, this time, the tube connected through his neck, not through his mouth. Dr. Hoopes, who was on his way down to do a heart/lung transplant, said to me as he left David's room, "This trach will prevent more injury to his throat and it will allow him to be more mobile. We have to get fluid off him."

"Thank you, Dr. Hoopes," I answered and returned to David's side, taking his hand in mine and praying for God to heal him. I prayed the Lord's Prayer, sat down in the chair to cry and thought, *What is God's plan? Why is this happening? Dear Lord, help us.*

Each day of the next week was the same routine. More medicines, more IV's, more a-fib. At least David could mouth words and write since having the trach. The ventilator was blowing air directly into his windpipe, bypassing his vocal chords.

His weight was down to 168 pounds and the skin fell in loose folds around his face, neck, and arms. He tried to eat, but said food had no taste. I was now being told that I could not sleep in David's room any longer.

I shared this information with our Trinity family and God provided an answer. Chris, a man who had served on the Board of Parish Education with me called with the answer: Aunt Margie and Uncle Don.

His Aunt Margie and Uncle Don lived only a few blocks away from the hospital and would be happy to let me stay at night in their home. I was overcome by their hospitality and readily accepted. They came to see David and meet me, and I believe to this day that they were both angels.

Margie was the aunt of a fellow teacher of mine named Sandy at Trinity. I had taught her son in my band classes. Sandy and Chris conveyed our story to them. They opened their home to me as if I was their daughter. Each night around 9:30 p.m., Margie and Don would drive to the hospital entrance and pick me up. Margie had told her neighbors about David, and they had organized a plan to take me back to the hospital by 6 a.m. each morning. They were a Godsend and little did I know what important role they would play in our lives.

Memorial Day weekend arrived. It was dreary, rainy and cold. By this date, word had spread that David had the 'Murphy's Law' syndrome. If something could go wrong, it would go wrong with him. One orderly, while delivering supplies to David's room said, "Oh! You're the guy they call Murphy."

David smiled.

The doctors had decided David needed a stomach wrap since he had horrific bouts of acid reflux. In fact, over the past several years, information showed that many patients who had been placed on the lung transplant list had injured their lungs from acid reflux. With as much trouble as David had experienced already, the doctors didn't want to take any chances he might have reflux acid get down into his lungs and start the scarring process over again.

A stomach wrap is where the upper part of the stomach is wrapped around the end of the esophagus to strengthen the esophageal sphincter valve, to prevent acid reflux, and to repair a hiatal hernia. The procedure is commonly done using a laparoscope, which requires tiny incisions in the abdomen so as to insert a small camera. The pulmonary doctors had decided it best to keep David in the hospital until he could recover from the procedure.

Several tests had to be done before the gastro surgeon would perform the operation, though. David needed a 24-hour ph test which required a long tube to be inserted through the nostril and down into the stomach to measure the amount of acidity over a twenty-four hour period. This test was only done in the facility located across the street from the hospital, however.

On May 30th, with rain lightly falling on us, a nurse and I pushed David in a wheelchair, equipped with oxygen, across the street to have the tube inserted. Or rather, the nurse was pushing David and I was trying to cover him with an umbrella.

We had stopped to wait for the traffic light to turn

when David grabbed my hand and mouthed the words, "Let the rain hit me." I realized it was the first time David had been out of a hospital in two months. I lowered the umbrella for a moment while he closed his eyes and turned the palms of his hands upward to feel the rain. The nurse reminded us that David was immune suppressed and probably shouldn't be playing in the rain, so I put the umbrella over him once again.

The ph test was completed and the surgery was set for the following day. The gastro surgeon came by our room to meet David and answer any questions we might have. He seemed pleasant until he began reading David's medical chart. His tone changed to a deeper, more concerned tone.

David and I had a strange feeling after he left the room. Sure enough, after seeing the many complications David had experienced, he wanted one more precaution put in place to protect himself should anything happen to David. He decided David needed a filter placed in his leg where the original clots had formed. The filter would prevent clots from forming during the procedure. There were many risks involved in the filter placement, none of which was small. Another obstacle in his recovery.

By this time, David was walking better each day and had been weaned off the respirator for a third time. He wore a clear, plastic bandage over the hole where the trach tube had been placed. Every time he tried to talk, the plastic cover would fill with air around the hole. He still had a terrible cough that always left him gagging. We were told that was because the old right lung had pulled his trachea so far to the right that it caused major irritation. He would have all the symptoms of pulmonary fibrosis until that second lung was transplanted.

David and I prayed that he could finally be released from the hospital and, on the morning of June 20th, one of the pulmonary team doctors who was checking David's status said, "David, I think you can leave the hospital, but you must be within a twenty-minute drive from here for at least two more months. What do you think?"

David's eyes began to fill with tears as he smiled, put his hand out to shake the doctor's hand and began nodding in approval. I couldn't believe it! David and I prayed and cried when the doctor left the room, and we began to make plans as to where we would go.

When we talked about it to Don, he mentioned a large apartment complex called Parkmerced Villas and offered to take me there to look. Later that day, I hugged David and climbed into the hospital bed beside him. We slept side by side that night, thanking God and praising Him for the gift He had given us.

CHAPTER 15

We woke up early, not due to our excitement that David would be leaving the hospital, but to a large mass sticking up from David's left thigh. It was the incision that was made when the doctors put David on life support during the transplant. The wound had not completely closed. It was a bright purple color and it looked like a baseball was under his skin. His and my heart sank as we knew this meant he would not be released as we had hoped.

This large mass was enough for the nurse to page Dr. Hoopes. He examined David minutes after receiving the page and said, "I think this might be a lymph gland that was cut in half at the incision sight. The fluid is most likely from the lymph gland." The mass suddenly ruptured when Dr. Hoopes pushed on it and lymphatic fluid shot into the air.

David and Dr. Hoopes looked at each other as if to say, "What could possibly happen next?"

It was decided that the risk of performing surgery on the gland was too great at this time. Dr. Hoopes was hoping it would heal itself. He looked at David again and said, "Better stay in for a couple more days since it is an open incision."

Horribly, this was not the worst news we were to receive that day. Around 10 a.m., a representative from the financial department came to our room. Her name was Sherry and she wanted to discuss our account with me. She and I stepped out of the room and walked a short distance down the hallway to the nurses' lunch area. As I sat down, I said, "Joanie is our transplant coordinator. Maybe you should be talking with her. She has been terrific through this entire transplant."

Sherry opened a black zipper folder and said without looking up, "I've already alerted her."

Alerted her? My stomach began churning. During the next few minutes, Sherry laid out some thirty or forty pages of billing statements, saying that this was only a partial bill Since his admittance on April 12th, David had accumulated a very long list of charges, more than a typical transplant patient.

"After all, Mrs. Bichler," she said, "your husband has

had many complications requiring highly specialized care."

I blinked my eyes and opened my mouth to speak, but Sherry continued by saying, "Now, our estimates show that as of the end of August, you will have maxed out your insurance coverage. How do you plan on paying for the remaining charges?"

My mouth went dry and I am sure I looked like someone had just thrown ice-cold water in my face. "What?" I said as I sat straight up in the chair. "That can't be! We have a transplant umbrella that gives us a reduced rate for the first ninety days after transplant. How in the world could we be close to our lifetime maximum of insurance coverage? There must be a mistake here."

Sherry dismissed my objection and continued talking with a monotone pitch to her voice. "You'll need to come down to my office first thing in the morning to put a payment plan in place. As you may know, all charges have to be cleared up before any patient will be considered for a transplant. They do plan a second transplant for your husband, don't they?"

For a moment, I was completely speechless. I found myself talking quickly and a bit louder. "I need to call Joanie right away. There is no way we can be close to that maximum. It's one million dollars!" I blurted out.

Sherry nodded and replied, "I'll leave this partial

statement with you. Please come to the financial office on the first floor tomorrow morning. We can discuss more at that time." She smiled, picked up her black zipper folder, and left the room.

I sat there staring down at the inch thick stack of papers. I flipped through one corner edge of the pages, listening to the noise they made as they flipped quickly by and thinking that Joanie would have the answer. I picked up the stack and headed back to David's room. He could see by the look on my face that something had happened and he saw the stack of papers I was holding.

"What's going on?" he asked in a raspy voice.

I quickly shared with him that the financial office needed a little more information and that I would be calling Joanie to help straighten it out. He didn't buy this answer at all. He motioned for me to give him the papers. I hesitated, knowing it would upset him. His eyes narrowed and lines began forming between his forehead and his eyebrows. His face became red, which made his blood pressure set off all sorts of alarms.

I explained to him what Sherry had said and tried to calm him. "Don't worry," I said as I put the papers into my backpack, "Joanie will have answers. Things will be fine. God loves us. Trust in Him. He'll help us." I tried to sound convincing, but my heart was not really in it.

When I spoke with Joanie, she confirmed most of what Sherry had said and told me she was working very hard to resolve any issues. It gave David and me a sense of peace. This would be fine. David would be fine. Our life together would be fine.

Don Elliott, still thinking David would be released soon, planned to take me to see the Parkmerced Villas later in the afternoon. The Parkmerced was a large complex of tower apartments, townhomes, flats, and single story rentals located immediately off Highway 1 and only a few minutes drive from the hospital.

David wasn't ready to navigate too many steps, so I found a small, one bedroom apartment in one of the many towers. It was called 55 Chumansaro Drive, and the elevator inside took us to Floor 1, Apartment A.

Each floor had two wings with a circle of four apartments in each wing. The smell of Chinese food was strong in this wing and voices from other residents echoed off the walls. The apartment was about six hundred square feet, completely empty and very close to the elevator. It would work for us and the elevator would help David get around. I knew that we would only need this space for a short while, so I signed the papers and agreed to the monthly rental rate of $1895.00. With the recent conversation about our insurance coverage running through my mind, my hand shook as I wrote out the check.

The next morning I was standing in front of the

financial office armed with Joanie's number and my cell phone when the doors opened. The office was a large room with many blue padded armchairs and several small round tables with magazines on them.

I gave my name at the front desk and said I had an appointment with Sherry. Immediately I was ushered through a small hallway between rows of cubicles. Sherry was sitting in the cubicle with the letters "A-B" on the outside wall. The workspace was only large enough for Sherry's chair, desk, computer, and one visitor chair. There was not much privacy in this maze of cubicles and the room was filled with people's voices and the sound of typing on keyboards.

I had prayed that God would give me strength and courage to calmly solve this insurance issue. Sherry didn't look up from her computer as I sat down in the visitor chair, but managed to say, "Good morning. I'll be right with you." I could see she was viewing David's account and I sat patiently waiting for her to begin the conversation.

After a couple of minutes, she turned her chair halfway from the computer screen, crossed her legs, and asked, "Were you able to come up with a payment plan or do you want to deprive your husband of a second transplant?"

Startled, my eyes began stinging and drops of tears fell on my cheeks. "What?" I managed to say, choking while trying to clear my throat. "I need a moment please," I muttered as I cried into the sleeve of my shirt.

"Sure," she said and handed me a tissue from the box on her desk.

Tears uncontrollably streamed down my face and I could not stop them. Didn't she realize I would do anything to save David? Couldn't she see that he was my life? I cleared my throat and through my tears I said, "Why would you say something like that to me? I would never stand in the way of a second transplant for David!"

Sherry, not responding directly to my question, continued by saying, "I'm sorry that your husband has had so many complications, but transplants are not cheap."

I was still stunned at the way this conversation was going and sat there dabbing my eyes while she spoke. "The umbrella agreement for the transplant will end after ninety days, which will be July 19th. We have projected what the average follow-up visits, blood tests, clinic visits, and so on, are for each transplant patient and, with the current charges your husband has incurred, we fully expected you to surpass the lifetime maximum of coverage by the end of August."

Tears were still streaming down my face like a water faucet filling a sink. "Our transplant coordinator, Joanie, is investigating this situation. Have you spoken to her?"

Sherry nodded 'yes.'

I pleaded, "How could we use up the lifetime maximum? It just isn't possible!"

She pointed to the computer screen and said, "As of today, your husband's bill is over $700,000 and many of the claims are yet to be processed. Medical treatment is expensive, as you can see."

I leaned forward, putting my head in my hands, still unable to stop the tears or understand how this could be possible.

Sherry patted me lightly on the head and said, "Oh, don't worry. You are not the first family to be in this position. You do have options."

Options? What options?

I raised my head up and sat back in the chair, blotting my tears while she began to lay out three options: We could use any or all of the savings we had accumulated over the last 23 years to pay the balance; we could try to raise around $400,000, which was the deposit required on a lung transplants for patients without insurance; or we could choose not to go through with a second transplant.

I tried to pray. I prayed that I would wake up and find this a horrible nightmare. I prayed to get out of that cubicle. I prayed to be in the room holding David's hand again. *Why was this happening?*

"Sherry, we have never been in debt. I will do anything to give David a new set of lungs and see him breathing easily again. Anything! This can't be happening." I shook my head as another stream of tears began dripping off my chin. The front of my shirt was wet where the tears had gathered.

Sherry sat back in her chair, looking into my face. She was quiet for a moment, then said, "Well, you have a little time. I'll keep in contact with your transplant coordinator and your account. Let's wait and see what can be done." She turned back to the computer screen as if she were dismissing me.

I left the cubicle to find the nearest bathroom. I couldn't let David see me this way. I had to be brave. David had always handled our finances, laughingly giving me a '$20 allowance' each payday. He'd smile and say, "Now, don't spend it all in one place," then give me a big hug. How was I going to find hundreds of thousands of dollars?

After I washed my face, I prayed out loud to the Lord, raising my hands in the air and saying, "Dear God, why have You put another obstacle in the way of David's recovery? Hasn't he suffered enough? We are faithful to You and our church. We pray for Your guidance. We don't drink or smoke or waste the blessings You have given us. Why God? Why? You are the great Healer! Why won't You heal David?"

David was sitting up in bed underlining a Bible verse when I sat down beside him. His look told me he was waiting for me to explain what I had learned. I smiled and said that we had options available to us, but first we had to concentrate on getting him released from the hospital. And that is what we did.

The lymph gland on his left thigh was still draining, and David was chomping at the bit to get released. Somehow, when the doctor came for his regular morning rounds the next day, David made his case that he would be at less risk outside of the ICU. He firmly told the doctor that he knew he could heal faster away from the hospital. The doctor looked closely at him while he talked and surprisingly agreed with him. He said, "Let me talk it over with the team. Maybe we can get you out of here this afternoon."

That was music to our ears!

David nodded his head and said, 'thank you,' his entire being seeming to relax just a bit.

The team agreed and, by 3 p.m., Don and Margie had parked their minivan in the circle drive entrance to UCSF and were waiting for David to be wheeled out the glass doors. David and I knew that the apartment was empty, but Margie was bringing over a blowup mattress for us to sleep on that night. Tomorrow I could look for garage sales to find just a few things we might need.

The day was June 20th and, as usual, the fog was beginning to roll in from the ocean, making things dreary and cool. Margie told us that when she saw David sitting in the wheelchair, his face glowed as he passed through the doors, making it seem like a sunny, bright day in San Francisco. He was so happy to leave that hospital!

The van was filled from top to bottom with green oxygen tanks (large ones and smaller portable ones), hospital supplies, David's toolbox and several other boxes full of medicines, three boxes of get-well cards, a backpack and a small suitcase, plus the four adults. It didn't matter how crowded we were; David was all smiles and his eyes sparkled as they filled with tears. All the jostling of the move had caused him to have a coughing spell and left him feeling a bit weak, but he said it was definitely worth any amount of coughing to be free from the hospital.

We pulled up in front of 55 Chumansaro and began the work of unloading the minivan. Don helped David out of the back seat and steadied him as he got his balance. Margie and I walked behind them as we entered the elevator to ride up to the first floor. When the door opened, I moved ahead to unlock the door for us. When I opened the door, I dropped my backpack and stared into the small room as, once again, tears began filling my eyes. Inside that empty apartment was a card table with two chairs, a throw rug on the floor, two lawn chairs, a lamp, a television, and a few pots and pans sitting on the kitchen counter.

"Oh my goodness!" I managed to say and turned to

see David standing in the doorway crying too. "Where did these things come from?" I asked.

Margie and Don were grinning, and Margie said, "Our street had a garage sale last week and these things were left over. Everyone agreed you should use them. When you get to go home, we'll donate them to the church." She laughed and smiled as she surveyed the room. "Don and I spent this morning readying your new home for you!" she beamed.

Don had the biggest grin on his face. "You know Margie is a go-getter," he laughed.

David and I were speechless. We hugged them both and said thank you many, many times. God sent Don and Margie to us during this time and we were so blessed by their kindness and love. Angels. They were both angels.

That night as we slept beside each other in the two lawn chairs, we held hands like we always did and prayed a prayer of thanksgiving for Margie and Don and for the many friends on their street who had been so gracious to us. And I prayed for God's mercy and forgiveness for the anger and frustration I had shown toward Him over the last days.

David squeezed my hand and said, "Joshua 1:9, Laura. 'Be courageous for the Lord your God will never leave you.'" He smiled and said before closing his eyes, "I know God is providing for us. He is in our lives. We need to remember that. What more do we need to ask for?"

For a few moments all the fear, frustration, and worry in my heart and mind subsided and I felt at home holding David's hand. With a big sigh, I closed my eyes, knowing that all would be okay. The worst was behind us.

Young married David and Laura Dec 1982

David, Linda, Mary in late 2003 just a few months before Linda's double lung transplant. (above).

October 3, 2005 - David's first day back at work in Wausau, Wisconsin. He went from 230 pounds to 150 pounds, size 38 to size 32, in two months time. (left)

David and I at Bamff in January 2004.

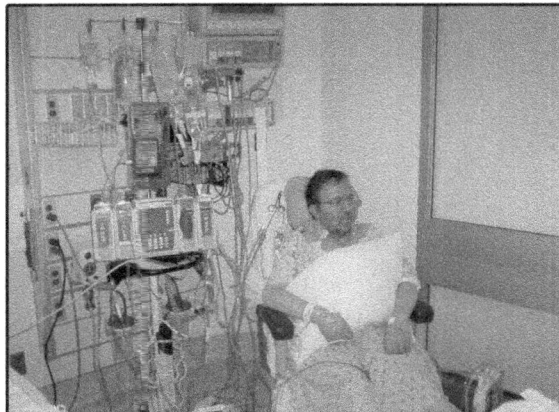

David one day after the second transplant in 2007.

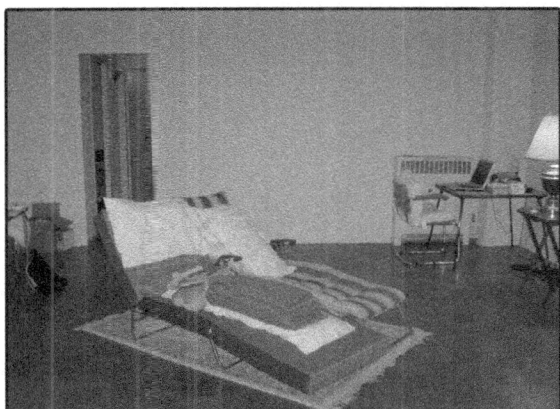

The apartment in San Francisco where we lived during the first transplant. Our bed was the two lawn chairs. (above)

David's first walk after surgery. (below)

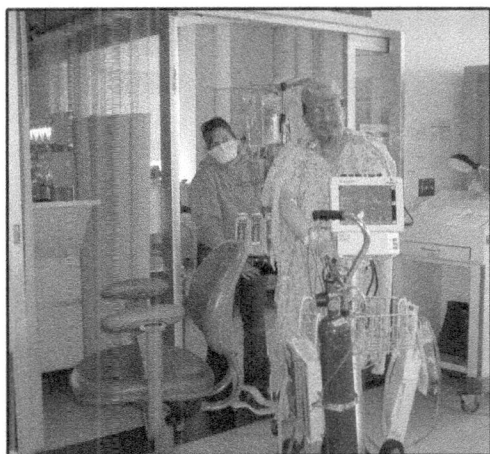

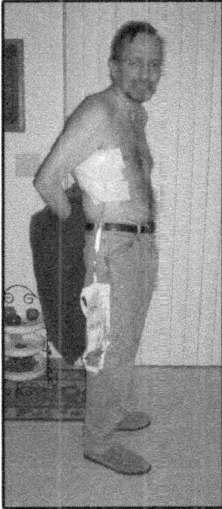

David's first bronch booboo.
Wausau, January 4, 2006
(left)

Laura and David
walking Spreckles Lake
(below)

CHAPTER 16

W e hadn't had a daily routine since David became ill four months before and waking up in Apartment 1A of 55 Chumansaro was the beginning of a new adventure for us: post-transplant maintenance.

For the next two months, our daily schedule revolved around appointments at the hospital, and the engineer in David took over the organization of the schedule. He drew a chart on a piece of paper that had every time, place, test, and doctor he was to see and he taped it to the wall next to the door of the apartment.

Blood draws and lab work by 8 a.m. each morning; bronch once a week; clinic appointments on Tuesdays; pulmonary function activities on Wednesday; home health care nurse on Mondays and Fridays; and he had written "Church" on Sundays.

David's employer sent, by FedEx, his work computer, files, drawings, etc., for David to begin working at the apartment as soon as he could. That was a Godsend because work kept his mind off his illness. His weight was just under 150 lbs. and he looked like a Hollywood version of a hillbilly as he tried to keep his size 38 jeans from falling off by using one of his neckties as a belt. His arms looked like toothpicks sticking out of his shirts. Even his shoes seemed too big!

A major part of David's post-transplant recovery was to walk and build up his lung capacity. He still took short, shallow breaths as his mind had grown accustomed to having oxygen pumped into his lungs instead of making his lungs work to expand and fill up.

In a way, oxygen had become his crutch. If he felt short of breath or became panicked that he couldn't breathe, he knew as long as he carried the oxygen tank, he would be okay. He still had bouts of coughing and choking when he exerted himself, caused by the diseased right lung. These bouts could last up to twenty minutes and always left him weak and exhausted.

The first walk David took after being released from the hospital was difficult for him as he had no oxygen tank to fall back on, and he was very apprehensive. It was a normal July morning in San Francisco – foggy and rainy, with the temperature around 50 degrees. As

I closed the door to the apartment, David, who had started walking toward the elevator, turned to me and said, "Now, don't push me. I'll walk as far as I can."

I smiled and said, "Okay. No worries. You are going to be fine. You'll see."

His crinkled brow and short breaths told me he was fighting a battle within his mind. He wanted to breathe normally, but his body just wasn't cooperating.

We left the building and began walking on the sidewalk toward the street. It was slightly uphill and, as we reached the street, David began coughing. His face turned red as the coughing caused him to gag. Choking and coughing, he sat down on the sidewalk. The coughing would usually subside if he became very still.

It was misting lightly on top of the baseball cap he was wearing as he sat there, trying to stop gagging and catch his breath. All I could do was sit beside him, patting his shoulder. How I wanted to cry and shout: "Why is this happening to him?" But I couldn't. I had to be brave for him.

After several minutes, the coughing stopped and was replaced by very short, jerky motions of his chest rising up and falling down, as his lungs tried to breathe with a regular pattern.

I helped him up and, as he stood there, wet from the mist and exhausted from the coughing, he said, "It's so hard to breathe."

I took his arm in my arm and we slowly made our

way back to the apartment. "I know, my love," I reassured him. "You did well for the first time. It will get better." My heart ached for him. He was so weak. Transplants aren't supposed to go this way. He was supposed to be happy, breathing, and back to his everyday life. I kept saying over and over again in my head, *Why God? Why? Can't you see he is trying so hard? Why?*

David rested in the lawn chair, and I tried to busy myself around the apartment. But I was watching him. *Was he breathing? Was he going to need oxygen?*

When he awoke, he smiled and said, "Laura, this breathing is a mind game. You know how the first time I helped Briana ride her bike? I walked beside her, holding on to her and the bike, making sure she felt confident and didn't fall?" He put his hand on the scar across his chest and continued, "When I did let go of the bike, she was terrified that she would fall. That's how I felt when we tried to walk this morning. Terrified." He rubbed his hand across the scar as I stood there listening. He said "I've been wondering why God let me live. Why did He let me live if I can't breathe or function?"

I couldn't hold back my tears and said to him, "Oh, my love, God is not punishing you. You have a purpose! You are here because God is not ready for you to come home." I hugged him as we both cried. "You will get stronger. I need you!" I told him.

Every morning and afternoon we tried to walk and each time David was able to go just a little farther than the last time, even though the coughing still plagued him.

One morning two boxes arrived from the pharmacy department. During the last bronch, the doctors found that David had a spot of aspergillus in his lung. Aspergillus is a fungus whose spores are present in the air we breathe each day, but it does not normally cause illness. However an individual with a weakened immune system is extremely susceptible to aspergillus infection and it can be deadly for lung transplant patients.

The pharmacy sent additional medicine to begin fighting the infection. David was to be on it for at least six months. When he opened the box of new medicine, he looked at the invoice and turned completely white. This invoice was for almost $5,000. The medication was in one box and there were thirty inhalation-tubing hoses in the other box. One tubing hose per day. And he was going to be on this for six months!

Since receiving the news from the financial office, David and I had been in constant contact with our insurance transplant coordinator, checking each day how close we were getting to the lifetime maximum amount. Transplant medications are extremely important to the survival of the patient and they are very, very expensive. The first set of medications we had received while in the hospital cost over $11,000. Most of the medications were not generic and had to be taken every single day.

Part of preparing for lung transplantation is becoming educated about the actual process of transplantation, going through pulmonary rehab prior to transplant to keep the body as healthy as possible, and committing to taking all medications exactly as prescribed. Organs are scarce as many people will not agree to become an organ donor. If a person was not willing to adhere to these requirements and take care of their transplant, then the organ would be given to someone else who would. The typical pre-transplant patient could be waiting up to two years for lungs.

Unfortunately, David became ill very quickly, and not realizing that he had pulmonary fibrosis, he did not go through the pre-transplant process or learn anything about transplantation. He never had to take any prescription drugs and rarely took aspirin. Suddenly, he was taking boxes of medications, none of which were optional.

His sister, Linda, had told him about a plastic pill container that would hold up to two weeks' worth of medicines and we had received one when we left the hospital. Every two weeks, we sat down and one by one, filled the individual sections with medicines. He took meds before breakfast, mid-morning, with lunch, before supper, and at bedtime. We had learned not only

the names of the meds, but what they were for and
what they interacted with. Why? His life now
depended on these medicines. They were part of our
new routine.

David felt strongly that we needed to be attending
church. He had looked through the phone book and
found a Lutheran church close to our apartment called
West Portal Lutheran Church. He called the office,
spoke with the pastor and explained his situation. That
very day the pastor came to the apartment and gave
David and me communion. He prayed for us and with
us. He was so very kind.

The following Sunday, armed with tissues in his
pockets and an oxygen tank in the back seat of the car,
David and I walked into the sanctuary of West Portal.
The pastor not only remembered our names but
welcomed us warmly by telling David's story to the
congregation before beginning his sermon. God was
once again providing for us and we attended every
Sunday we were in San Francisco. It didn't matter if
David had been up all night coughing, he would insist
that we attend.

Besides the shortness of breath and the coughing,
David had another issue that just wouldn't go away and
it was the lymphatic gland in his thigh that continued
to leak. We tried using gauze bandages. We tried
covering the wound with several thicknesses of sterile
cotton pads and wrapping an Ace bandage around

them to keep them in place. Within twenty minutes, the fluid had already leaked out through the bandage and soaked his pant leg. Nothing seemed to work. For once, my engineer husband was at a loss. What in the world could we use that would last longer than a few minutes?

Brushing my teeth one morning, I looked in the tiny medicine cabinet mirror and a light bulb in my head went off. Kotex pads! They just might work. But how to hold them in place? A big smiled came across my face and I put down my toothbrush.

David was sitting at the card table, and I triumphantly said to him, "Kotex pads! You need Kotex pads!"

The look on his face was priceless. He raised his eyebrows and replied, "Have you lost your mind?"

I laughed and explained that Kotex pads were made to be very absorbent and should keep his pant leg dry much longer than the Ace bandage.

He shook his head and grinned. "How do I hold it in place?" he wondered aloud.

Again I grinned and replied, "Spandex shorts like the cyclists wear. They are skintight and just might hold the pad in place."

A Target department store was close to our apartment, and I went there looking for the pads and spandex shorts. The pads were easy to locate, but the spandex shorts were more difficult. David had lost so much weight that his waist was down to a size 30. All I could find that might fit him was a pair of women's exercise shorts. The legs would be long enough to cover the pad.

The first time we 'padded' him up, as he called it, was a comedy of trial and error. We tried putting the pad vertically on his thigh and pulling the shorts on over it, but the spandex short would scrunch up the pad or move it. We tried putting the pad horizontally on his thigh, but it didn't cover the leakage from the wound. Finally, we put the pad on vertically again, this time securing it in place with one of his shoestrings lightly tied around his leg before pulling on the shorts. Dressed, he stood up, looked down at the lump on his thigh, shrugged his shoulders and said, "I hope these darn things don't give me a rash!"

We both laughed. I gave him a big hug and said, "Who knows? Maybe you can patent this somehow as a medical device!"

Before we knew it, the month of July had passed and we were getting used to seeing fog every morning and evening. Since David was on a blood thinner, he was constantly cold, and the dampness in the air seemed to trigger his cough.

Our dear Trinity Lutheran family in Houston was still sending him get-well cards and each one would boost our spirits. The hospital bills had been arriving and we would go through each one, line by line, to double check that the charges were accurate. The insurance coverage issue hung over us like a rope of a gallows and we knew that in a few weeks we would reach the maximum. About a third of the charges had been processed, which meant a very large amount would not be covered.

David had been suffering from bouts of depression, which was a normal reaction after transplantation. The body was recovering from mass trauma and being forced to be immune suppressed. His constant coughing, his leg wound that would not close, and the worries over money added to his depression. I had been sharing our situation with our church family, asking for their prayers to heal David. We had very little income, were making a house payment in Wausau and a very large rent payment in San Francisco, and David was scheduled for more surgery.

Suddenly, the wonderful cards from Trinity began to have something else inside besides the prayers of encouragement. They were sending us money to help us pay our bills. We were overcome with emotions. Worry about the hospital bills, embarrassment that we were no longer able to keep up with those bills, and sadness that David was still not healing, we were overwhelmed that our dear friends at Trinity cared that much for us. David and I were humbled by each one's love and kindness. Each time an envelope arrived, we would open it together and cry.

Our daughter, who was going to be a junior in college, had been working during the summer and was flying in the first weekend of August to see her dad. We were so excited. The day before her arrival, David had been scheduled for a routine clinic visit, which included a CAT scan, blood work, and other things. One of the doctors, while checking him over, discovered a lump in his left calf. It wasn't very large, but the doctor ordered an ultrasound to check it out. The ultrasound was done that afternoon and we were asked to wait in the lobby while the doctor viewed the results. David was feeling better and we didn't think much about it until the doctor came out to speak with us.

"I think you may have a blood clot in your calf and we are going to admit you in order to treat it," the doctor said.

David looked over at me, then back at the doctor and said, "I'm not going into the hospital today. My daughter is flying in tomorrow. Can it wait till Monday?"

The doctor didn't waver and replied, "I'm sorry, David, but a room is being made ready for you. I don't want you walking anywhere till we can reduce the clot."

David balked. He stiffened his back and said with a not-so-nice demeanor, "I'm not going into the hospital today. I've been there for several months and I will not spend the only weekend I have with my daughter in a hospital room." He was upset and disappointed, and it was the first time he had bucked one of the transplant doctors.

The doctor was silent for a moment. Then noticing how upset David was, he said, "David, you must not be on that leg and we need to monitor you. I'll make a deal with you. If by Saturday the clot has dissolved, I'll release you to go home that afternoon."

David was silent for several minutes before agreeing with the doctor. He was not happy, not one bit, and as he sat in the wheelchair that was to transport him once again to the 10th floor of UCSF, he glared at me with much anger in his eyes. His mouth was clenched closed, and I knew it was all he could do to remain calm.

Our daughter arrived the next day and we played cards, retold funny family stories and tried our best to cheer David up. She was attending the same engineering college that he had attended 25 years earlier and they talked about how she was staying in the same dorm he had stayed in and compared his freshman experience to hers. It was good to see both of them laughing together again.

David was still angry about being in the hospital and he was very cool toward the doctor who had admitted him. We tried to keep his spirits up, and the nursing staff helped too. They laughed as we described how we 'padded up' David's leg with Kotex pads and the spandex shorts. Most thought it was a pretty ingenious way of covering the wound.

Saturday morning arrived, and David had decided he was going back to the apartment. When my daughter and I arrived at 7 a.m., he was already dressed and sitting on the edge of the hospital bed.

"Has the doctor been in early?" I asked.

He said, "No, but I am going home this morning, clot or no clot. I've had enough." And when David decided enough was enough, no one could change his mind.

The doctor didn't make his rounds till almost 10 a.m., and David was still sitting in the chair waiting for him.

"Well, David, looks like you are ready to get out of here," the doctor said as he put his hands in the pockets of his white lab coat.

David was silent, only nodding his head in agreement.

"The pulmonary team has been reviewing the ultrasound pictures and we do not believe you have a clot after all. It appears it may be a small amount of scar tissue," the doctor said quickly. "You understand that we have to take precautions since you have a history of blood clots," he continued as he eyed David's reaction to the news.

David never took his eyes off the doctor and

replied, "I understand. I assume I am being released at this time."

The doctor smiled and said, "Yes, you are free to go. The wheelchair will be here in a moment to take you downstairs. Enjoy your weekend and we will see you on Tuesday at the clinic."

My daughter and I glanced at each other, wondering what David was going to say about this new turn of events. We didn't have to wait long as he rolled his eyes toward the ceiling and asked, "Think he knew I was angry?"

My daughter and I both nodded 'yes,' and he said, "Good. Let's get out of here."

The rest of the weekend went by quickly and it felt good having the three of us together again. Our daughter left late Sunday afternoon, and David was visibly tired from the excitement of the past few days. I noticed his face looked flushed, but he brushed it aside, saying he had a slight headache and needed to rest. He had several coughing bouts that night, each one a bit worse than the one before. I felt something was wrong but didn't know what. He slept through most of Monday and I was glad we had a clinic appointment scheduled for the next day.

Tuesday morning he woke up still feeling tired, checked his temperature just like always, and noticed he was running a fever of about 100 degrees. Our appointment wasn't until the afternoon, but I remembered the list of precautions given to us as we left the hospital after his transplant. Running a fever was a bad sign for a lung transplant patient and could mean that rejection or some type of infection was setting in. We needed to get to the doctor as soon as possible. We decided to go early to the clinic and try to get in.

CHAPTER 17

The staff at the pulmonary clinic knew David and me very well and when we arrived several hours early for his regular clinic, they knew something was wrong. As David stood at the registration desk, his face was flushed and his breathing was labored. The attendant at the desk immediately called back to the doctor and David was in an exam room within minutes.

Usually, he had to weigh in, get his blood pressure and temperature taken, and then go back out to the waiting area until his appointment time. None of that happened today. He sat down in the chair beside the exam table, put his elbows on his knees and rested his head in the palms of his hands.

Dr. Hoopes was not normally one of the doctors in the clinic, as he was either in surgery or attending to a newly transplanted patient. Thank the Lord he was in the clinic today and he was the first one in the small exam room.

"David, how are you feeling?" he asked as he shut the exam room door.

"I feel like I have the flu," David answered. He raised his head to look at the doctor and his eyes were bloodshot.

Dr. Hoopes quickly took his blood pressure and temperature, and then listened to his chest. This doctor was extremely intelligent, and I could see by his demeanor that he was very concerned. He looked straight into David's eyes and said, "I need to see what's happening with the lung. I know you are not happy about going back to the hospital, but that is where I need you to go for a day or so."

David's flushed face never changed expression as he replied, "I thought you were going to say that."

In the blink of an eye, David was once again in a wheelchair being taken to UCSF hospital, floor 10, Moffit wing. He had begun having chills as they transferred him to the hospital bed. The nurse on shift had been assigned to David many times before and she kindly said, "Now don't you worry, David. Dr. Hoopes will have you fixed up in no time."

After a CAT scan, blood tests, PFT's and x-rays, we found out that the aspergillus had worsened and David was anemic. IV's went into his arms, and four different medicines filled the bags hanging from the IV poles. David felt so bad he couldn't keep his eyes open. I could tell he was so disappointed. He almost seemed resigned to the fact that he could not stay off the 10th floor. I was once again holding his hand and I realized how disheartened he was. I prayed that the Lord heal him and not let this lead to his body rejecting his new lung.

Four days passed before David felt better. Another problem with being immune suppressed is that the body doesn't heal very quickly. It would be months before the aspergillus would be cleared from his lungs and that meant months of inhaling Amphotericin B, the very expensive medicine used to fight the infection.

He was given some good news the morning of the fifth day, however. Dr. Hoopes had been by to say that the gastrointestinal doctor would be able to do the stomach wrap on David while he was in the hospital.

"David," Dr. Hoopes said, "I'll be there during the procedure and I'll try to cauterize that lymph gland in your thigh. If we are lucky, it will close off and you won't have to wear menstrual pads anymore." Dr. Hoopes and David chuckled together. "And, boy, if anyone deserves some luck, you certainly do!" Dr. Hoopes said as he left the room.

The following afternoon while David was in surgery for the stomach wrap, I was called down to the financial office. My heart was heavy as I knew that this hospital stay probably put us over our lifetime maximum of medical insurance. I checked in at the desk and expected to be taken back to Sherry's cubical just as I had been before. But this time when I gave my name, the clerk at the desk was silent and took several minutes searching her computer before speaking to me. She said, "Someone will be here in a moment to help you."

Okay. I sat down in one of the big blue padded chairs, wondering when David would be out of surgery.

About thirty minutes later, a short older woman walked over to where I was sitting and said, "You need to follow me." She turned and I quickly followed her out of the financial office, down a long hallway, and into what looked like an emergency room waiting area. She never spoke to me again, but went straight to the front desk, gave some paperwork to the attendant, and then walked back the way we had come in.

Confused, I walked over to the front desk and asked, "Hello, I think I am in the wrong area. I'm supposed to meet with Sherry." A small, young Asian lady answered without looking up: "Have a seat. It's first come, first serve. When it's you turn, someone will call you."

Huh? I stood there for a moment, not quite knowing what to do, then turned to find a seat. There were no big blue padded chairs in this area. Only regular metal-type folding chairs occupied with people of all nationalities, many of whom looked like the homeless people that the UCSF front lobby security guard had been hired to keep out.

People were speaking in Spanish, Chinese or Mandarin, and all were talking to their families at the same time. Some were visibly ill, coughing and lying down across several chairs. One woman had vomited in a trashcan.

Why was I in emergency? My eyes grew wide and filled with tears. I couldn't understand anyone who was talking. No one. I felt so alone. *Why was I here? Was David out of surgery?*

One hour later, I heard my name called and I walked back into a very small area that had three window openings along the side of one wall, much like a ticket window at a sporting event. I walked in front of the middle window and the woman sitting across from me asked, "What is the patient's name?"

I told her, and she continued asking me questions, including our address and nearest relatives, and then ended by requesting to see my driver's license.

"What is this about?" I asked. "I was supposed to be seeing the financial advisor."

She had a blank look on her face and replied, "This area is for people without medical insurance. Fill out these forms to see if you qualify for Blue Shield of California."

I stood there for a moment, looking down at the stack of forms, and tried to gather my wits about me. I started to ask the lady a question, but she had disappeared into a hallway behind her chair. Stunned, I took the papers and found my way back to David's hospital room.

He was still in recovery and the surgery had gone well. This procedure would prevent David from having any acid reflux seep into his lungs again. I kept praying to God: *How am I going to tell him about these papers? He is depressed enough now. Dear Lord, how am I going to tell him?*

Over the next few days, David recovered quickly and, to our great joy, the cauterization of the lymph gland was a success! The incision was no longer leaking. Such a tiny victory, but to us it was like winning the lottery. Finally, a procedure with no complications!

We were discharged on the 19th of August and, on the way back to the apartment, I drove to the small, neighborhood grocery store in Parkmerced and bought David four of his favorite type of candy bars: Halvah! He always loved the sesame seed treat, and we had discovered this tiny grocery store carried the candy. He had a huge smile on his face as he immediately opened one of the bars and took a big bite. For the first time in months, I saw the familiar sparkle in his eyes and, for a brief moment, I had the old David back.

Our transplant coordinator, Joanie, called to tell us about the termination of our insurance coverage before I had the chance to show David the paperwork we needed to fill out. He became very quiet and studied the paperwork carefully. Since we had not been California residents earning an income, we were not eligible for the Blue Shield of California (which would have given us coverage throughout the state). David had been on short-term disability through his company since April 4th and was drawing a small portion of his regular monthly income. It was not enough to cover our expenses of rent, house payment, medicines, and now hospital bills.

That night we prayed together, lying side by side in our lawn chairs. David tried to pray, but tears choked him.

I prayed: "Dear God, we love You and have tried to follow Your will. Thank you, dear Lord, for putting David in my life. He is my soul mate. You are the Great Healer. Please heal him!" I began to cry and had to stop to gather my voice. "Help us to keep our faith strong. We know You will provide for us. Amen." I couldn't continue. I held my husband's hand close to my heart, kissing it and telling him again, "I love you, David. God will heal you, I just know it."

A few days later, after walking almost four blocks, we stopped at the large group mailbox to see if we had any mail. Along with one card from Trinity, there was a letter from David's company. We waited until we were back in the apartment before opening the mail. He opened the one from his company first and I noticed he was moving the paper back and forth as if he were trying to focus on it.

"Something wrong with your eyes, dear?" I asked.

He replied, "I can't read this. My glasses must be dirty." He took them off and I quickly washed and cleaned the lens. He was still looking at the letter when I handed the glasses back, and I noticed a frown forming on his face. He looked up and said, "I have be back at work on October 3rd or I will lose my job."

Stunned, I said, "What?"

As he put his glasses back on he continued, "The company has done away with long term disability. Once the six months of short term disability is used up, the employee is let go."

We both looked at each other in silence. *Let go? No job?*

He slowly put down the letter, took off his glasses and sighed. He stared out the apartment window for several minutes, and I noticed tears running down his face.

I hugged him and said, "Don't worry. We will be back in Wausau well before October 3rd."

He didn't move or respond. I sat down beside him and he turned to me and said, "I think I am going blind.

I can't see anything but black in the bottom part of my vision."

My mouth fell open. He gazed at me and said, "I noticed it when I was trying to read the letter. It's in both eyes. It's like I can only see the top half of everything." Again he sighed and slightly slumped down in his chair.

That evening when I knew he was asleep, I walked out of the apartment and into the small yard behind the apartment building and sobbed. I yelled up at God.

"Why his eyesight? Why can't he be healed? Why have You allowed this to happen?" I was angry and hurt and I lashed out at Him. "We've been praying. All our family and friends have been praying for him. Why God? Why?" I walked and cried. I cried and yelled at God some more. "He is a good man. Why does he deserve this illness?" In my heart I knew it was wrong to yell at God, but I couldn't help it. I had nowhere else to turn.

A week later, David had an appointment with the head of the cornea and external disease department at UCSF. He read through David's history, shook his head and said, "You've been through the ringer, haven't you?"

David nodded and replied, "That is an understatement."

After an extensive exam and several highly specialized tests on David's eyes, the doctor told him that the medication he had been taking for the arterial fibrillation or a-fib, called Amiodarone, was the culprit. "One rare side affect of Amiodarone is loss of vision due to the swelling of the optic nerve." He showed David a few pictures taken of his left eye and continued, "Patients almost always lose the bottom portion of their vision."

David looked at him and asked, "How long will the swelling last?"

The doctor said, "Once the swelling occurs, it never goes away. You are fortunate that you didn't lose your sight completely."

Silence. I watched David's expressionless face as he asked, "This is permanent?"

The doctor nodded. "Yes. I will contact your pulmonary doctors and recommend they change your medication. That will prevent further damage."

David was quiet as we walked back into the apartment. He had said nothing since hearing that his loss of eyesight was permanent. His mind was preoccupied with thoughts of bills mounting, no long term disability, loss of his eyesight, and the disease that started all this mess… pulmonary fibrosis. All I could think of was to try to cheer him up, but how?

I made the excuse that I needed to go to Target to pick up a few items and prayed I could figure out something that might make him feel better. I walked the aisles of Target, looking for anything and everything that might help him. Suddenly, I stopped dead in my tracks. I was standing in the toy department and there was a huge, round magnifying glass in a box with a boy scientist on the front. *Perfect!* Maybe it would help him to see.

I slipped into the apartment, trying to prevent David from seeing the magnifying glass, and headed into the kitchen. I wrapped it in a kitchen tea towel and proudly walked over to the card table where he was sitting.

"This is for you, my dear!" I said proudly as I handed him the tea towel.

He looked at me, then down at the tea towel. He pulled the magnifying glass out of the towel and held it in his hand. For a second, I thought he was going to cry. Then he held it up to his right eye, blinked a few times and said, "This just might help! Thank you!"

The end of August was approaching quickly and, surprisingly, the temperature was getting warmer. The foggy time was about over, and there were days when the sun shone brightly. David had been progressively walking farther each day and we had found a small beach area, called Rockaway Beach, that had paved walking trails.

We would drive to the beach, walk down the paved path as far as he was able, then sit outside the car and watch the waves. Sometimes David would recline the passenger seat of the car, roll down the window and listen to the soothing motion of the waves going in and out. It became our place of peace during this turbulent time.

September arrived and our regular schedule changed a little bit. David only had to have blood draws twice a week and bronchs two times a month. That meant he was improving, little by little. We continued to attend West Portal Lutheran Church on Sundays and our prayers were now for healing and patience.

The October 3rd deadline was weighing heavily on David's mind, as well as the mountain of medical bills we were collecting. Thankfully, our dear friends at Trinity were still sending get-well cards and some still had money in them. David always handled our finances and had begun withdrawing retirement funds to pay as many of the bills as possible. Each clinic visit or PFT test or x-ray or prescription was suddenly a financial burden.

His weight was still around 150 pounds and he said food still had no taste to it. That was another normal reaction from a major trauma to the body. The coughing episodes continued and nothing seemed to prevent them or stop them once they began. It was very hard to watch this strong man that I loved struggle so to catch his breath while coughing and gagging. Sometimes the least movement brought on the coughing. A sudden turn of his head to the right would trigger it. If he bent over to tie his shoes, that would trigger it. Lying on his back would trigger it.

The third Tuesday of September, David woke up knowing that he had a bronch and clinic scheduled for that day. I could tell that he seemed more determined today about something, but he wouldn't say what. Sitting in the clinic exam room, I found out what that was.

The doctor came in as usual and read the results of the bronch and labs. He talked to David about changing the amounts of a few medications and then told him to make an appointment around the first of October.

David looked at him and said, "I'm afraid that is not possible. We are going to go back to Wausau the end of this week. Will you make arrangements for a doctor in Wausau to do the next visit?"

The doctor leaned back in his chair and thought for a moment before responding. He said, "Well, David, you have been through so much these last months and I realize you want to go home. But I will have to get clearance from the pulmonary team before releasing you to go back to Wisconsin." The doctor grinned and added, "David, we all pray that you can go home. Let's make sure it is the right time, alright?"

David firmly replied, "I have to be back at my job on October 3rd or I will be let go. My short-term disability runs out on that day."

The doctor and David locked eyes for a brief moment before David added, "We have to make arrangements in Wausau. I have no choice."

The doctor nodded and said the team would discuss it in the next Wednesday meeting. He shook David's hand and then said, "It has been a pleasure seeing the love between you and your wife. Even through the multiple complications you have experienced, you have been an example of faith for everyone who treated you. We'll call you with the team's decision."

The following Monday afternoon we received a call from the pulmonary transplant team. They would release us to go to Wausau and they would send orders to the pulmonologist there. But David would need to fly back to UCSF at least once a month if a proper medical facility could not be found in the area. David gave me a big hug and said, "Let's get out of here."

CHAPTER 18

I n a matter of days, we were driving from San Francisco to Wausau, Wisconsin. The car was packed, but this time it was full of nebulizers, medicines, blood pressure monitors, plastic hospital pitchers, pillows and the few articles of clothing.

We stopped in South Dakota long enough to see David's family and visit our daughter. His family was shocked to see how frail he looked, but so glad to see him alive! I took a picture of David and our daughter, Briana, before we continued on to Wausau. David had tears in his eyes and seemed so terribly sad. As we drove away, he said in a teary voice, "I wonder if the Lord will let me live to see her graduate next year?"

Startled, I replied, "Of course you will see her graduate! I just know it! God has blessed us and you are going to live a long, long life."

He wiped the tears from his face and then laid his head against the headrest and tried to sleep.

We arrived in Wausau on Saturday, October 1st, 2005. It had been almost six months to the day since David had collapsed on the bathroom floor and our transplant journey began. It had already turned cold in Wisconsin, and the trees had lost most of the leaves. Our home had a musty odor, and I began to open a few windows to let some fresh air in. David stood in the front room, looking around as if he had never been in the house before.

"Is everything okay?" I asked him.

He nodded 'yes.' Then he walked into the bedroom and stood in the bathroom where he'd fallen. The glass had been cleaned up and there were small holes in the wall where the mirror had once been attached. Once again his eyes began filling with tears and he said, "I can't remember anything except walking in here to get ready for work."

I choked back tears and asked, "You don't remember falling down? The ambulance ride to the hospital? Mayo clinic? The airplane ride? Anything?"

He shook his head 'no.' There was silence between us for a moment, and then he said, "I remember getting ready for work and then waking up in the hospital at UCSF, feeling pain along my chest from having the transplant."

We hugged each other, and I was so thankful he

didn't remember the terrible feeling of suffocation or not being able to hold his head up by himself. I said, "God is truly merciful, my dear, and He knows you do not need to remember."

The weekend passed quickly and I noticed that David's coughing had worsened as the colder fall air seemed to irritate his throat. The blood thinners were doing their job and he constantly felt cold, putting on layer after layer to try to warm up.

"I've never been sensitive to the cold," he said as he stood by the fireplace to get warm.

I smiled and answered, "Well, you have me and as many blankets as you need to keep you warm, cutie!"

He grinned. It was so good to see him smile!

We both felt nervous when Monday morning came and he readied for work. "I feel like a first grader getting ready for his first day of school!" he said as he tried to shave. The steroids made his hands shake and he had to be very careful not to cut himself.

I had gone to town to buy him a few clothes since the ones in his closet swallowed his now frail frame. When he put on his size 30 slacks and size medium shirt, he held up one of his favorite old dress slacks, size 38, and said, "Do I look too thin?"

"You look fabulous!" I told him as I gave him a big hug. "Let's take a picture of your first day back to work and send it to our family and Trinity. They will all be so happy to see you."

I took the picture as he stood on the stairs that, only a few months ago, he could not catch his breath to climb. Tears filled my eyes as he stood there with his lunch sack filled with his ham sandwich and the pills he had to take.

"Good luck today, my love," I said as I kissed him goodbye. "Everyone will be so glad to see you." The date was October 3rd, the last day of his short-term disability. It was a huge milestone he would always remember. I prayed he had enough stamina to last the entire day.

Later that day, I stood by the phone and looked up at the clock. 12:28 p.m. *Would he call like he always did?* I soon had my answer. The phone rang as the digital clock read 12:31 p.m. I picked up the receiver and heard those wonderful words: "What's going on?"

I grinned. *Yes! Finally our lives will get back to our normal routine.*

David said he was a bit tired and had been coughing several times, but he was glad to be back in his office. Most everyone had stopped by to visit with him, wishing him well. After he hung up, I raised my hands in the air and said, "Thank you, dear Jesus, for getting him back to work!"

Between 2:30 and 3:00 p.m. that same day, I received a call from David's boss. He was telling me that it was good to see David back at work, but he had been coughing a great deal and seemed very tired.

They were sending him home to rest and wondered if I would mind if one of the other engineers drove him home. His boss explained, "I'll bring his car by later this evening."

I was waiting by the front door to give him a big hug when he came in. He looked so very tired and had dark circles around his eyes. "I'm so proud of you!" I beamed as I hugged him. "It must have been good to be back at work."

He looked so thin, so pale, so tired. "I think I need to take a short nap," he said as he slowly walked up the stairs. He lay in the recliner and slept soundly for about an hour before a coughing spell jolted him awake.

After catching his breath, he said, "It's cold in here. Can you turn up the heat?"

I wrapped him in a blanket and turned the heat up to 80 degrees.

"It's not like me to be cold," he said, shaking his head.

"Don't worry," I replied. "It's just the blood thinner. You'll be warm in a minute."

He went to work each morning and came home each day exhausted, cold, and coughing. October was gone and November came in like a lion. As the weather grew colder, the coughing spells came more frequently. A few days before Thanksgiving, David came home from work and I noticed something was wrong. He was pale, but his eyes seemed glazed over. "I think I've got a cold," he said as he collapsed onto the bed.

I felt his forehead and it was burning up. We got him undressed and into bed, and then I checked his temperature. It was 101 degrees. High temperature is extremely dangerous to a lung transplant patient as it could be a sign of rejection, which can be fatal. I got my cell phone and called one of the UCSF transplant team's cell number. Getting the answering machine, I said, "David is feverish and cold and feels as if he has the flu. What do we need to do?"

It was several hours before I heard back from the doctor and, by that time, David was shaking with chills as his fever was going up. "He probably should go to the emergency room," the doctor said.

I told David that and he shook his head 'no.'

"He doesn't trust this little hospital. Is there anything else we can do? Does he have another option?" I asked the doctor.

The doctor spoke with David and asked many questions before deciding to call in a prescription for Tamiflu.

"If he is not better by morning, he must go to the emergency room," the doctor told me. "Call me anytime during the night if his symptoms get worse," he said as I hung up the phone.

The night hours went by slowly and I watched David for any sign of improvement. Every half hour I would wet a washcloth and gently wipe off his forehead and face.

"I've never been a sick person," he said, "and I don't like being sick."

I sat beside him, holding his hand and responded, "Remember, your immune system is gone now. You are more likely to catch germs floating around."

He tried to sleep and I prayed that God would take the temperature away.

At 5 a.m., the doctor from UCSF called to see how David was doing. I reported that his fever had gone down slightly to 100.6 and he seemed to be resting.

"Have him take the prescription and make him stay in bed today. If he is still running a fever by tomorrow morning, get him to the emergency room."

I told the doctor I would do that, but I did not tell David that was the plan. He told me more than once he did not want to see the inside of a hospital again for a long time.

David's temperature slowly went down and, within a few days, he felt like going back to work. "It's not easy being a sick person," he said.

I smiled and said, "No one likes being ill, but it sometimes happens. You're going to be fine now."

December brought freezing temperatures and snow to Wausau. David still had not gained any of his weight back, but he was gaining a bit more stamina. He was looking forward to Briana coming home for the

Christmas break. December was also the first month that a bronch had been scheduled with the Wausau doctor and we both were apprehensive about it.

The doctors at UCSF had given all of David's records, procedures, and information to the pulmonologist in Wausau. It was the same pulmonologist who had first treated David and sent him to Mayo clinic back in April.

I had begun working and had no vacation time, so Briana, who would be home for the Christmas break, said she would go with her dad to the bronch appointment. After all, it was routine and should only take about an hour.

The morning of the appointment, David and Briana were having breakfast, and as I left for work, I said, "The appointment is at 11 a.m., so be sure to get there around 10:30."

David looked up and said, "Yes, dear." He smiled and Briana was laughing under her breath.

"I know, I worry," I said as I tapped him on the shoulder, "but Briana, call me with the results when the bronch is finished. It should only take about thirty minutes."

She nodded 'yes' and then gave me a hug goodbye.

I went to work not worrying. It was just a routine bronch. Everything would be fine.

I kept looking at my watch as the second hand ticked by. 11:30 a.m. No call. 12:15 p.m. No call. 12:30

p.m. No call. 12:45 p.m. No call. Something was wrong; I could feel it. 1:00 p.m. No call.

I had just gone into my supervisor's office to ask to leave work early when my phone rang. It was Briana. She was upset and still at the hospital.

"Mom, you need to come right away. They punctured Dad's lung."

I raced out of the office and sped to the hospital where I found Briana in the surgery waiting room. She tried to explain but was confused. I went to the nurses' station and said, "David Bichler is my husband and I want to know what happened. He was supposed to have a routine bronch. Where is he?"

The nurse could see I was worried and upset and stated, "He is in recovery. The doctor will give you details."

I stood there and tried to be calm as I asked, "When can I see the doctor?" but nothing about my voice was calm. The nurse left to see if she could find the doctor. I paced back and forth in front of the station desk. Briana was watching and had a very concerned look on her face. The nurse came back and said, "The doctor will be here in a few moments."

Minutes passed like hours before I finally saw the doctor making his way toward us.

"Mr. Bichler has to be the albatross around my neck," he began. "Everything that could go wrong does!" the doctor said with a slight chuckle.

I was not laughing. "What happened? This was a routine bronch. What happened?" I questioned.

The doctor explained that during the bronch, he looked into the new lung and things looked fine. Then he decided he wanted to look into the old lung to see what a fibrotic lung looked like.

My mouth fell open.

He said, "We inflated the old right lung with oxygen in order to see it and we must have punctured it during inflation."

Inflated the old lung? What? I couldn't believe I was hearing this.

The doctor continued, "David's throat began to close around the breathing tube and I thought I was going to have to perform a tracheotomy or lose him."

Tears were flowing from my eyes as the doctor continued, "He gave us quite a scare, but I think he will be fine. He will need to have a drain tube in the lung for several weeks though."

I could feel the blood rushing to my face and my hands were trembling. I said, "You looked into the old lung? Didn't the UCSF doctors give you instructions?"

The doctor, with no expression on his face, simply said, "He will be in recovery for another hour or so, then you can take him home." With that, he turned and walked away.

Stunned, angry, and scared, I looked at Briana and said, "We're going to the recovery room now." We walked down the hallway and into recovery where David was in one of the curtained-off areas. No one was there to stop us, so we opened the curtain and stood by his bedside. He had begun to wake up and felt the pain in his right side from the drain tube.

"What happened?" he asked.

I forced a smile and said, "Don't worry. I'll tell you about it when we get home."

Needless to say, David was mad when he realized what had taken place during the bronch. We called UCSF to tell them what happened and sent pictures to them of the drain tubing. They could not believe it. Now David would have to deal with the drain tubing and the threat of infection from the incision. The UCSF doctors called in a prescription antibiotic for him and told him to rest. It was the last time David had a bronch at Wausau. From that point on, we flew back to San Francisco for everything.

January brought the infamous 'below zero' temperatures and winds that are common in a Wisconsin winter. Wind gusts blew in straight from the cold north and would chill David to the bone.

He struggled with horrific bouts of coughing when he had to breathe the sub-zero cold air and would wear a mask over his mouth and nose between the car and office or home. He could no longer shovel snow or clear our driveway and sidewalk, so that became my job.

I would get up a 4 a.m., put on many layers of clothes and wobble outside to start up the massive red snow blower he had purchased only a year ago. After getting covered in the snow that I was trying to blow away, I figured out how to move the 'snout' of this monster machine from side to side.

It was a slow process for me as most of the time the machine drove and I followed it, trying to hold on for dear life. After an hour or so, I would wobble back into the house, covered in snow, where David was always waiting for me with a warm blanket and a big hug.

His eyes would tear up and he would say, "This should be my job. I hate that you have to do it." He was always such a gentleman and he felt as if he was worthless now, unable to do the small task of blowing snow off the driveway.

Giving him a hug, I said, "God is giving us the opportunity to appreciate the things we have done for each other. I thank you for all the times you did the snow-blowing for me. And as soon as you are healthier, I'll be glad to let you drive that big red monster again!"

He smiled, but there was still sorrow in his big brown eyes.

Soon, God once again blessed us through David's work. As we had maxed out the insurance coverage in August of that past year, we had spent many hours worrying about how to get medical insurance now that David was a post transplant patient. The prescription costs alone were staggering. Our dear friends at Trinity Lutheran in Spring, TX, had been continually sending us money and cards. Trinity Lutheran School students had dedicated their chapel offerings to us and we were so humbled by their generosity. Without their help and prayers, we would not have survived.

Then, late in December, the human resource department at David's company had given us the good news that they had another insurance plan David would be accepted on! As of January 1st, we would have coverage! *Praise God! He does provide for us.* It wasn't as good a plan as we previously had, but it was coverage and we were so thankful.

On February 5th, David's 47th birthday, I baked his favorite dessert – a red velvet cake with sour cream icing – and we thanked God, praying that this year would be so much better than the last one. He had gained about five pounds and was beginning to get his appetite back.

"Food is beginning to taste good again," he said as he devoured a large piece of birthday cake.

Silently I thanked God that my husband was sitting beside me after the struggle he had been through a few months ago. I prayed that the worst of times was over, that he would gain strength and eventually receive two good lungs.

Despite the signs of improvement with his weight and appetite, David's eyesight had worsened slightly and he depended on the magnifying glass I had found in San Francisco to help him see the tiny lines of print on his work laptop. He had figured out the best way for him to read paperwork or text: he would take off his glasses, tilt his head downward, raise the text upward with his left hand and hold the magnifying glass in his right hand. Since the bottom half of his vision was gone, he could look upward through the large glass and be able to read entire words.

One of his engineering friends had started calling him 'Sherlock,' as he looked like the fictional detective with his magnifying glass. David would laugh, but he was extremely frustrated and it was exhausting for him to read through numerous manuals and specifications. He didn't complain. Not one time. Work kept his mind off the struggles he had each day to control the coughing or the prospect of having another transplant surgery, and it enabled him to feel that he was providing for his family.

CHAPTER 19

March came in, bringing tons of new snow and more freezing weather. David had been struggling with aspergillus in the new lung and had begun another six months of breathing treatments in order to kill the fungus.

Once again we had boxes and boxes of disposable breathing tubes stacked in our bedroom and the expensive, thick, yellow liquid that he had to inhale twice a day in the refrigerator.

He seemed to continually have a cold or the flu and the coughing spells had been increasing. As he sat in front of the fireplace, wrapped in two blankets, and trying to catch his breath after coughing, I wondered if the weather would ever warm up so he could feel better. In my nightly prayers that month, I asked God to bring warmth to Wisconsin so David could breathe easier.

Toward the end of March, my heart felt heavy as I looked back on the year that had passed. David's one-year transplant anniversary was approaching and I sat down at my computer to write to my friends at Trinity. Here is what God put upon my heart to write:

One Year of Blessings

March 21st, 2005 began as a very quiet day. Little did we know that it would become both a beginning and an ending of our routine way of life. Sitting in the doctor's office that afternoon, David and I seemed to be in a daze. Pulmonary Fibrosis... 2 years to live... lung transplant. We heard the words but couldn't comprehend them. All we could do was stare at each other and shake our heads.

My mind was racing with all kinds of thoughts: ope, this must be a mistake. David has always been the healthy one, and we just moved to Wisconsin. The plan was to travel every weekend, go camping, skiing, and enjoy being empty-nesters. 2 years to live? No way! I'm not buying it. God would not bring us up here to let David get sick. We are good people, faithful churchgoers. God loves us! We need a new doctor because this one has made a huge mistake. I do not believe it.

Over the next two weeks, David went from a strong, confident, happy, and slightly overweight mid-forties man to a weak, frightened, sad, extremely thin older man. In a matter of days, this disease had completely destroyed the David I married and left in his place a scared, dying man who had to gasp for even the smallest amount of air. I felt so helpless, so lost. We prayed and prayed. We called Garry Stuhr and asked for our Trinity family to become prayer warriors for him. We read Scripture and cried and cried together. Each day his condition worsened.

4:30 a.m., Monday, April 4th, 2005: David had been lying in bed the past weekend too short of breath and too weak to sit up. He had a strange, dull look in his eyes. I will never forget his words to me. "Laura," he said, "I don't want to die. I'm not ready. What is going to happen to me?" I told him we would get him two new lungs and he would be back to his old self in no time. "God loves you," I said. "He has plans for you. Don't worry! He will help us."

I helped him up to use the bathroom and turned away to straighten his pillows when I heard this sound. It was an eerie, long, low growling sound that made my back stiffen. I turned around to see him fall to the floor. He was grey all over. I heard myself saying, "God where are you? What is happening? Help him! Please God help him!" I called 911 and his long battle – our journey – was just beginning.

The next days felt like an eternity of no information, no one helping, God not answering. Two days in the Wausau hospital, then a four-hour ambulance ride to Mayo Clinic. A week of hearing them say David was an oddity. Pulmonary Fibrosis never progresses this quickly. Doctor's saying they had no clue why he was going down hill. He needed new lungs right away and the waiting list for the Midwest was 2-3 years. No hope. We saw twenty-one different doctors, interns, residents, experts. Each one told me to call in the family as soon as possible.

David had been on every kind of breathing/oxygen machine they had at Mayo. His weight was still dropping. He was not able to walk or stand. I would sit and sleep by his bed in ICU, just holding his hand… praying. But my prayers were turning harsh and angry. I was frustrated, scared and I wanted an answer now. I wanted him to be well. In my head and heart, I knew God was there, and that He would answer in His time. But my feelings were on edge and all I wanted was two new lungs…and David needed them now. So, I wasn't just praying to God, I was TELLING Him to get lungs for us. I was yelling at Him, arguing with Him, begging Him.

As a last-ditch effort, the Mayo doctor agreed to

contact the University of California San Francisco transplant surgeon, Dr. Charles Hoopes, to see if they would consider taking David as a patient. UCSF takes the most gravely ill patients… the ones no one else will mess with.

Since David's younger sister had a double lung transplant there in 2004, we had the surgeon's name and phone number. The call was made and the surgeon said, "We will find something for him. Get him here as soon as possible." I said a prayer of thanks to God, and I told David, "All is well… God does love you and is sending us to UCSF to get your new lungs."

8 p.m., California time, April 12th: We arrived in a medical transport plane at San Francisco airport and were whisked away in yet another ambulance. The hospital was waiting for us. The next hours were spent trying to stabilize David, retelling all of the past weeks events to yet another team of doctors.

David was still getting weaker. Unable to eat or stand up, with his oxygen level dropping to gravely dangerous numbers, his eyes developed dark, almost black circles around then. He had no color, just pale, almost transparent, skin. His breathing was so labored, he had to prop his head up and rest it on his hand.

He looked so small lying in that hospital bed with all the tubes and machines constantly beeping, pumping and humming. Still, I sat and slept by his bedside, holding his hand and crying.

My prayers were desperate pleas for healing. Why is God letting this happen to him? Why? Where are the lungs? Where are the doctors? Have we been so arrogant that God is teaching us humility? Why David? Why is he suffering so? I need him! He is my soul mate! God, why don't you make him well?

2:30 a.m., April 19th: The surgeon was watching David's breathing from the hallway. In my heart, I knew he only had a short time left to live. He looked so sad, so tired.

Around 5:00 a.m., the transplant team came in to tell me they were moving him to another room to monitor him more closely. The surgeon told me that David would only be able to survive a few more hours without being put on life support. And once a patient is put on life support... they never recover.

My head was spinning and I was sick to my stomach. Tears streamed down my face.

The doctor told me he has found one lung that, while not a great match, would allow David to live without life support. It was a damaged lung, but still better than his current situation. The surgeon would transplant the lung, wait a few months, and, hopefully, find two good lungs for David.

As you know, David did get that single lung transplant on April 19th. I prayed for forgiveness for all the demanding and yelling and pleaded with God for the new lung to function normally. I prayed for the donor family to have peace, knowing their loved one gave David life. I thought soon we would be back home with David going about his normal activities. I thought all the stress and worry were over. I was wrong.

During the next six months, David went through many, many many complications, and procedures. Every time a new problem would arise or he would again be in surgery or the lung collapsed, I prayed angry prayers. I pleaded with God. I demanded healing from God. I questioned His purpose. Still I knew God was holding David up. He was with us.

Today, March 14th, 2006, David continues to struggle with everyday life as does every transplant patient. We have talked many times about the events of the past year and, thankfully, he doesn't remember much from the time he collapsed at home until after the transplant. God is kind not to let him remember and He has taught me so very much.

I always thought I was a strong and faithful Christian, kind, understanding and sympathetic to others who have struggles in their lives. But He taught me I was wrong. When God tested me through David's illness, I failed miserably. Even though I knew the Lord was carrying David and that He was with us, I became angry with Him. I questioned where He was and why He LET this happen. I argued with His judgment and wanted answers now…not waiting for His timing.

When I had to be interviewed for financial aid,

becoming classified as a 'non-insured risk', I never had such a feeling of humiliation. Sitting in a room full of people in my same situation, taking a 'number' and waiting...waiting...waiting for my number to be called. Having the social worker treat me with a forced kind of courtesy, hurrying to get on with her own daily tasks, and talking down to me as if I couldn't understand her words...I thought about how often I had walked through the Main Street area in front of Trinity's church office and had seen people waiting in the chairs for help from Linda or Jean, and breezed right on by them with a big smile and a "How are you today?" How uncaring I was each time! I was doing nothing to help them, simply going about my own business.

The reason I wanted...no, needed...to write you is to share how much your prayers and cards and thoughts have meant to David and me. We have grown so much through this experience and, God willing, will continue to grow. He has also grown each of you through David's illness. You have come together in prayer and praise for us, and possibly met another member of Trinity's family you may not have known. God has heard your prayers and will continue to bless Trinity through you each day. I am glad the Lord brought us to Trinity... and I know He was using our time at Trinity to prepare us for this time in David's life. I thank God for each of you and my prayers will always, always include asking God to continue to bless you.

My love always, Laura.

The last Friday in March, I was cleaning up the supper dishes and David was working on his computer when the telephone rang. I answered "Bichlers!" as I always did, and then listened intently. David saw my expression change and my eyes open wide when I said, "Why, hello! How are you?" On the other end of the line was the principal from Trinity Lutheran School and he was calling to offer me a teaching position for the upcoming school year. *My goodness!*

Stunned, I listened to the information and told the principal that David and I would pray about it. As I hung up the phone, I turned to David, who had been listening to my end of the conversation. I explained about the teaching position and how surprised I was to receive the call. The teaching position wouldn't be enough income for the two of us to live on if we moved back to Houston, but what a wonderful thing for the school to do.

David had a strange look on his face as he watched me talking. I didn't know whether he was shocked or happy or confused. He didn't say anything immediately, but then his eyes opened wider and he said, "My boss told me today at noon that they want me to move back to Houston to head up a new office there."

I stood looking at him with a blank look on my face. "What?" I replied when I could speak.

David was smiling and said, "I was going to pray about it to see if it was God's will for us. But with you receiving a teaching position at the school, too...the same day I was asked about moving...I believe that is God telling us to head back to Houston!"

We were jumping for joy! No more cold weather for David to endure. No more tiny hospitals and doctors. Houston had a terrific medical community and had a respected lung transplant program. *Thank you, God!* For the first time in over a year, David and I held each other, smiling and dancing to the music on the radio. We were going home!

CHAPTER 20

The next few months were filled with excitement that we would be moving back to Houston at the end of May. David's health had stabilized, even though he continued to battle aspergillus. We listed our home and it sold within a few weeks. On May 22nd, 2006, we left Wausau and headed south to Houston. We had decided to stay in an extended stay hotel until we could find a house and move our things in. The two-day trip was tiring for him, but the thought of being close to friends and medical facilities was worth the strain.

A new medicine, Caspofungin, had been added to David's regimen since the fungal infection was not responding well to the inhaled medication. This new medicine was given twice daily through a 'PIC' line the doctors surgically placed in David's left upper arm. I was soon an old pro at starting the infusion, cleaning the 'PIC' line, and sterilizing everything. We had a small, portable IV pole that ran by gravity. I would set up the IV pole on the bed and David would sit beside it for the 45-minute infusion before work and again before bedtime.

A few weeks later, we found a home very close to Trinity Lutheran Church with easy access to the freeways, so David could travel to and from work without any trouble. Our belongings had been placed in storage by the movers, and on June 22nd, 2006, Jean Smith, my friend from Trinity, and I helped them unload the nine crates of our 'stuff.' It was a typical June day with the temperature in the upper 90's and the humidity in the same range. David wanted to help, but since moving back to the area, he had struggled with the heat and humidity. It was difficult for him to breathe and it zapped his energy very quickly.

David came home from work that day to find a fairly large pathway through moving boxes of all shapes and sizes in each room of the house. He grinned. "Well, Laura, this looks like one of our typical moves! Did we lose anything while it was in storage? Are all boxes accounted for?"

I didn't have the heart to tell David that I hadn't used the extensively detailed and color-coded Excel spreadsheet of inventory he had made for me. Instead, I had simply counted the boxes and checked them against the packing slip. "I believe we may have one box unaccounted for, sweetie, but I don't think it had anything valuable in it," I said as I gave him a hug.

"Humph," he answered as shook his head sideways. "Didn't use the spreadsheet, did you?"

How did he always know?

I smiled. "It was a terrific spreadsheet, but the movers were so fast, I couldn't keep up with marking all the little squares on it."

He nodded and smiled.

Before we left Wisconsin, the doctors at USCF decided that David to see the lung transplant team in Houston and our appointment was scheduled for Thursday, July 6th. I was glad to have a good doctor close by. David was a week past the regular schedule for his bronch by this time, and the pulmonologist scheduled one for the following Tuesday morning. *Great!* David would be finished in time to be at work by noon.

We soon found that the protocols used by UCSF and Houston were a bit different. At UCSF, bronchs were done with patients awake and the recovery time was between 20-30 minutes or so. At the Houston facility, a bronch was done with the patient sedated and secured to an operating table that tilted. The patient was to rest for at least 8 hours afterwards. I sat down to read a magazine in the surgical waiting room, thinking that David would be out in a few minutes.

One hour passed before the doctors came to get me. Something had gone wrong.

The doctors took me into the procedure room where David was strapped onto the table. He was still groggy from the injection they had given him prior to beginning the procedure.

The pulmonologist began speaking to the both of us, saying, "Mr. Bichler, we have a problem here. We can't seem to find the right lung."

My face scrunched up with a confused look and I said, "What do you mean you can't find the right lung?

The doctor replied, "We always do a CAT scan prior to any bronch and the scan shows nothing where the right lung is supposed to be. We cannot proceed with a bronch, as it would be too dangerous for Mr. Bichler."

David looked at me and his eyebrows grew close together.

I said, "That can't be possible. The lung is there. What could have happened to it?"

The doctor was quite upset as he answered, "We are notifying your transplant team in San Francisco. Mr. Bichler will have to been seen there because they are familiar with his case history and the surgery that was completed."

I stood beside David in disbelief. *No right lung? Of course the right lung was there, wasn't it?*

David was quickly unbuckled and, within a half hour, I was driving home with a very sleepy husband sitting in the passenger seat. After getting David settled in the recliner for a nap, my phone rang. It was one of the transplant doctors from UCSF.

"Laura, we have no idea what is going on with David. Houston is sending us the CAT scan pictures, but we need to see him. How soon can you get a flight out of Houston?"

"We can get there as soon as you need us to," I replied. That turned out to be the following Monday.

After learning that we would once again be flying to UCSF for a couple days of testing, I had called our dear friends Margie and Don to see if we could stay with them for a few days. They were such wonderful people and quickly agreed that we should stay with them rather than pay for an expensive hotel room. David and I packed lightly, as we expected to be back by the end of the week. He took his computer with him just in case he had time to read his emails. We boarded the plane and were in San Francisco that weekend.

Monday, we made the familiar trip to UCSF. By this time we knew the heavy trafficked streets to avoid. We kidded each other that we had a designated parking space in the large parking garage. That spot was open when we pulled in that morning and we laughed about it. We took the elevator to the second floor where the bronchs, labs and day surgery were typically performed. The nurse at the registration desk looked surprised to see us and said, "Why, David! Why are you back here so soon?"

David explained briefly, and then sat down to wait for his name to be called. He knew the routine. Change into a hospital gown, opening in the back, put your clothes in the plastic bag, and then sit in the waiting room till it was your turn.

David's name was called, and I went back to wait with him in the recovery room while an IV was started. We knew all of the nurses on duty and visited with them, talking about their families, the weather, and such. When the pulmonology team was ready for David, I kissed him and went back into the lobby area. They would call me when he was back in recovery room.

After the bronch, we were to walk over to the medical building across Parnassus Street and ride the elevator to the sixth floor. That was where the heart and lung clinics were located. The doctors would go over David's results and let us know what, if anything, was wrong. We waited in the clinic lobby for almost an hour before we heard his name called.

The transplant team doctor showed us the CAT scan from Houston and the CAT scan from earlier that morning. He said, "We are not sure what happened when the CAT scan was done in Houston, but it doesn't clearly show a right lung."

We strained to look at the computer screen where the CAT scan was displayed.

The doctor continued, "The lung is there, but we think that it may have changed position slightly when it was inflated back in Wisconsin."

David looked at me, rolled his eyes, and then looked at the doctor and asked, "So everything is all right?"

"Well, your PFT's have gone down quite a bit since we saw you and we are concerned about your oxygen levels." (Pulmonary function testing was another regular test that showed how much oxygen a patient's lungs were inhaling and exhaling.) The doctor continued, "I think the team wants you to speak with Dr. Hoopes about your options."

I thought to myself: *Oh, no. It can't be a good sign if we are seeing Dr. Hoopes.*

The next day we were sitting in Dr. Hoopes office, waiting for him to finish another heart/lung surgery. He came in and was very cordial. He spoke to David about what he thought was going on within his lungs and what his options were.

"David, we can put you on the transplant list today. Right now, the demand for lungs is not great. You might get lucky and have two new lungs within a month."

David shook his head. "I need to make arrangements with my work and let them know what the plan is."

Dr. Hoopes stood up and shook David's hand. "We will get you listed this afternoon. You know you have to stay in San Francisco while you are listed."

I nodded 'yes.' I prayed that God would give David new lungs very quickly and then asked for Him to bless Dr. Hoopes.

We explained our situation to Margie and Don and they said we could stay with them until his transplant, which we hoped would only be one month away. David once again made an office upstairs in Don's den. He used a card table to put his computer on, and I bought two plastic tubs to put his files in. The doctors had put David back on oxygen, so large, green oxygen bottles filled their entryway closet. Margie and Don were angels sent to help us. We loved them as much as if they were our natural parents.

Everything was in place. Now was the hard part. Waiting. Carrying your cell phone with you everywhere. Placing it on the nightstand by your bed. Keeping it on the sink when you showered. The phone was our line to new lungs for David.

August 1st arrived and so did the San Francisco fog. Each morning the grey fog would be thick and slowly burn off by noon, only to return around 3 p.m. like an old ship returning home to shore. Don said he welcomed the fog. He had grown up in San Francisco and, for him, the fog was like an old friend. He would build ship models in his den while David worked on the computer. Days passed, then weeks passed. But no calls from the transplant team.

Since we had flown to San Francisco with only a small suitcase, we needed some way to get our car and belongings from Texas to San Francisco. Once again our dear friends from Trinity Lutheran came to our rescue. My friend Jean walked through our Texas house, talking with me on the cell phone to see what things needed to be sent to California. One man, Gerhardt Pipho, was going to drive our car, packed with our clothes, from Houston to San Francisco. He had a brother in California whom he would visit and then he'd fly back to Houston. What a blessing! I remember telling Jean, "Hopefully David will get new lungs this month and we can be back in Houston by Thanksgiving!"

She and several others from church had offered to check on our house every so often. Since we were in the house only two weeks, we hadn't even unpacked our things. We didn't want someone to realize the house was vacant and break in.

At first, the days passed by quickly with David working diligently on his projects in France and sending email after email after email. I tried to help Margie and Don around the house and then would read or write to pass the time. It was the middle of August when I received a call from my sister in Littlefield, TX. My dad, who I had called Poppo for years, had been diagnosed with bladder cancer, and I needed to come to Texas. I was very close to my dad, always being his shadow as a child and wanting to do everything he did.

At 84, he had been very healthy until the last few months. He buried my mother in 1998 after 53 years of marriage and still missed her every single day. I always called him when I felt scared or needed advice. He had been so good to check on David during the first transplant. Now he was the one who needed me. But how could I go? David was on the transplant list!

David, Margie, Don, and I talked about the option of my leaving for a few days. They could get David to the hospital if the call for a transplant came through, but I would not be able to get back in time for the operation. I prayed to the Lord about what to do.

David gave me a hug and said, "Laura, Poppo has always been there when we needed him and I think you need to go for a few days. I'll be fine. Margie and Don will get me to the hospital if I get the call. You need to go."

So, I booked a flight to Littlefield, Texas for the following weekend.

I was in constant contact with Poppo while waiting for my flight. The doctors were going to scrape his bladder in the hope that they could clear away any cancer cells, as they felt he was in Stage 1 cancer. I prayed that the Lord would let the procedure be a success and that Poppo could continue to be my rock for many years to come.

The procedure was scheduled for Friday and I would be flying in late the evening before. I loved my dad so much. He was a retired Phillips Petroleum employee and had been the staunch Missouri Synod Lutheran of our family. I remember him holding my hand as I walked downstairs to Sunday school class. He patted my hand and told me he would be standing in the hallway waiting for me after class. I smiled. Strange how little memories fill your mind when a loved one is ill.

Bright and early Friday morning, my sister, her children, my son and his wife, and I sat anxiously waiting for the doctor to tell us he had gotten all of the cancer cells and that Poppo would be fine. After a short time, the doctor called my sister and me into a different room where he told us that he had been mistaken.

Dad was in Stage 4 bladder cancer and the scraping and chemo would not be enough to kill the cancer. We had two choices to make for him: we could talk him into have a surgical procedure which would remove his bladder, in the hopes that the cancer had not spread to his kidneys, or we could do nothing and within a few weeks, the cancer would destroy the kidneys and he would pass away painlessly and quietly.

I began sobbing. *Dear Lord, how can you take my dad*

away now? With David needing a transplant, Dad is my rock, my safety net. He is my sounding board and comforter. He is my dad. Please do not take him out of my life now!

My sister and I tried to compose ourselves before going to recovery to talk with Poppo. I could tell by the look on his face that he knew things were bad. My sister told him what the doctor had said while I stood by his bedside, stroking his face and holding his hand.

After hearing the options, Poppo asked, "What do you girls want me to do?"

Tears were once again flowing down my cheeks, and my sister said, "Dad, they think they can get all of the cancer if the bladder is removed. It sounds like the only option you have."

He closed his eyes for a moment and then said, "If you feel that is the best thing, then I will say okay."

I squeezed his hand and bent down to kiss him on the forehead.

The doctor said Poppo would need a week to heal, and the procedure was scheduled for the first week of September. I stayed by my dad as long as I could before having to fly back to San Francisco.

During those two short days, I shared with him memories I had of silly things that had happened, things I remembered from long ago. We laughed a little bit and we cried a little bit when we talked about David and about Mom.

My heart was aching when I said goodbye to him. I

didn't want to leave him, but I had to go back because
David needed me. He understood and gave me a strong
hug. He said, "Baby doll, I love you. Be safe going back."
I told him I loved him cried all the way to the airport. I
kept wondering why would God take such a good man
from my life? Why now?

The three-hour flight back to San Francisco seemed
to last for days. I wanted to hold David, to tell him
about Poppo, to have him hold me. I needed him to be
there for me. I needed him to tell me things were going
to be fine.

And there he was, in the car waiting for me when
the plane landed. He had grown very close to my dad
over the almost 25 years we had been married. He and
Poppo had built onto the first house we had owned. He
helped Dad anytime Dad needed it. David and I both
cried when I told him about the hospital and about the
cancer. We prayed together that the Lord would heal
him if it was His will. Then we sat together, holding
hands and being silent for a while as memories and
thoughts about Poppo ran through our minds.

The surgeons did perform the surgery and found
that the cancer had spread from the prostate to the
bladder to the kidneys. They removed not only Dad's
bladder, but the tiny tubes called ureters that
connected the kidneys to the bladder. He would have
several bags connected to his body to replace the
cancer riddled parts that had been removed. He stayed

in the hospital until the insurance said he had to be moved to an intermediate care facility. The surgery had left him in pain and dependent on skilled nursing care.

During the next few weeks, I called my sister several times a day to see how Dad was feeling or if anything had changed. One day she put the phone next to his ear, and I said, "Dad, I love you very much. Thank you for the many wonderful things you did for me. I love you. Keep fighting." When he tried to speak, all I heard was a garbled growl. I began yelling into the phone so my sister would hear: "Something is wrong! Dad can't talk! Get the doctor! Something is wrong!" The doctors found that Poppo had a severe infection, most likely cancer that had settled in his jaw and ear. Even though they tried to drain the area, he was still in pain.

I talked to David after learning about this latest infection in Dad's jaw and I remember what he said to me, "Laura, Poppo is a Christian and believer. Heaven is waiting for him. Don't be selfish by keeping him here for you. Life is about quality, not quantity." I knew he was right, but I still prayed that a miracle would happen to heal my dad.

On October 16th, 2006, Dad lost his battle with cancer and the good Lord took him home. Once again I made a flight reservation, but this time it was to attend his funeral.

David was still on the transplant list and still could

not leave San Francisco. I cried the entire flight back to Amarillo. Even though I knew my dad was in Heaven, my heart was missing him terribly. I felt so very alone and sad. Who would I talk to now when I needed a shoulder to cry on?

CHAPTER 21

November had arrived and the holidays were only a few weeks away. During the last month, we had learned that our dear friend Margie had been diagnosed with Hodgkin's' Lymphoma. She and Don had been so gracious, treating us like family and providing us with a home in San Francisco. After hearing this news, David and I felt we needed to move back to the Parkmerced Villa apartments so Don and Margie could concentrate on her cancer treatments and recovery.

Once again, I moved the few belongings we had into the apartment complex we had become familiar with less than a year prior. This time our apartment was not in one of the towers but in a row of apartments on Cardenas Street. This created a new problem... parking. The apartment complex was filled with college students, each one owning at least one car.

Since our tiny one bedroom apartment didn't have a parking garage attached to it, finding a parking space remotely close to the apartment became a daily challenge. In addition, I soon found out that the city of San Francisco has rules about which side of the street and which day of the week one could legally park the car.

Tuesdays, I could park on the right hand side of the street if a spot was available. Thursdays, I could park only on the left hand side of the street and only during certain hours. Whew! Most of the time, I dropped David off at the door of the apartment and found parking several streets or blocks away.

We began settling into a strangely familiar routine of driving to and from UCSF from the apartment. We thanked the Lord for the work David's company was supplying him and continually prayed for new lungs to become available quickly. Each time David had tests at the hospital or clinic, his results would be a bit lower or worse than the time before. I could see that he was becoming more and more disappointed and depressed.

Thanksgiving passed and Christmas was around the corner. Our daughter, Briana, would be graduating from South Dakota School of Mines and Technology on December 16th, 2006 in Rapid City. David's eyes filled with tears when she called to say she had been asked to give a speech at her graduation ceremony. She had become quite a leader during her years at her dad's alma mater and had been inducted into their Leadership Hall of Fame. Now she would be a featured speaker at the graduation and David would not be able to attend. He was still on the transplant list and still not able to leave San Francisco. He was still waiting. David was so very proud of Briana, but devastated, disappointed, and angry that he was forbidden to attend.

"Laura, am I asking for too much from God?" he asked me. "Should I be satisfied with the lung I have been given?" His eyes, once strong, confident, and bright were now filled with tears and clouded with worry. He continued, "I wasn't there for you when your dad died and now I will not be there for my daughter when she graduates. Have I been so selfish that God will not allow me to at least see her graduate?"

I put my arms around his neck and wanted to hold onto him forever. My eyes filled with tears too as I said, "My dear, I know this is difficult, but God is not punishing you! We have nothing if we lose our trust in Him." I sat down beside him, holding his hand. For a long time, we said nothing. We simply held hands and cried.

That night, after David and I prayed, I silently questioned God. "Why, dear Lord, why? You took my dad home and now the love of my life is suffering so.

Why are You waiting to heal him?" Part of me felt ashamed that I would dare to question God. Yet, I was so frustrated, so stressed, so confused, so hurt that I could only reach out to Him with angry pleas.

As if to answer my prayers, our daughter called the next morning. "Hey, Dad," she said over the phone. "I've been working with the dean to get the college to broadcast my graduation ceremony LIVE online. I could call you on my cell phone, put my earpiece on, and you could not only see me live, but would be able to hear me give my speech!" She was excited and I could see the sparkle in David's eyes as he listened to her. "We are going to work it out, Dad, you'll see!" Briana exclaimed.

David and I wrestled with the idea that I fly to Rapid City for the graduation while he stayed in San Francisco. Once again I would not be able to get back to him in time for the surgery if the call for a transplant came in while I was away. I was torn and worried about David having such a serious surgery and not being able to get to him. Suddenly, I began praying that God NOT send lungs to David the few days I would be in Rapid City for the ceremony.

December 16th came and as I sat in the auditorium watching my daughter graduate with honors as a Metallurgical Engineer, David sat alone in our tiny apartment watching the ceremony live online. As Briana walked up to the podium to begin her speech, she said to the audience, "My father is in San Francisco awaiting a lung transplant. I have my cell phone in my ear so he can hear me and he is watching this live via the web."

The audience was silent for a brief moment then began clapping. She nodded and began her speech, which she had fittingly entitled "Time."

Emotions were washing over me as if I were standing underneath a huge, powerful waterfall. Tears streamed down my cheeks because I was so proud of our daughter. Yet my heart was aching because I knew how badly her dad wanted to be healthy and sitting next to me, holding my hand.

I flew back to San Francisco the day after the graduation and let David know that Briana would be coming to visit us over the Christmas holiday. As I walked into the apartment, David was sitting at his computer working as always. When he glanced up, I noticed that his eyes seemed hollow and had dark circles surrounding them. His face was pale and he seemed extremely tired. I dropped my suitcase by the door and walked over to give him a hug. He felt unusually warm. I asked, "David, what's wrong? How are you feeling?"

"Fine", he said gruffly, "just fine."

I knew better. "How long have you been running a temperature?" I asked him.

He shrugged his shoulders.

"I'm calling UCSF," I said.

David rarely had a temperature and the few times he did, he was seriously ill. I left a message and, within a few hours, was talking directly with one of our transplant doctors.

David rolled his eyes as I told him the doctors wanted to see him.

"Let's be smart about this, dear," I said to him as we readied the portable oxygen tank to take with us.

"I am so tired of all this," David said. His voice was deep and without emotion. "I've missed so much these past two years," he continued.

I opened the car door for him and helped him inside. *Dear Lord* I thought to myself, *help us.*

After a CAT scan, pulmonary function tests, and a blood draw, we were sitting once more in front of one of the team doctors and hearing him say that the Aspergillus fungal infection appeared to be back.

"David, I'm upping your antibiotic dosage for two weeks and you will need to start back on the Amphotercin B," he said.

David asked, "How long on the inhaled Ampho B?" The thick yellow liquid that he had been forced to inhale since his first transplant was disgusting and very inconvenient. I had to leave the room David was in during the inhaled treatment to avoid my becoming immune to the drug if the situation ever arose that I needed to take it. Usually, I went for a walk during the 30-minute treatment.

The doctor leaned back in his chair and said, "You know, David, that it is a six month treatment time." He continued, "Since you have had a very strong immune system, you know that we have to keep you immune suppressed in order to avoid rejection of the new lung. As your immune system is weakened, it takes much longer for you to fight off infection. The fungal infection in your lung, aspergillus, is something that is found everywhere in everyday life. Most likely it is something you will battle from now on."

We were completely silent as we walked through the long hallways, into the elevator and rode down to the garage parking level. When the doors opened, we heard the echoing sounds of cars driving around the parking area, either looking for a parking spot or for the exit.

David broke the silence by saying, "This is not living. Going from the doctor's office to the apartment and back is not what I call living."

Over the last year and a half David had suffered through a few down times when his disease tried to get the best of him. I always tried to talk him through the despair, trying to make him laugh just a bit or make him see that he was beating this terrible disease called Interstitial Pulmonary Fibrosis. We prayed a great deal.

Today, as we drove out of the parking garage and

headed back to the apartment, I tried once again to reassure him. "I can't imagine how difficult it was for you not to be able to attend Briana's graduation ceremony. But God allowed you to view it and hear her speech live. That is another gift He has given you!" I said.

David nodded in agreement before speaking. "Laura, since I was told that I have IPF, not one thing has gone according to the doctors' plans," he stated coldly. "All of the complications, getting one lung for transplant, the blood clots," he continued and sighed. "Maybe I'm fighting against God's will by trying to stay alive."

His words startled me and, for a moment, I didn't say anything.

After getting him settled back into the apartment, I saw my unpacked suitcase standing where I had dropped it several hours earlier. As I picked it up, I said to David, "God tells us that He alone knows how long we have on this earth." I lifted up the suitcase, pointed to it and continued, "He says to be prepared. To always be prepared and ready to go. But only He knows when. Sweetie, if God were ready for you, I would not be standing here talking to you. He would have taken you home."

He nodded and tried to smile, but it was a half-hearted smile.

"Besides," I added, "God knows I would be

completely lost without you. Who else would balance my checkbook for me and eat my grilled peanut butter and jelly sandwiches?"

He chuckled and gave me his crooked little smile, the expression he knew would make me smile.

Our daughter came to our apartment right before Christmas to spend a brief few days with us. That made David very happy. We kept as many of our Christmas traditions as possible those few days. We watched part of the 24-hour marathon of the movie "A Christmas Story". We played the black and white version of the movie "It's A Wonderful Life" and laughed as Briana mimicked the little girl at the end of the movie who says the line about when a bell rings, an angel gets its wings. We played cards and ate turkey and dressing, and David helped Briana balance her checkbook, too!

This holiday was also the first time Dad and daughter could truly talk what I called "engineer" talk. Now that she had graduated and was working as an engineer, she had many questions to ask her dad since he had been in the engineering field for more than 25 years. She was looking forward to having an experienced reference anytime she needed him. It was so good to hear them discuss project management issues, mathematics, and general engineering stuff.

I watched in wonder as my two engineers laughed, hugged, and fought over the last of the chocolate brownies. I had to turn away when tears suddenly filled my eyes as I thought, "Dear Lord, thank you for this day."

Never once did the thought enter my mind that this would be our last Christmas together. Not once. I knew God would heal David. All we had to do was pray and wait for His timing.

CHAPTER 22

The new year arrived, and our hopes were renewed that our dear Lord would bring new lungs to David very soon. He had been on the transplant list for almost six months and had only had one call about a possible lung, which didn't work out.

Each day, David sat diligently at the card table he used for his office, writing emails, reviewing specification sheets or conducting kick-off meetings via conference calls. Each night we thanked God for allowing David to be so busy with work. It kept his mind off his deteriorating health.

We had hoped his eyesight might return, but gradually we realized that it would not. He had become quite good at using the magnifying glass to view the tiny computer screen emails and had even created a 'stand' for the magnifying glass out of a cardboard box. Ever the organizer, David kept track of over 11,000 emails sent for just one of the projects he was working on. His lungs may not have been working, but nothing was wrong with his sharp mind!

Over the next few months, we received updates from Don about Margie's cancer battle and her chemo treatments. She was such a brave soul! Always putting on her smile and caring for others much more than she cared for herself. Sometimes, when she felt good, she would call and laugh with David about how badly she and I had beaten them at dominoes. She was truly an angel and always brightened up our day no matter how badly she felt.

January was passing by when we received a call from our social worker at UCSF. She had been trying to get David and me to attend a monthly meeting of transplant survivors who were giving encouragement to patients waiting for transplants. We had always declined. But this time, for some reason, we decided to attend. Two days later, I wrote a letter to my friends at Trinity describing the meeting:

Dear Trinity family and friends,

Friday, January 26th, 2007…5 a.m.…I reached over to turn the off alarm on the telephone. These past seven months we have awakened every hour or so…

waiting for 5 a.m., waiting to get up...waiting to start another day of... waiting.

The humming sound of David's oxygen concentrator is as familiar now as the voice of an old friend. The ocean fog covers the city like a blanket of grey cotton balls. The wind is moving the fog slowly by, almost as if it is hesitant to go away. Yet, it, too, is a familiar part of our daily routine. Routine is such a strange word. Regular? Everyday? Normal? It has been so long since we knew the meaning of routine. Perhaps it means unexpected, or unreal, or ordinary. Maybe it just means...waiting.

You would be so proud of David. Wearing an oxygen cannula under his nose, he drags the fifty some feet of tubing behind him and sits at the little card table each day, dutifully logging onto his computer and trying to review any drawings or emails his company graciously sends him. He eats a little breakfast and I fix him a nice cup of hot chocolate with that wonderful whipped topping you squirt out of a can. It's his favorite and it makes him smile.

The bare white walls of our 600 square foot apartment are only dressed with a couple windows and a picture of Jesus that once hung over David's late grandmother's bed. We are blessed that this apartment has carpeting, which helps with the echo sound that occurs in a semi-empty room.

Each day David's coughing spasms seem to increase

in both frequency and length. Sometimes, these spells last twenty minutes or more. They tire him so much that he needs to lie down and rest. But lying down causes more spasms and the coughing begins again. It is an unending cycle for him as it is with all pulmonary fibrosis patients. I can only watch him, see him struggle to walk, breathe, cough.

Thoughts about the transplant operation he survived… how it was supposed to solve everything… bring back his health…bring back his dreams…the jumbled images ramble through my mind like an instant replay that refuses to go away. Images of the hospital stays, the IV infusions, the doctors shaking their heads in disbelief that he can't breathe, the surgical procedures, the sarcastic jokes from the Wisconsin pulmonologist about David being his 'albatross,' his 'patient that the worst would certainly happen to,' his 'worst nightmare'. All these memories run through my mind as I watch him, and my admiration for him and his faith grows each day.

The lung transplantation group has a monthly discussion group for pre-transplant patients and post transplant patients and their families. I suppose it is meant to be UCSF's effort to help educate patients. For several months, the social worker has been asking us to attend in order to encourage pre-transplant patients, ease their fears, and tell them everything will be okay. David and I have struggled with this idea, knowing that our emotions are like frayed wires, spurting out fountains of sparks and looking for the slightest motivation to ignite into a raging fire of frustration and anger.

For that reason, we had decided not to attend any of these meetings...ever. We have prayed for the Lord to give us contentment, give us strength to keep hoping...keep waiting for Him and His timing. Some days are easier than others to keep our eyes and hearts looking toward Him. But, yesterday was the January monthly meeting and, for some reason, the Lord put it in our hearts to attend that meeting.

With great reservation, we loaded our portable oxygen tank into the car and headed for UCSF. Strange how familiar the parking garage at the hospital is. Just as if we are walking into the Trinity sanctuary to look for our 'regular pew for church,' we look to see if someone is parked in 'our regular spot.' And grumble if we have to move to another less desirable space.

We hardly notice any of the surroundings of the hospital hallways or corridors anymore. Just routine... thinking about our plans or problems or just walking without thinking of anything at all...walking and waiting.

The awkwardness and anxiety of walking into the conference room, pulling a clanging portable oxygen tank, was abruptly elevated with the look of astonishment and surprise on the face of the social worker.

As with most small conference rooms, the large, heavy table was engulfed by too many over-sized, legal-looking swivel armchairs squeezed tightly around it. We clumsily made our way to a couple of empty chairs at the far end of the table and sat down. For several minutes, people sat silently waiting for someone to open the meeting or be brave enough to say something.

As we sat there…waiting…I looked into the faces of the others trapped in a seat around this big table. On one side were three people. Two were pre-transplant patients. One was a small, Hispanic lady who looked to be about our age. She was alone and clutched a little package of tissues that she periodically used to dab her teary eyes and her nose. Only once, for a very short glance, did her eyes look up. Goosebumps spread throughout my body like lightning when I looked into her eyes. Fear. The same fear I had seen in David's eyes was now glaring at me through her swollen eyes.

The other two people on that pre-transplant side were men. One of them was an Asian man with COPD being evaluated for a transplant. His eyes rotated around the room, stopping only to look into the hallway or at the man seated next to him. The man next to him appeared to be his significant other. They were perhaps a little older than David and I. They had no tissues or tears or runny noses. The significant other appeared to be uncomfortable, looking down mostly, as if this was meeting was an unnecessary distraction.

On the other side of this table were two post-transplant patients and one social worker. The first post-transplant was a healthy looking young man in his 30's. He was Caucasian, wearing a t-shirt, and baseball cap, and chewing gum like a first-baseman waiting for the next inning to begin. He had one of those faces that would never look older than about 15. He was looking around the room, rocking back and forth in the chair, smiling at people. Very polite. Very happy.

The black lady next to him was also a post-transplant patient. Again, about our age, very well educated and well spoken. She was wearing an Ace bandage around her right hand, wrist, and arm. Very pleasant smile and graciously greeted everyone.

David and I sat at the end of the table. A fitting place, I suppose, since David is both a pre-transplant and post-transplant patient. We looked at each other, wondering what to say, if anything. I have no trouble talking to people or strangers, as you know, but I found that I was having an unfamiliar feeling of shyness.

The conference began with the social worker saying, "Okay, does anyone have anything to say or any questions to ask?"

I thought: Hmm, that's it? That's how a social worker eases people into a conversation?

After a few moments of awkward silence, the Asian man asked what experiences any of the post patients had. David and I looked at each other...I thought: Oh, no...here we go.

But the happy young Caucasian man answered that he had waited only one week for a transplant and it was almost his one-year anniversary. He had no problems or complications. In fact, he stayed in the hospital only 10 days with the transplant. He went back to work after 4 months. He felt great. In fact, he had recently gone on a cruise and had a great time. Life was good.

I watched the two pre-transplant people while he talked. The Asian man was smiling, even nodding a couple of times. The Hispanic lady dabbed her eyes and nose but looked up and smiled. Perhaps she was having a moment of hope, a moment when the fear subsided just a bit. I've seen David have that look too.

The black lady's story was not quite as rosy. She was anticipating her 4th year anniversary from transplant. The first year or two were spent in and out of the hospital. She was a talented, successful attorney with a thriving practice. She tried to go back to work part time, but her health failed her. She planned to go back in the near future, though. Complications from medication had also been a problem for her. But, she was still here, with two good lungs. She felt good most days.

Again, I watched the two pre-transplant patients. The Asian man's smile was not quite so wide, and the Hispanic lady's fear had returned with vengeance and she was dabbing her eyes again. I took a deep breath and looked at David. I reached over to hold his hand. My heart began beating quickly as he started to speak. *Lord, please guide his words. Help him.*

As David began to speak, I could see the confusion on the faces of both the pre and post patients. If this man was a post-transplant patient, why was he wearing oxygen and short of breath? Why isn't he just fine? Did he not take care of his transplant? If this is what happens after transplant, why go through it at all? You could see these questions going through their minds like an LCD messaging billboard.

David did a good job of explaining his story, his experience. God allowed him to not be overcome by the deep anger or frustration that had become part of our lives. But He did give David the words to share that faith is the only constant source of his healing, the reason he has not lost all hope, the reason he can cope with this disease. The people that were sitting around that very big table learned about a man and heard a story they could not have anticipated.

I looked at the faces around that table as David shared his experience. The happy Caucasian man was no longer rocking in his big chair, and he had stopped chewing his gum. He had leaned forward on the table with his hands together, alternating between watching David and looking down at his hands. The black lady had leaned back in her chair with her chin resting on her bandaged right hand. She kept her eyes on David the entire time he was speaking.

The Asian man and his significant other were both looking down. They fumbled with their fingers while he talked, but neither one looked in David's eyes. There was no smile, no emotion of any kind. Just silence between them. And the Hispanic lady, who was alone, had tears gently falling from her eyes. She looked at David once in a while, dabbed her eyes and sat quietly. She too was wearing a portable oxygen cannula, and also had pulmonary fibrosis.

David was such an inspiration. He was honest with them about the things that sometimes happen with transplant, about his heartbreaking times, and about how much he valued the doctors at UCSF. But he ended by expressing how much faith, prayers, and support from family and friends had meant in his life. No one said anything for a moment. But everyone knew of his strength and faith. God led us to that meeting yesterday, and I pray that those who needed it received the message He wanted to send.

Dear friends, you have been such a blessing to us. Your continued prayers and cards are the highlight of our days. Even though many of you have your own trials, illnesses and disappointments in your life, you make time to include us. How can we ever tell you what that kind of love means to us? Thank you, thank you, thank you, dear Trinity family. We love you and pray that God continues to touch each of you and your families with His loving kindness and blessings.

Love always,

David and Laura

CHAPTER 23

The month of February passed by slowly and the first week of March brought the yearly battery of tests at UCSF for David. Pulmonary function tests, CAT scans, bronchs, and blood work were some of the tests done yearly for transplant patients. As David and I sat in the lobby of the sixth floor pulmonary clinic waiting for his test results, we were both amazed and stunned how our lives had changed in only two years. Two years. Had it really been only two years since he first collapsed at home?

"It seems like a lifetime ago, Laura," he said to me as he put his right hand on the scar that graced the left side of his chest.

I patted his arm and replied, "Yes, it has been two

years of challenge, but we are still here, still together!" I smiled at him, hoping he would, in turn, smile back.

He did not.

We were called back into the office area for what we thought would be the results of the yearly tests. We were very surprised when Dr. Hoopes walked into the room instead of one of the pulmonary doctors.

David glanced at me with a look of dread and said, "Why, hello, Dr. Hoopes. How are you today?"

Dr. Hoopes shook David's hand, sat down at the computer, and logged in. "Hello, David," Dr. Hoopes began. "We've got to stop meeting like this or people are going to talk," he kidded.

David and I laughed.

Then the doctor continued, "David, you've been on the list for some time now. Your pulmonary function tests are steadily decreasing, and we are going to redo a few tests to try to get you moved up on the list. But what disturbs me is your creatinine level. Your kidneys are functioning at about 50 percent of normal."

I looked at David who began to frown as he heard the news. I took hold of his hand and asked Dr. Hoopes why.

"Medicine is great and keeps transplant patients alive," Dr. Hoopes began, "but we haven't figured out how to keep that same medication from destroying other organs. Most likely the Caspofungin IV's you were on for the Aspergillus fungal infections caused damaged to your kidneys."

Although David didn't speak, I could see in his face what he was thinking: Not another complication.

Dr. Hoopes told David that he would be setting up an appointment for him to see the kidney transplant team on the seventh floor for evaluation and to get entered into their system.

David asked, "Am I understanding that you think I will need a kidney transplant at some point?"

Dr. Hoopes answered, "I'm not sure at this time, which is why I want you checked out by our group. Once you lose kidney function, it cannot be restored. We can't get you a pair of lungs if your kidneys are functioning below a certain level." With that, Dr. Hoopes shook David's hand and got up to leave. "Don't worry, David, we will find you lungs. You are on the top of my list."

As David and I waited to hear when his appointment would be with the kidney transplant team, one of our friends on the pulmonary transplant team sat down beside him.

"It's a good sign that Dr. Hoopes has you on his short list. I'm guessing it won't be too long before you get a call that he has found lungs for you," she said, trying to comfort him. He nodded and she gave him a hug.

"Thank you," I said. "We are a little bit shocked

about the kidney transplant though. What is going to happen?"

She said that they were trying to get David into the kidney groups' system for if and when his kidney function dropped to a dangerous level. "Don't worry. Dr. Hoopes knows what he is doing and all he wants is the best for David," she said as she smiled at me. I shook my head that I understood.

David's kidney group appointment was for the third week in March. "Boy," he said, "when Dr. Hoopes wants something, it gets done in a hurry!" We giggled. It usually takes weeks, even months, to get an appointment with the kidney transplantation group. "It is a blessing that he is my doctor," David stated. I agreed.

Walking out of the UCSF elevator, we could see that the seventh floor kidney clinic looked much different than the sixth floor pulmonary clinic. There were several rows of upholstered chairs that were filled with people either waiting for appointments or for family members to finish appointments.

David pulled out a small, pocket-sized notepad from his shirt pocket and his favorite mechanical pencil.

"What are you doing?" I asked.

"Writing down names. This is a new transplantation group and I want to be able to call them by name," he replied.

I smiled and squeezed his arm. *That's my engineer husband that I love so very much! Always paying attention to details.*

The head of the kidney transplantation department met with David and, after reviewing his rather large file sent up from the pulmonary department, said "My goodness! You have certainly had a rough couple of years, haven't you, Mr. Bichler?"

David grinned and nodded 'yes.'

The lady doctor continued, "Well, from the preliminary results, I can say that down the road you will most likely need a kidney transplant, but that may be looking several years ahead."

Again David did not answer but nodded.

The doctor continued, "The good news is that we are currently developing new medication for transplant patients that will not have an adverse effect on the kidneys. We are hoping to have it approved for use sometime next year."

I knew that was meant to be good news, but David and I looked at each other, politely smiling on the outside, but greatly disappointed on the inside.

Once more the doctor spoke. "Right now, Mr. Bichler, I believe we do not need to change your medication, but we will need to monitor your kidney functions more closely the next few months. I am giving you some material concerning kidney transplants to read over before our next visit. If you have any questions, do not hesitate to contact us." She handed David several brochures, shook our hands and left the room. His next appointment was set for mid-June.

I could tell that he was deeply disappointed with the thought of yet one more transplant and, as we drove from the hospital back to the apartment, I told him again how much I loved him, how much I admired him, how much God was in control of our lives, and loved us dearly. He never spoke, but only nodded his head in agreement.

He slept for a couple of hours after we returned to the apartment as the walking and coughing had tired him out a great deal. I sat in front of the television mindlessly watching whatever happened to be on at the moment, while he slept. The hundreds of prayers I had been saying the past two years were whirling around in my head. *Why, dear God? Why has this happened? Now a kidney transplant too? How can we continue to remain strong? Why?*

When a coughing spell woke him up, David sat down beside me, and I knew something about him had changed.

He looked at me and said, "I'm not going to live to be an old man, Laura. I realize that."

I began to cry.

He put his arm around me and continued, "Over the last years, I prayed that God let me live long enough to get you back to Houston where our friends at Trinity could take care of you and that Briana graduate and have a good job that would take care of her."

I looked into his face and saw something I had not seen in years. Peace. He wasn't angry or disgusted. He wasn't disappointed or scared. He was simply at peace. I buried my head in the shoulder of his shirt and sobbed.

"Laura," he said, "God has given me those two things. We were transferred back to Houston and Briana has a great job and she has a wonderful young man in her life that loves her. God answered my prayers." There was a long pause. He sighed and said, "I'm ready to go home whenever He is ready for me."

It took me a long time to stop crying enough to speak. David sat there, holding me the entire time. Finally I said, "I need you! We have prayed that God heal you and we have come so far. God knows I need you and I believe He will heal you and we can live out the rest of our lives together."

He smiled at me, but I know he didn't believe me.

That night as we lay down to sleep, David said our prayers for the first time in two years. He asked only that God's will be done in our lives and gave thanks for the lives of all the donors who allow others the gift of their organs and for the many doctors who had treated him. All I could do was silently shout at God to not take this man out of my life and not to listen to David's prayers.

Before we knew it, April had arrived and David's coughing spells were increasing. He had begun to lose weight once again, and I could see that his breathing was more and more labored. He continued to work diligently at his computer, trying to finish up the project he had begun two years earlier. I noticed that he was quietly finishing up several things and it bothered me a great deal. We didn't speak again about the day he told me he was ready to be taken to Heaven and I tried everything I could to prove that we would live together well into our retirement years.

One day in late April, the UPS man arrived at our apartment with several large boxes from David's employer. He was being put on a new project! *Hurray! Just what he needed to help him realize he would be around for a very long time,* I decided.

David diligently opened each box, thumbing through the 800 pages or so of new specifications for some oil/water-processing unit he was in charge of getting built.

I said with a smile, "Guess you'll be having another kickoff telephone conference soon!"

His answer took my breath away for a moment. He said, "I've created an index file for you of names, phone numbers and addresses of people from my office. I'll keep the files I'm not working on in their original box. It will make it easier for you to send back to Houston."

Huh? I swallowed hard. "What? Are these the wrong files or something?" I questioned.

He smiled but didn't respond to my question. I was frightened and got busy fixing him a nice cup of hot chocolate in order to keep from crying once again.

A few nights later, I had trouble sleeping and couldn't figure out why. Something was bothering me, weighing heavily on my mind, but for the life of me I didn't know what. I got up and quietly went into the other room to check emails or read or watch television until I became sleepy. I surfed the internet, watched television, read a little bit. But nothing seemed to help. I felt extremely anxious for some reason. I prayed for a bit and lay back down to try to sleep.

Still restless, I finally got up around 5 a.m. and decided to get dressed. I was as quiet as possible in order not to disturb David's much needed sleep. But by 7 a.m., he was up and our day was beginning. He liked to have hot oatmeal for breakfast and I was pouring it into a bowl when he walked into the small kitchen area.

"Morning, my love," he said.

"Morning, sweetie," I answered, setting his bowl of oatmeal and glass of milk on the card table.

He said, "I don't feel right today, but I can't put my finger on it." He paused for a moment then continued,

"Think I'll check my email schedule to see if there is a deadline or something I've missed."

I nodded and said, "You know, I didn't sleep at all last night either. Maybe it was too warm in here or something." With that said, I dismissed it and poured milk into my bowl of oatmeal.

David remarked, "Well, today is April 30th, but I don't show any deadlines I need to be concerned about." He shrugged, repositioned his nose cannula, and began eating his oatmeal.

By 9 a.m., David was steadily working on his computer and I had gathered our few towels together and walked over to the shared laundry room in our group of apartments. Each time I walked, my cell would bang against my leg, reminding me that it was in my pocket. This morning was no different.

I always took a deck of cards with me to the laundry room and played Solitaire while the washers ran through the short cycle. I had lost two games when my phone rang. Not thinking much about it, I figured it might be David needing me to walk to the store and bring him something. I looked down at the caller ID and it said UCSF. My heart skipped a few beats. "Hello?" I answered.

"Laura, hello! This is David's pre-transplant nurse. What are you guys doing this morning?"

I thought to myself: *Why would she ask what we were doing this morning?*

"Not much," I replied. "David is in the apartment on his computer and I am down at the laundry room, washing towels. Do we have any appointment with you today?"

I heard her chuckle slightly when she said, "Yes, we would like to see David. How would he like to get new lungs today?"

I stood there with my heart beating so hard my head was pounding! "What!! What!! New lungs!! Are you sure?" I was talking so fast that I couldn't understand what I was saying.

The nurse on the other end of the phone was laughing. "Yes, Laura, Dr. Hoopes thinks he has a pair of lungs for David. How soon can you get him here?"

I shouted into the phone: "We'll be there in 20 minutes or less! Thank you, thank you!"

Not thinking about the clothes in the washer or the sack of other dirty laundry, I bolted out of the room, running and jumping and shouting, "Thank you, Jesus!! Thank you, Jesus!!" I almost knocked the apartment door down trying to get it open and I burst through it, saying, "David, David! They have lungs for you! They have lungs for you!"

He was startled at first, then began to understand what I was excitedly trying to tell him. This was the call we had waited ten months for! God was giving David a new pair of lungs! He was going to get new lungs today!

CHAPTER 24

❧

"They called?" David excitedly asked.

"Yes, yes, and we need to be there by 10 a.m.!" I quickly answered. "I'll pack the overnight bag; you get dressed, okay?" I continued as I went into the bedroom to pack.

David began notifying his office and sending emails to take care of the projects he was working on. Within a few minutes, we were in our car heading towards the familiar UCSF parking garage. "Oh, my dear, you are getting new lungs! Wow! I am so thankful. I told you God would heal you! I knew he would!" I chattered as I drove toward the hospital.

David smiled, but was strangely quiet, or maybe I was just doing all the talking. I was overjoyed that soon he would be able to breathe, talk, walk, and laugh again without choking and gasping for air.

We reported to the tenth floor ICU unit and were greeted with many congratulations from the nurses and doctors on the floor. I was sent down to admitting and David was put in the floor's waiting room. I was happy and felt like screaming out to everyone I saw, "God is giving my husband new lungs today!"

The admission office was full of people waiting their turn. I added my name to the registration list and sat down beside an older Hispanic woman who was holding onto a beautiful string of prayer beads. I said hello to her as I sat down and she nodded. "I pray all goes well for you today, ma'am," I said. Her eyes briefly looked up from the prayer beads and again she nodded. My mind was racing.

When would the operation begin? How long before I could see him again? When could we finally go back home to Houston? I checked my watch. 10:15 a.m. I couldn't sit still and kept shifting my position in the chair. Eventually I began pacing the tiny space around my chair. I checked my watch again. 11:01 a.m. *My goodness! When are they going to call me up to register David?*

Suddenly my cell phone rang. It was the pre-transplant nurse calling to see if David had been admitted yet. I told her no, that David was on the 10th floor, and I had been waiting in Admitting for almost an hour. She said she would take care of that and hung up. It wasn't five minutes later that my name was called!

I walked up to the registration desk, told them David's information and that he had received the call for a lung transplant today. The young lady at the desk smiled and said, "Yes, we know. The transplant team called us. We are to rush you through to the financial aid officer."

My jaw dropped open. *The financial officer? Oh no,* I thought to myself. *I don't have to talk with her again do I?* But that is exactly the financial person who was in charge of David's case once again.

"Hello, Sherry," I said as I sat down in front of her small desk. Her cubical hadn't changed since I'd met with her the year before. That's when she'd coldly confronted me with either paying my bill or letting my husband die.

"Hello, Mrs. Bichler," she stated as she typed on her computer keyboard. "I see Mr. Bichler is getting another transplant."

I nodded, wishing and praying that I could get away from this interview as soon as possible.

"I also see that you have different insurance coverage this time. That's good. Otherwise I would need around $200,000 from you before we could perform the transplant."

Her monotone voice and matter-of-fact statements were uncaring and harsh.

Again I nodded and tears began to form in my eyes.

"Now, Mrs. Bichler, don't cry," she began as she handed me papers to sign. "I'm sure things will go well for your husband this time. No one can be that unlucky two times in a row."

Teardrops fell on the paper I was signing. I said, "I pray you are right," and handed her back the papers.

She finished typing, handed me a couple of wristbands for David and without looking up said, "Thank you. Have a good day."

I quickly stood up and walked down the narrow hallway, out of the admission area and into the nearest women's restroom where I dried my tears. I couldn't let David see my eyes red. Not today! He was getting new lungs today!

I checked my watch as I got out of the 10th floor elevator. 11:55 a.m. I hurried back to the waiting room area only to find that David was still sitting there. He asked, "Were you able to check me in?"

I smiled and assured him that everything was great and he had been admitted. I presented him with the wristbands that had his identification on it. He smiled and said, "Hmm, just my size."

We chuckled.

"Have you seen Dr. Hoopes? Have they said when the surgery is going to start?" I asked him as I sat down beside him.

"No, but I expect one of the transplant doctors to come in anytime now."

I grabbed his hand in mine, kissed it and held it close to my heart. "God is so good, sweetie. He is answering our prayers." He looked at me and smiled.

I had packed a deck of cards in my backpack and we played Gin to pass the time and to keep our minds occupied. Around 1 p.m., one of the transplant doctors walked through the door. "Well, are you comfy in here, David?" he asked and smiled as he sat down across from us.

David shook his hand and said, "It's been quite the morning, to say the least".

I told him, "We are so excited! When will the surgery begin?"

The doctor smiled and said, "We always call at least two people to come in when an organ becomes available. The process of matching a donor lung to a patient is a greatly detailed procedure that can take several hours. You are the first in line for these lungs, but the second person on the list is here also in the event you are not a complete match."

David and I looked at each other, both listening intently.

"We are not sure you will get these lungs, David, but from the preliminary tests, Dr. Hoopes believes they will be a good match for you. Have you called your family yet?"

I replied, "Yes, but I told them not to come until we know for sure that David will be getting the lungs."

The doctor nodded and said, "That's a good idea." He turned to David and said, "We are going to take some blood, get you into one of our executive hospital gowns" (he and David both laughed) "and put you in one of the intermediate care rooms until we hear from Dr. Hoopes."

Both David and the doctor stood up and David, always the polite gentleman, shook his hand and said, "Thank you. Tell all the doctors thank you."

For the next five hours, David and I sat in the intermediate care room waiting to hear something. My cell phone rang just about every hour. It was either our daughter or one of his sisters, checking to see if we had heard anything. Each time I would answer, "Nope. Not yet."

We tried to play cards, but our hearts weren't really in it. David had been unusually quiet, closing his eyes to pray or trying to rest. The excitement had worn off and the reality of going through as serious an operation as a double lung transplant was weighing on both our minds.

He had been staring out the window for a while, when he suddenly turned to me and said, "Laura, am I asking God for too much? Why should He grant me a second pair of lungs when the second person on the list hasn't had one?" On his face was a look of uncertainty and fear. It scared me.

I knelt down in front of the chair he was sitting in, took both his hands in mine and said, "Remember, my love, God will decide who best matches these lungs. He loves you, David, and I know He has a plan for us and our future." I squeezed his hands.

But he questioned again, "Should I be satisfied with the gift He already gave me?" His next sentence brought tears to both our eyes. He said, "Laura, someone died to give me the single lung I received two years ago and I'm alive because of it. Someone died today to provide these lungs, too." I blinked the tears back as he continued, "I want people to know that Jesus died so they all could live. Make sure people understand that, okay?"

I cleared my throat and said through my tears, "Oh, my love! God is going to bless you. You are going to be all right. Our loving Savior will grant our prayers to heal you. I just know it!"

He wiped the tears from his eyes and nodded. We hugged each other for a long time. We didn't speak, but I knew we were both praying.

A gurney suddenly appeared outside the room and a nurse came through the door, saying, "Mr. Bichler, it's time to get ready. Looks like you just might be getting new lungs this evening!"

Startled, we looked at each other. The nurse helped

David from the chair and said, "Things are going to start hopping around here. When Dr. Hoopes is ready, things move quickly."

David grinned and I nodded. I followed the gurney down the hallway and into the elevator. David was being taken down to the pre-op where IVs would be started. I held tightly onto his hand, taking fast steps to keep up with the gurney.

Once in the pre-op area, an operating room nurse started an IV drip, went over his vital signs, then said, "Nothing more to do but wait, Mr. Bichler. Dr. Hoopes is still determining the match for the donor lungs."

I stood by his bedside, holding his hand and kissing him every now and then. We were in a holding area surrounded by a curtain and could hear movement all around. Nurses talking, IVs beeping, and occasionally a laugh or two. David asked what time it was. "It's 6 p.m.," I told him after checking my watch.

No sooner had I finished my sentence than Dr. Hoopes threw open the curtain and walked over to David. "Well, David, I have a pair of lungs waiting for you. What do you say?"

I was smiling and David nodded as Dr. Hoopes added, "Remember, David, this will not be a piece of cake. Any number of things could happen." He was sitting on the side of the bed, looking David straight in the eyes. He continued, "For instance, I'm not sure if I can get the old lung out cleanly or if the cavity will open up again." He paused, still looking David in the eyes. "David, it doesn't matter what Laura wants or what your family wants. This is between you and me. Period. I am the one who will take the credit for giving you new lungs and you will get to live a long life. But I am also the one who must take responsibility and sign the death certificate if things go badly." Again the doctor paused. I watched David's face and he was listening very closely to each word the surgeon was saying. Dr. Hoopes ended by saying "So, what is your decision? I'll respect whatever you decide."

David's eyes never left the doctor's gaze and he said without hesitation, "I'm ready. Let's do this."

"Great. My team will be coming for you in a few minutes," Dr Hoopes replied. He shook David's hand then said to me, "This is where you kiss him and tell him you love him. I'll come to the 10th floor waiting room and talk to you when the surgery is over." And... he was gone.

I bent down to kiss my husband and assured him that God was watching over him and that he had the best surgeon in the world.

"I will be here the entire time you are in surgery. I'll never leave you, my dear. God is with you."

Before he could answer, the team came and wheeled his gurney down the hallway. Tears filled my eyes as I watched him disappear through the surgery doors. I began praying the Lord's Prayer as I walked toward the elevator.

I called our daughter and David's sisters. They were praying also and would be coming to UCSF the next morning. I called my friend Jean Smith at Trinity and she spread the word to our church family.

The waiting room was completely empty. I pulled two chairs together in order to stretch my legs out. 6:30 p.m. The nurses said a double lung transplant could take between 6 and 8 hours. I tried watching television. I tried reading. I tried praying. The hands on my watch seemed to be moving in super slow motion. Every hour the nurses would check on me to see if I needed anything. Sometimes they would play a hand of Gin with me. They knew the trials David had gone through the last two years and they, too, prayed that the surgery would be a success.

Around midnight, I walked over to the ICU nurses' desk to see if they had heard anything about how the procedure was going. The night nurse said, "I think well. It looks like they are finished. He got a single right lung."

Wait. Did she say single lung? "Are you sure that it's David you checked on? He is getting a double lung transplant," I said.

She frowned for a moment, checked her charts and said, "No, it says here they only did a single right lung transplant."

My heart sank. What had happened? *Dear Lord, don't let him suffer through pain again!*

I asked, "Do you know when Dr. Hoopes will be coming by to talk with me?"

She said it would be in about an hour or so. I thanked her and went back to the waiting room where I began to question God. "Lord, he was supposed to get two lungs. Please let him be all right. Please let him be able to breathe." I sat by the door and did the only thing I could do…I waited for Dr. Hoopes.

CHAPTER 25

My arms and legs felt strangely heavy as I sat watching the clock on the wall tick slowly by. The only light in the vacant waiting room was an eerie glow from the streetlight below that outlined each windowsill. My stomach had turned sour and dread engulfed me. Something must have happened. But what? My mind was racing and all I could do was try to recite the Lord's Prayer over and over again, trying not to cry or panic. I strained to see my watch. 1:30 p.m. It was now May 1st and, for some reason, my thoughts turned to what my dad used to say: "May-Day." He would always shrug when the first of May arrived and say that "May-Day" means that summer and the hot weather are just around the corner!

My Dad was not a person to sit around idle. He

was either walking, playing dominoes, selling antique cars, going to the store, or something. But he rarely sat around doing nothing. I had to smile. "Thank you, dear Lord, for giving me these memories to make me smile." It is strange how God gives you tiny things like memories to help calm you during the troubled times in life. How when everything looks dark around you, He is there to carry you, to wrap His arms around you, to bring a glimpse of His light in your sorrow, and to love you when you feel most alone.

I stood up when I heard footsteps coming toward the waiting room. I reached the hallway as Dr. Hoopes came through the ICU doors towards me. His eyes looked tired and he was still wearing his operating scrubs and hat. My heart was beating loudly in my ears and I didn't know whether I felt relief or fear.

"Dr. Hoopes, how is David? When can I see him?" I blurted out. We both leaned against the wall of the hallway, facing each other.

He said, "He's doing pretty well. I was concerned about the right lung cavity not opening up big enough to get a lung inside, but when we took out the old scarred lung, it popped right back into place. It was beautiful."

Here stood a six-foot surgeon who had just held my husband's life in his hands. I was in awe of the talent God had blessed him with.

"The nurse told me he only got one lung. Is that right?" I asked quickly.

The doctor answered, "We did an incision across the entire chest and had intended to do a double lung. But the donor's left lung was in worse shape than the current lung David has, so I decided not to transplant it again. I think he will better recover with the lung he has."

He must have seen that I was discouraged or disappointed because he continued, "Laura, if David were being born today, this new lung would be the one he would be born with. It was almost a perfect match." He smiled just a little.

I felt relieved and smiled back at him. "Thank you, Dr. Hoopes, thank you," I said as I reached out my hand to shake his.

He shook my hand and assured, "I think David is going to do very well with his recovery. He was not as ill as he was with the first one. I am praying he has no complications this time. Poor guy has been through so much." Then he added, "God is the one who provided this lung for David. I am only the one who sewed it in."

I couldn't help myself and began crying again. I nodded and asked, "When can I see him?"

"My team is checking his vitals, getting him stabilized," Dr. Hoopes said. "In about an hour you should be able to go to his room. I'll have the nurse come get you."

As he turned to leave I said thank you once again.

He stopped, turned around and said, "He will be in some pain and perhaps a bit mad at us for cutting an incision across his entire chest. Even though this lung was a good match, there are still many things that could go wrong. We won't be out of the woods for several days."

I nodded that I understood. He also nodded, turned, and walked by into the ICU. I breathed a huge sigh of relief and said aloud, "Thank you, Lord! Soon our lives will be back to normal. Thank you!"

I stepped back inside the waiting room and thought about calling my daughter and David's sisters, but realized it would worry them if I called at two in the morning! *I'll wait till around 6 a.m.*, I thought to myself, and settled into the chair to wait for the nurse to come. Finally, David would be breathing, laughing, traveling, working... living again! I felt a renewed sense of comfort and I knew that the many prayers said for us had been heard by our Father in Heaven.

Around 5:30 a.m., I was in David's ICU room, which happened to be #12, on the left wing of the ICU floor. Even though the room number was different, the room looked exactly the same as the other rooms, right down to the mechanical ventilator standing next to his bed.

It felt strangely familiar. David was still sedated with a breathing tube down his throat, and the double

IV poles at the head of his bed were filled with eighteen or so different bottles, all feeding into his arms. In his neck was another large arterial line where they would be able to draw blood easily without poking him. Each room had its own nurse's station just outside the glass doors of the room. This time we knew all the nurses, their hobbies, and their families.

There were two stark differences, though. David had two drain measurement boxes for his lungs, one that hung on each side of the bed, which were quickly filling with a bloody, red fluid. And he looked great! He had color in his face and arms. He really looked good!

Our daughter and David's two sisters arrived by noon and he was already off the ventilator and was quite alert. For Linda, it was like a homecoming as she knew all the nurses and doctors that treated her only three short years ago. She gave us hope that lung transplant patients actually do get their lives back and had been a kind of poster child for the lung transplant program. We all prayed David would have the same remarkable recovery as his sister.

The first day after the transplant was terrific, with David taking his first walk that afternoon. He was very sore, but he was breathing! And not labored breathing either. He was taking regular breaths, in and out, without coughing! We were all astonished and amazed and happy. You could see a sigh of relief from the nurses and doctors as David steadily got better and better. I took pictures of him as he walked, emailing them to Trinity with shouts of wonder and praise that God was healing him.

The morning of the fourth day after surgery, David was laughing and joking with his nurse and beating me at Gin. Linda, Briana, and Mary had gone home, knowing that he was well on his way to recovery. It happened to be a Friday and David mentioned that he was hoping to get out of ICU. He had gone through the daily bronchs, x-rays, CAT scans, and blood work with flying colors. Not one complication. His oxygen saturation levels were steady around 95 without wearing his oxygen cannula.

David called his office to say that he hoped to be able to start working on his computer again within a couple of weeks. He was smiling and planning for the future. Things felt great. I had no worries and was looking forward to having my old husband back in tip-top form.

He was sitting in the chair beside his bed early that same afternoon, dozing while watching some television movie. I was reading a book, sitting across the room from him. He was still hooked to the heart monitor and the IV machines and still had the arterial line in his neck. He snorted loudly, waking himself up and chuckling about it. As he started to shift his weight in the chair and stretch just a little bit, the alarms on every single monitor and IV in the room began screeching and beeping. David's eyes popped open and I threw my book to the floor. Several nurses bolted into his room and began checking him. Their frantic actions told me there was something terribly wrong.

I could tell David was as confused as I was. The nurses got him back into bed, shut off the alarms and began their systematic regiment of checking his vitals. Within a few minutes, two of the lung transplant doctors were in the room, listening to his chest and talking to the nurses. David and I looked at each other, almost afraid to ask what was wrong when one of the doctors asked, "David, are you experiencing any pain?"

David said, "No."

The doctor continued, "How is your breathing? Do you feel any pressure in your chest?"

Again David shook his head 'no.'

Then the doctor said, "What happened while you were sitting in the chair?"

David told them that he woke himself up snoring and had shifted his weight to stretch a little bit when the alarms began to blast.

The doctor replied, "We have a call in to Dr. Hoopes because you have gone into a-fib. Hoopes is doing a heart transplant, so it will be a while before he gets here."

His heart was racing at 185 beats per minute...and that was extremely fast.

The doctor said, "We're going to give you amiodarone to get you back into a sinus rhythm."

I could see David's smile turning into a frown and I said to him, "This will be okay. It's just one dose and then things will be fine again." Amiodarone was the medication that caused him to lose a portion of his eyesight, and I knew David was balking at having to take it once again.

Within a few hours, David was back in sinus rhythm and the doctors had given him the go ahead to be transferred over to 10 Long. His smiled returned and for the first time since his daughter was born, he was truly giddy with excitement! How he wanted to get out of the hospital and get back to his life. He asked the nurse, "Does this mean I might be released tomorrow?"

The nurse studied his orders and, with a look of surprise, he said, "Well, Dr. Hoopes has orders that you could be released tonight."

I looked at the nurse with a questioning look of uncertainty and he returned my glance with the same uncertainty.

David, however, was pleased. He announced, "I'm calling Linda to let her know that I am being released one day sooner than she was!"

I was more concerned about what had happened just a few hours earlier.

While David talked to Linda on the cell phone, I caught the nurse in the hallway just out of his hearing range. "Have you told Dr. Hoopes what happened this afternoon?" I asked the nurse.

The nurse shrugged and said, "No, Hoopes is still in surgery. He made these order this morning."

I paused and said, "Do we know what caused the a-fib?"

Again the nurse shrugged. "The doctors will be back in around 7 p.m. tonight. Right now my orders are to move you guys to 10 Long." He had a concerned look that matched mine. I desperately wanted to get out of the ICU, but after what happened this afternoon, I was frightened to be dismissed late on a Friday evening with no Dr. Hoopes close by.

I went back into the room to talk with David. I knew he should look happy, but there was something very wrong about his expression. There was something he wasn't telling me or the nurses.

"Hey, sweetie, shouldn't we wait to hear from Dr. Hoopes before moving our stuff to 10 Long?"

He didn't say anything or change his expression.

I tried again. "We don't really know what caused the a-fib this afternoon. Are you comfortable with leaving tonight? Maybe we should wait till tomorrow morning, just to have Dr. Hoopes check you out."

David looked down at his hands but didn't say a word.

An hour later, the nurse was in to transport David out of ICU, down the long hallway to the wing known as 10 Long. The nurse said, "Laura, I'll get David situated in the room. Why don't you collect all your belongings and we will meet you in his new room."

I nodded and began gathering the things we had accumulated during this week's stay in ICU. Kleenex boxes, pillows, cards, toothbrushes, pink water pitcher and plastic glass with the ounce measurements on the side. I put the things into a large black trash bag the nurse gave me. I resembled Santa with his huge backpack.

As I walked out of ICU, each nurse that had attended David hugged me and said, "We wish the best for your husband. He has been through so much. God bless you." I felt like I was leaving home and moving far away, not just down one hallway corridor.

David was in a room toward the end of one of the sides of 10 Long and a good distance from the nurse's station that was centrally located on the floor. 10 Long was also shaped like a horseshoe, the central point being a large nurses' area.

I walked through the door with my heavy black trash bag on my shoulder to see David standing by the small white board hanging on the wall directly across from the head of the bed. He was grinning like a boy who had just gotten his first kiss and his cheeks were rosy red.

I dropped the trash bag and asked, "What's going on?"

His smile widened and he said, "Guess when I am being released from this place?"

I shook my head and said hopefully, "Tomorrow?"

He proudly picked up the red marker attached to the side of the white board and wrote "5-4-2007." He drew too big lines underneath the date.

"TONIGHT?' I said in a concerned voice.

"Yep! I could be released as soon as Dr. Hoopes comes by to check me out," he replied confidently.

I hugged him and said that was terrific, but in my heart I knew I would be more comfortable if we left early the next morning. Since he had gone into a-fib earlier that day, I needed to be assured by Dr. Hoopes that he was going to be all right. So many things could go wrong that I just wanted to know I had a direct line to Dr. Hoopes if David needed him. And being in the hospital was that direct line.

CHAPTER 26

David settled into the hospital bed, waiting for Dr. Hoopes to come by, and I sat beside him, holding his hand. We watched the television that was mounted on the wall without talking. For some reason, I felt uneasy. David was holding something back. I couldn't put my finger on it, but I just had a feeling of dread.

The respiratory therapist that had been working with David in ICU stopped by his door and said, "Well, Mr. Bichler. I see we have moved uptown!" He smiled and David acknowledged his smile. "Do you feel like taking a walk? Maybe trying to walk up a couple stairs?" he asked.

Both David and I knew it wasn't a request, but almost an order. David grinned and said, "I hope you can keep up!"

The therapist smiled. "Take it easy on me, okay? You're supposed to have just had a lung transplant, you know." The therapist walked over to the bed to help David to his feet and then out the door they went. I followed as usual.

There was a stairwell close to our room and David stood before it, looking very small, like the biblical David standing before Goliath.

The therapist after checking David's vitals, asked, "Do you feel strong enough to try a step or two?"

David didn't nod or hesitate. He simply took off and almost raced up the entire flight of stairs. Stunned, the therapist jumped over two steps to catch up with him. No sooner had David gotten to the top of the stairs did he turn around and walk back down.

He was breathing hard when he reached the bottom and his therapist said to me, "Boy! I thought he would go up one at a time. Maybe do a total of three steps. This guy thought he was in the Olympics!" He was pleasantly surprised, but I was intently looking at David's face. It seemed swollen and red. I noticed he had a few drops of sweat beginning to form on his forehead. The therapist also noticed the beads on his forehead and said, "Well, that's enough for now. How about let's head back to the room for a cold one?" They both grinned as the therapist added, "A big cold glass of water!"

David had barely gotten back into the bed when Dr.

Hoopes and one of his Fellows poked their heads into the room. "Dave," the surgeon said, "you caused quite a bit of excitement this afternoon. How are you feeling?"

David said 'okay.'

Dr. Hoopes paused a moment and asked, "Does your chest feel heavy? Any sharp pains when you breathe?"

Again David shook his head 'no.'

Then I asked, "Dr. Hoopes, are you releasing him tonight?"

"No, I want to run a CAT scan on the new lung just to be safe. If everything checks out, he can probably leave in the morning."

David gave me a grimace, and I said, "It's probably for the best. It's just one night more." I wiped the sweat from his forehead and noticed that he was once again breathing rather shallow, quick breaths. Not the longer, relaxed ones I had seen earlier in the day. I looked into his eyes and asked, "Are you telling us the truth? Are you having trouble breathing?"

He stared straight ahead as if he was sulking. After a few moments of silence, he said, "This afternoon I felt a heaviness in my stomach, like I needed to pass gas. When I tried to push out the gas, the alarms went off." His eyes had a cloudy, far away look to them. He sighed and said, "Laura, I'm not going through all that pain again. If this transplant has gone bad, I just want to die quickly."

As if someone pushed a button that said cry, tears began streaming down my face. "Oh, my love! Don't say that. We don't know what happened this afternoon. Is it hard to breathe?"

Finally he admitted that he had felt a heaviness in his chest that had grown stronger throughout the day.

I questioned, "Why didn't you tell the doctors? Why didn't you tell Dr. Hoopes?"

He answered very quietly, "I don't want to die in this hospital."

I began to tremble, feeling sick to my stomach. My throat began to hurt. "You are not going to die! God has given you this perfect match! This is just a minor setback!" I crawled into the bed with him and held his hand. That familiar strong grip was no longer in his hand. He looked so very sad. "You've got to tell Dr. Hoopes so they can see what it is and fix it!" I told him, trying to reassure him. He didn't answer.

I sat up to give him a hug and noticed that his entire face was drenched in sweat. I knew he was running a fever. "I'm going to call the nurse. We need Dr. Hoopes as soon as possible."

Again he didn't answer.

I pushed the nurse's call button and said, "We need a nurse right away. David is sweating profusely and I'm sure he is running a fever."

No more than a minute later, the nurse came in to take David's temperature. "You have a fever of more than 102 degrees, Mr. Bichler. I will let the transplant team know right away," she said as she walked out the door.

I took his hand again and began praying for the Lord to let the doctors find what was causing the fever in order to cure it. David had simply laid his head back against the pillow and closed his eyes. He said nothing, but I could see the deep disappointment on his face.

Once more I began pleading with the Lord. "Dear Lord, please do not let this be serious. Please let Dr. Hoopes see what it is to correct it. He has done so well! Please give him courage to fight this one more setback."

Before long, the radiology team came by to take David down for a CAT scan. I began calling everyone to have them start praying about this new setback, not realizing that it was past 10 p.m. Pacific Time. After the calls, I waited for what seemed to be an eternity for David to return from radiology. I could tell his breathing was becoming more and more labored. I was becoming frantic but didn't want to let David see my fear. I asked the radiologist as he was leaving the room, "Have you seen Dr. Hoopes? Does he know what has happened to David?"

The young man, seeing my fear and concern, said, "I heard that Hoopes is doing another lung transplant. I'll tell the nurse's station for you though."

What? I stood there stunned and scared to death. *Dr. Hoopes is doing another lung surgery? Dear Lord, why?*

Don't you see that my David needs Dr. Hoopes? These things kept running through my head, over and over and over again.

I'm not sure whether David was silent because he felt so bad or whether he didn't have enough air to speak, but for the next few hours, he lay in the bed, eyes open, staring into space. I would hug or kiss him or hold his hand. I tried to talk about the great things that were waiting for us when we got home. He would only blink, but never smile. My scared prayers were now becoming angry ones. *Don't you hear me, Lord? I yelled out in my mind. Is the devil causing this to happen to him? Are you testing him? What can I do? Help me. Dear God, you know I need him. Heal him! Don't let him suffer again! Please heal him!!*

Around 3 a.m., the head of the ICU unit came into David's room. She was a very matter-of-fact person and immediately said, "Mr. Bichler, my staff has been monitoring you and I believe we need to take you back to ICU in order to stabilize your breathing."

One tear fell from his eyes and he looked at me and shook his head 'no.'

I said to the doctor, "Dr. Hoopes is his doctor. Is he through in surgery? He will know what to do because he knows David's history."

The lady doctor said, "I'm the head of ICU and I can see that Mr. Bichler is in trouble. Dr. Hoopes will come by when he is out of surgery, but that will be several hours from now. We must do something or your husband will be in a desperate situation by that time."

Again I looked at David who had such a dreary look on his face that it scared me. His eyes pierced through mine as I said, "David, I don't think we have a choice. I don't know what to do."

He said nothing but closed his eyes.

The lady head of ICU said, "Mr. Bichler, my team is going to transport you back to ICU and we are going to stabilize you till we talk with Dr. Hoopes."

She left and at least ten people came into David's room, gathering IV poles, oxygen meters, and putting yet another nose cannula around his head. He was put on a gurney and was out the door before I could blink. I said, "Wait! Wait for me! I want to go with him!" as they almost ran down the hallway with his gurney.

One of the nurses instructed, "Gather his things and come to Room 23."

I started bawling. Simply bawling. I tried to find the big black trash bag I had just the night before packed to move from ICU. My heart was racing and, through my tears, I found my backpack and asked one of the floor nurses to bring whatever I left behind to ICU Room 23. I ran through the hallway and through the doors of the ICU only to find the curtains drawn in Room 23. I was sobbing and asked one of the nurses, "Where is David? I need to see him."

The entire 10th floor ICU nursing staff was shocked to learn that David was once again back in ICU. One of them came to me and gave me a big hug and said, "David's in trouble, Laura. They are trying to put in an arterial line in his neck. He may be back on the ventilator."

I stood there, sobbing and shaking my head in disbelief.

She said, "Sit here in my chair till they let you in his room."

I sat on the director-style chair and the blood rushed from my head to my toes. Everything seemed to be moving in slow motion. All I could do was cry out over and over and over again, "Why, Lord? Why? Why is this happening? Don't you care? Why?"

It was only an hour, but it seemed like a lifetime before the head of the ICU came out of David's room. She walked past me, saying nothing. She was followed out of his room by the nurse who would once again be taking care of David. The nurse was familiar and knew all about us. She told me, "We don't know what has happened, but we had to stick him more than fifty times just to get an IV started." Tears were filling her eyes too. "They have inserted another arterial line in his neck along with a trach tube," she continued. He had been put back on the ventilator. "His breathing became very shallow and we had to." She hugged me again. "Come on in. Dr. Hoopes will come by when he is out of surgery."

I slowly got off the chair. My legs felt like lead posts and it took almost all the energy I had to get to David's bedside. There he lay with a ventilator tube coming out of his neck. What was wrong? Less than 24 hours ago he had almost jogged up a flight of stairs! Now he needed a ventilator to breathe? I put my head on his bed, holding his hand in mine and cried. I tried to pray, but all that came out were tears.

The lights came on in the hallway at 6 a.m., and I began making phone calls to our family. They, too, were shocked and stunned. Only a few days before, David was laughing and playing cards. Was he bad enough that they needed to fly back in? I told them to wait until I heard from Dr. Hoopes before making any decisions. He would know what had happened and he would be honest with me about the prognosis.

I finally saw Dr. Hoopes around 7:30 a.m. the morning of May 5th. He and several transplant team doctors came to David's room. He checked out the charts, questioned the nurse, and talked to the transplant team before talking to me.

"Dr. Hoopes, what has happened?" I said, trying to bravely hold back any tears as I stood by my husband's beside, holding his hand.

Dr. Hoopes shook his head and said, "I don't know for sure. The lung has whited-out on the CAT scan. I don't know if it was blood clots or what. I'm as confused as you are. I will be running tests today.

When I know something, I will let you know." He left the room.

I nodded and one of the transplant doctors gave me a hug. He said, "The best thing you can do is pray."

Again I nodded, turning to look into the closed eyes of the man I loved more than anything in the world. I gulped and asked, "If the new lung is whited-out, does that mean it is dead?" I knew the answer before I asked it, but I was desperately praying that answer would be different.

The doctor said, "We just don't know."

Nothing changed over the next two days. When David wanted to talk, he would lift his right hand and motion with his fingers. I would place a pen in his hand and hold the paper for him to write on. He kept writing over and over again, "Mind games. Is new lung dead? Mind games now."

I would assure him that the new lung was not dead and that the doctors were trying to figure out what had gone wrong. "My love, this will not last forever. God will heal you, I just know it!" I would say in his ear every time he questioned. But I could not figure out what he meant by 'Mind games.'

On Tuesday, May 8th, he woke up looking better. In fact, he had color and his red blood count was up. By the end of the day he was sitting in a chair, breathing on his own!

I said with a smile, "See, my dear one! God hears

our prayers and you are back on the road to recovery. Just a little setback, that's all."

He nodded, but I could see in his eyes that he was not as convinced as I was.

Dr. Hoopes came in and was pleased to see him up without the ventilator. "You don't do anything the easy way, do you, David?" he said smiling.

David grinned and answered, "Just trying to keep you on your toes!"

Dr. Hoopes told him that he wanted to keep him in ICU for a couple more days because he was concerned about the new lung and the fact that his creatinine levels were dropping. David grimaced, but nodded that he understood.

I had been updating our family and friends, and Mary had decided to come back to San Francisco the following week. When I told them that David was better and was breathing on his own, everyone thought he was out of the woods. We all relaxed a bit. Except for David and the transplant team of nurses and doctors. I think they knew something was still not quite right.

Each day that week, David was able to sit up in a chair for a few hours, breathe on his own, and even walk around his hospital room. I could tell he was not happy about this setback and he was much more quiet than normal. He never answered my question about what he meant when he wrote "Mind games."

I knew he was tired and I tried to cheer him up, but he was distant. I could tell he was thrashing out thoughts in his mind that he wasn't ready to share with me.

Just when we thought David was out of danger, Saturday morning brought a drastic change in his condition. Once again he was struggling to breathe and his red blood count plummeted. By 7 a.m., he was once again put on the ventilator.

He wrote, "My arms and legs feel extremely heavy. I don't think I can lift them."

I hurriedly took the note to the nurse and asked her to page one of the doctors ASAP. Soon, a transplant doctor came and sat by the bed, listening to David's breathing. He asked him to raise his right hand. David tried to lift it, but it was shaky and he was only able to raise it a few inches off the bed. The doctor looked into his eyes and told him that they were going to draw more blood. David nodded. I followed the doctor as he left the room because I had questions to ask him that David didn't need to hear.

"What is happening? Is he in rejection?" I asked the doctor.

He replied, "We're not sure if it is rejection or some sort of infection. We are going to do a bronch in his room later today. We need to see the lung."

My heart was hurting. Why would David get better,

then worse, then better again? *Dear Lord, let them find what is wrong.*

I stood in the hallway watching as one of the young doctors training under Dr. Hoopes began a routine bronch on David in his hospital room. I could see the oxygen monitors, the nurses assisting, and the image on the computer screen, showing pictures of his lungs. This younger doctor was not moving as quickly as Dr. Hoopes, and I noticed David's oxygen level beginning to drop. 85, 80, 78. The nurse attending said to the young doctor that David's level was down to 68.

You must hurry, I said to myself. I began to feel sick to my stomach. Just as the attendant finished his sentence about David's number, bells and alarms began screaming their loud, high-pitched alerts. Nurses came from all over the floor and the curtain surrounding David's room was quickly drawn. Even though I couldn't see, I knew what was happening. He wasn't able to breathe and his oxygen had dropped to a deadly level.

Tears filled my eyes and I tried again to pray. Dr. Hoopes came running down the hallway and into the hospital room. I could hear frantic voices saying, "We're losing him. We're losing him!" More doctors came running into his room and I felt fear grabbing onto me so tightly I couldn't breathe. My brain was shouting: "Dear God! No! Please don't take him! Please! Oh my God! No!"

After what seemed like years, the doctors came out of his room and opened the curtain. I could see him. He was on the ventilator and once again sedated. I tried to be brave and not cry, but my face was stained with tears.

"What happened? Why did they wait so long to finish the bronch?" I questioned Dr. Hoopes.

The young doctor who had performed the bronch was visibly shaken and she was in tears too.

Dr. Hoopes replied, "We took a little too much time getting the bronch done." He went on, saying, "David is a difficult case. I should have realized that he needed a more experienced doctor to do this bronch. My young trainee doctor feels terrible. This has really shaken her confidence."

I glanced over to see that she was as white as a sheet. "Is David okay? Was there damage done?"

Dr. Hoopes shook his head. "I need to get more fluid off him. What may be happening is that every six or seven days he starts to feel better because his red blood cells have regenerated. Then his white cells begin attacking and killing them and his condition worsens." He stopped long enough to glance back into David's room. "He is sedated right now and he needs to rest." He patted me on the shoulder before heading down the hallway.

I walked into the room and sat beside my husband, holding his hand and being careful not to disturb the

IV line that was taped to it. Many of the veins in his arms had hardened and stood out stiffly. I knew that we needed our prayer warriors and so I began making calls to update family and friends, asking them to pray... hard.

Mary flew back into San Francisco the next morning. David was awake but still had the ventilator blowing oxygen into his lung through the opening in his neck and he was visibly weakened. His eyes had dark circles around them.

"Hey, bro!" Mary said, trying to cheer him as she walked into the room. "Just can't live without me, can ya!" She grinned and leaned over to give him a kiss. David rolled his eyes, smiling just a bit.

I hated to leave David's side, even for a few minutes. But Mary convinced me that I needed to shower and rest a bit. I was thankful that she had come back for a few days but was still worried that something would happen while I was gone. When I went to the apartment to shower and sleep, I found myself restless and felt I needed to hurry back.

Just as Dr. Hoopes had said, over the next few days David seemed to be getting better, although he was not able to get up and walk. Mary and I played cards or sat and talked with him, doing what we could to cheer him. She stayed for almost a week, leaving when he seemed to be well on his way to recovering.

The morning after Mary left, David asked me what day it was.

"Thursday, May 17th," I told him and leaned over to kiss his forehead. Still unable to speak, he mouthed the words that his foot hurt. I nodded and got up to check his feet as I thought he might have been cold. I loosened the sheet at the foot of the bed and raised it only to have my breath taken away. Both his feet and ankles were purple, black, and blue. *Oh my Lord!* I thought to myself *I can't let him see this!* I put the sheet down and told David that I would ask for more blankets for him. He looked into my face and frowned. He knew I was hiding something. I'm sure he knew it.

I walked out of the room and motioned for the nurse to follow me down the hallway. She followed and asked, "Is something wrong?"

My voice cracked as I said softly, "His feet and ankles are turning black. Does that mean his circulation is bad?"

She paused before saying, "Laura, we are aware of the discoloration in his feet. We think his white blood cells are destroying the red blood cells and he's not able to circulate enough oxygen through his body."

I heard what she said but stood there in shock. "I've always heard that when people begin turning purple and black, they don't have long to live. Is that right?" I mumbled, gazing into the room where David lay.

"The doctors are working very hard to help him."

CHAPTER 27

I pulled my chair up to David's bedside and said, "God is protecting you, my love. He will heal you."

He tried to put his hand on mine but clumsily hit the bedrail. I laid his hand on mine for him. He grunted at me and mouthed the words "Mind games."

There it was again. Mind games. What did he mean by that?

I said, "What do you mean when you say mind games? I'm sorry, but I can't figure that out. Do you need something?" I looked straight into his eyes and saw that they were not cloudy, but very clear and determined.

He stared at me for a moment and then mouthed the words, "All I have to do is pull out this trach tube. My suffering will be over."

My eyes grew wide and I almost shouted, "No!! David that is NOT an option and you know it! God will heal you. We must be brave. Do you hear me? We must be patient!" His words frightened me. His eyes never left my face and he motioned for a paper and pencil.

It was difficult for him to hold a pen, but he managed to scribble a few partial sentences. "Devil playing mind games with me. Body has given out. I am trapped inside." I began to cry as I read the words, and he began trying to write again. "Mind games tempting me to end this. This is not living."

I leaned over the bed, taking his face into my hands and said, "I can't imagine what you are struggling with, but I love you and need you! Please, don't give up! So many prayers are being said for you. I know God will make you better. Please keep fighting!"

Once more he took the pen and wrote, "Job. I'm like Job. Why am I being tested so?" He dropped the pen and tears began falling from his eyes. It broke my heart to see him suffer so.

He closed his eyes and I looked around his bed. On the right hand side were two IV poles with monitors and bags hanging from them, oxygen monitors stacked on a shelf in the corner, tubing hanging all over the walls. On the left hand side stood the ventilator with a long tube running from it into the hole in his neck. Beside it stood a large, menacing machine. A dialysis device that resembled an old 8mm movie camera. It had eight different tapes that were turning independently from each other. These tapes were laced with tubing that contained a red fluid. His blood. The doctors were desperately trying to clean his blood, get fluid off of him, and try to stop the white blood cells from destroying the red ones.

I looked back down at the man I had loved for almost 25 years and prayed, "Dear Lord, why have you let this happen? He is a good man. He believes in You. Does he deserve this?"

I stayed by his bed until midnight when the nurse made me leave.

"Please call me if anything changes," I pleaded with her.

"Of course we will," she said. "I will make a note to call you immediately."

I kissed David on the forehead and said, "They are making me leave for a few hours. I am not far away. You will be all right. I love you."

The parking garage was lighted, but deserted, and my footsteps echoed loudly. I cried all the way to the apartment and, exhausted, I lay down to sleep. I set the alarm for 5:00 a.m. I wanted to be back in his room well before 6 a.m.

I'm not sure how long it took me to fall asleep and I kept my cell phone beside my ear. Its loud ringing startled me and I jumped up, grabbed it, and answered.

It was UCSF. David's temperature had spiked to 105. I grabbed my backpack and ran to the car.

Lord, I prayed, *please help me get there quickly.*

I knew I was speeding, not stopping at signs, but there was little traffic at 3 a.m. and I was thankful for that.

When I reached David's room in ICU, one of the lung doctors stopped me before I went in. "Laura, the nurses tried to raise David up in the bed because he had slipped so far down. When they lifted him, they accidentally pulled out his arterial line and he lost a lot of blood."

I stood there, stunned. "What? Oh my Lord! Is he okay?"

"Yes, we have put the line back in, but he is gravely ill. We have had to use the defibrillator on him several times."

I swallowed hard. "You mean he stopped breathing? His heart stopped?" My eyes were teary as the doctor nodded 'yes.'

As I sat down beside David, I took his hand in mine and he turned his head to look into my eyes. He looked very tired. He mouthed the words *I love you* and I choked back tears as I said, "I love you, too." He closed his eyes and I sat there holding his hand and crying. Dr. Hoopes was once again performing a lung transplant, so the interns and Fellows were on the floor. David was being heavily monitored, so there was always someone else besides me in the room with him.

I decided to call family and let then know what had happened. I tried to be as positive as I could, but I told them that he was gravely ill and, for the first time, I didn't know if he was going to make it. My heart was breaking and my mind was trying to process what had occurred over the last two years. We had such a normal, wonderful life! We had looked forward to being empty-nesters and to traveling and to planning for retirement. Thoughts flashed through my mind quickly and randomly. I thought about all the times I had seen him laugh. I remembered the first date we had and how we had fallen in love with one another from day one. I cried when I realized our 25th anniversary was only a few months away and that he might not be with me to celebrate it.

It was Monday, May 21st. David's feet, ankles, and legs up to his knees were purple and black. The ventilator was turned up to the highest level, sounding very loud as it forced air into his lungs. Several times that morning the alarms sounded and David was in cardiac arrest. The nurses scrambled to get the paddles out and the defibrillator would shock his heart into beating again.

Our daughter and his two sisters were making flight arrangements to come the next morning. It was after noon when I received a call on my cell phone from someone in UCSF. It was the financial office. They needed me to come to their office at 2 p.m. I tried to explain that I wasn't leaving my husband's bedside for even a second. The person on the other end of the line said, "It is imperative that you come. It won't take long."

As sick as David was, his mind was as sharp as a tack and I didn't want him worrying about finances, so I told him that I was going to grab a few crackers from the cafeteria and would be right back.

Scared and tired, I walked into the financial office, expecting to see the same person attending to our account. But it was a different young lady. She greeted me, saying, "I've been assigned to your account, Mrs. Bichler."

I was thankful that Sherry was no longer on David's account. I sat down in a chair beside this new financial officer's desk, and she turned the computer monitor so I could see it.

"Mrs. Bichler. I realize this is not a good time for you, but I am required to let you know where you are concerning your husband's bill."

I slumped in the chair and nodded that I understood.

"Your husband has reached the maximum level of benefit from you health insurance carrier and we need to find a payment plan for you to setup," she continued.

I looked down at the floor and saw the drops of tears that had fallen from my eyes.

"My husband is gravely ill and I need to get back to his room. We will pay you, just please set up something and let me know. I have to get back to his room."

She apologized for the timing and said, "Well, I can come to his room tomorrow afternoon with a plan for you. Will that be all right?"

I nodded and got up to leave. As I left the office and headed back to ICU, I was having a difficult time processing what just happened. *I don't care what it costs, I just want my husband to live. Lord, please, please let him live.*

David's condition didn't change throughout that night and into the next morning. Around 7 a.m., he went into cardiac arrest once more. The defibrillator was used several times before his heart began beating again. Dr. Hoopes was paged and, when he arrived, he took me outside of the room so David couldn't hear. "David is hypoxic, meaning he isn't able to send adequate oxygen to his body through his bloodstream." I was numb. I was hearing him, but I was numb.

Dr. Hoopes continued, "I've got to get more fluid off of him and I need a few more days. I've got one more thing I can try."

I nodded and said, "Our family is flying in today."

He nodded too and said, "I will be checking back in on him soon."

I returned to stand by David's bed, watching him fight to breathe, when he began mouthing words to me. He said, "I know what is happening. Don't keep me here just for yourself."

I blinked tears back.

He tried to hold my hand and said, "Heaven is waiting for me. I will have a new body there. Please, let me go."

I sat down in the chair next to him, devastated, confused and sad. For some reason, God put it in my mind to call our daughter, his sisters, and his mother so they could say goodbye to him. He was not going to live long enough for them to make the flight here.

I stood up and asked David, "I want to call everyone and let them talk to you, okay?"

He looked at me with those big brown eyes, nodded yes, and then closed his eyes.

I walked out into the hallway and began calling. I told each of our family members that I would give them about 20 minutes to think about what they wanted to say to him and then call them back, one at a time. Briana was at the Minneapolis airport. Mary, her husband, and her mother were at the Rapid City airport. Linda, his youngest sister, was getting ready to drive to San Francisco.

David had gone into cardiac arrest once more during those 20 minutes and the room was now filled with nurses and doctors. All of them were watching

David. One by one, I called our family. I held the phone close to his ear and they would talk. He understood each word and would nod at times. His eyes were closed, but I knew that he heard each heartfelt *I love you.*

Dr. Hoopes had come back into the room and sat once more on the bed beside David. He leaned over to look him straight in the eye. "David, I'd like to try one last thing. I know you have suffered a great deal and I can't tell you that this will cure you."

David nodded, never taking his eyes off the doctor.

Dr. Hoopes continued, "I told you that if something happened, it would be you and I that make the decisions. I am asking you. What do you want me to do?"

There was a brief hesitation then David mouthed the words "I'm tired."

Dr. Hoopes looked into his eyes and said, "I understand." He got up and stood at the foot of the bed.

The room was filled with nurses, doctors, interns, and aides and each one had tears in their eyes. I looked at David, still holding his hand and saw his head lie back, his eyes glassy and fixed.

"David," I said and then my voice stopped.

Dr. Hoopes told everyone in the room to do nothing. The alarms began sounding and a nurse shut them off quickly.

I stood there, holding his hand, wanting to speak. I couldn't. I physically couldn't open my mouth. I tried, too. I tried to say the words I had been taught to say: "May the Lord's angels take you home to be with Him." I tried to say, "I love you!" But I couldn't move or breathe. Nothing in the room moved. I wept as I watched David's mouth drop open and suddenly I felt his hand completely relax. It startled me and I gasped. I couldn't speak or move. All I could do was stand there and cry. It was a God moment. I had witnessed the presence of God taking the love of my life to his Heavenly home.

After several moments, Dr. Hoopes said, "I'd like to do an autopsy on the new lung only. If we don't do it quickly, we will never know what killed him."

I looked at Dr. Hoopes and said, "It's okay to autopsy the lung…only if you promise to find a cure for this dreaded disease. No one should have to suffer the way he did."

Dr. Hoopes nodded. Everyone slowly left the room. The curtains were drawn and I was there, crying and holding the hand of the body that gave out on the love of my life.

For next few days, time had no meaning. I didn't know if it was day or night, if it was morning or evening. David had told me what his wishes were and I had one mission: to make sure I followed them to the letter.

He had asked to be cremated and to have Briana and I scatter his ashes over a hill close to the school where he and Briana had graduated. I found myself making arrangements to have his body flown to Deadwood, South Dakota, so the family could say goodbye and have some closure before his memorial service.

Mary had made flight arrangements for me, and her husband, Larry, picked me up from the airport in Rapid City. He took me to the funeral home where it was my duty to make the arrangements. I tried to be so brave. I tried to do exactly as David had asked. There was to be time for only family on Sunday evening and then his body would be cremated. The memorial service was to be held in Grace Lutheran Church in Deadwood, South Dakota. He was baptized and confirmed in that church and now he was to be remembered there.

One task was weighing heavily on my mind. I had to talk with the Pastor of Grace Lutheran to tell him what David's wishes were. Once again, Larry drove me to the church and I sat down beside Pastor Goldammer to talk about the message David had requested. The pastor had met David several times and had known his mother for many years. He prayed with me, and then I told him what David had asked me to say.

"David does not want this to be a service of sadness. He doesn't want this to honor him. He wants every person to know the Easter story. That God has risen and is the Way, the Truth, and the Life." Tears began falling, and I tried to keep my chin from trembling. "Would you please tell people how important it is to believe in Jesus Christ as our Savior? That they need to trust in Him now more than ever?"

The pastor nodded.

I wiped my tears and said, "He wants us to be happy that he is not suffering in this world anymore. He is home." My voice cracked as I said *home*.

And Pastor Goldammer did just that. His sermon was one of hope and joy and salvation. Just what David had wanted.

The day following the service, Briana, Wayne (her fiancé), and I picked up his ashes and drove the 50 miles to Rapid City. As I sat in the backseat of the car, holding a small black container filled with ashes, I felt at peace. I felt that David was there with me. I felt like this bad dream was going to be over and things would be right again.

We scattered his ashes as he'd wanted and I felt as if a weight that had been pushing down on my shoulders had fallen off. I took a deep breath and thought, *Ok, David. I did what you wanted.* But tears suddenly gripped me and I asked, "Dear God, how can I live without him?"

I never knew how much I would miss David. Looking back, I think I lived in a fog for more than two years. I didn't know who I was or what my purpose was or how not to be Mrs. David Bichler. Many nights I sat up crying, unable to sleep. I thought about the conversations David and I had during the two years of his battle with IPF and how our idea of *transplant* had changed.

David and I assumed that, with the advanced medical technology in our world today, a person could pause his life for a brief time, heal from the transplant procedure, then un-pause his life and continue with his plans for the future. How wrong we were!

While God assures us that we will be made anew in Heaven and we no longer will need our earthly bodies, people refuse to be organ donors. At times people forget that the body is just that... a body. Once our Father has called us home, we no longer need this earthly shell. Why not give the gift of life to someone God has not called home yet? Across the nation, organ procurement centers are begging people to become donors. Thousands of people are hanging onto life and waiting on long lists for one organ that could prolong their life.

David told me during one of our long conversations that, had he not gotten so sick so quickly in 2005, he might have chosen not to receive a transplant.

I was shocked when he said that and I questioned him further. "Why on earth would you say that?"

He replied, "If I had been able to go through the preparation for transplant, the training about what transplant truly meant for my life, I might have chosen not to go through with it."

I'd sat beside him for moment, trying to grasp what he was saying.

"Laura, there are only so many organs available while many more people, young and old, are needing them. If God had given me the time to learn how my life would be changed with the transplant, I think I would have chosen to live out my days with my family and let nature take its natural course."

I had stood up and said, "Now, you are just having a tough day. I know you had many complications with the first transplant, but you are alive!"

He nodded and said, "Life is about quality, not quantity."

I could see he was thinking about what he wanted to say next.

He continued, "I don't have my life back. I can't travel to other countries with my job anymore. My days are filled with taking pills all day long and having blood draws and CAT scans."

I sat back down beside him and hugged him.

"I catch every germ that is floating around and I never used to get sick! I've seen more doctors in the last few months than in my entire lifetime. I can't eat or talk without coughing and I couldn't even go to my daughter's college graduation." He stopped long enough to cough a few times. "I had a great job and was planning for my retirement. I know that when I die, I am going to Heaven."

I said, "Yes, and when you were gasping for each and every breath, I would have given you my lungs to keep you from suffering. I am glad you received the first transplant!"

We were silent for a while and the subject of *choice* didn't come up again.

Now that he is gone, I see better what he was talking about. Life after transplant is nothing compared to what it was before. It is a lifestyle and lifetime change. Sometimes for the better. Sometimes for the worse. I thank God that Dr. Hoopes gave David the chance to choose and that God kept his mind healthy so he could choose. He was tired of fighting his body that didn't work anymore. He wanted to go home. He wanted to be with Jesus forever and suffer no more. He had a choice and he made it.

Several months after his death, I received the death certificate in the mail and called back to UCSF to ask a few questions. There were several things listed as causes of death with hypoxia as the first one and pulmonary fibrosis as the second. I asked one of the transplant doctors, "What actually killed David? Was his body rejecting the new lung?"

The doctor on the other end of the cell phone said quietly, "Laura, when Doctor Hoopes took out the lung, it was filled with clots. David would never have recovered, no matter how long he battled."

I started crying and felt a small amount of relief. I had been wondering if David had given up too soon, if only he had let Dr. Hoopes try one more thing. If only. David had thrown blood clots again and most likely on the day when he thought he was passing gas. When he pushed, the clots spewed through his system, the mass of them landing in his new lung.

People have asked me what message I wanted to get across by writing this book. Several things come to my mind. I wanted people to see how very important a life of faith and prayer is. In a way, this book is part of my healing process as I still miss my husband each and every day. David wanted me to share his love for Jesus with everyone. He wanted me to spread the Gospel news of forgiveness and salvation. And I believe he wanted me to share that nothing in this life compares to the joy of living in Heaven with our Father. God had many purposes for David's life and I am thankful that he was in my life for almost 25 years. As hard as it isto live each day without seeing him or hugging him or talking with him, I know I will see him again... when God is ready to take me home.

In December of 2007, about seven months after his death, I had a dream. It was so real I will never forget it. I was standing in the living room of Don and Margie Elliott's home in San Francisco, looking across into the dining room, when I saw David sitting on a tiny chair in the corner. He was wearing his favorite plaid shirt, the one he wore the first time I saw him! His hair was dark and full and he was wearing jeans and his work boots. He didn't wear glasses and he looked exactly as he did the day we married. I felt tears streaming down my face as I walked toward him. I felt him near me. I could smell him. He was there. He leaned forward in the chair, putting his elbows on his knees and folding his hands together. His smile was big and bright and he said, "We are praying the same things, Laura."

I was so happy to see him! I asked, "Can I hug you?"

He shook his head no, and then I woke up, crying with my heart beating so hard it almost came out of my chest. I called his name because I knew he was there. I looked for him and realized I had been dreaming. I still believe that God gave me that dream to help me continue to pray and to know that David is happy and well among the servants in Heaven. It was a gift.

My prayer for you and your loved ones is that you are never touched by pulmonary fibrosis and a cure can be found for this dreadful disease before more must suffer and battle to breathe. If you or someone you love is facing a serious illness, whether or not they are waiting for a transplant, pray hard every day. Ask your church family to pray too. God listens and He hears prayers. Ask Him about the choices you need to make. He is our strength and our Savior. Ask Him for guidance in those difficult times of your life. David did. God answered him. God answered my prayers, too. He gave David the ultimate healing – Heaven. Who could ask for more?

ACKNOWLEDGMENTS

I believe thousands of prayers were said for David and me during his two-year battle with Pulmonary Fibrosis. Many dedicated doctors and nurses spent hundreds of hours trying to save his life. There are so many that I need to thank, to express how much their prayers and efforts meant to my family and me. Please forgive me as I am sure simple words alone can't possibly describe my eternal appreciation and gratitude for each person. I pray that God blesses each one of you!

Thank you to my dear friends at Trinity Lutheran Church and School in Spring, Texas for their thoughts, prayers, cards, and emails. David and I read each one, and they brought smiles to his face during times he had nothing to smile about. Your prayers are still with me, and I will keep each card and letter forever. They are so precious. Thank you to Jean Smith, who served as my liaison at Trinity. Jean, you prayed in our home when

David's transplant operations were occurring, and you prayed for me as you took his favorite Sunday suit out of his closet to send me for his burial. That meant so much to me!

Thank you to the University of California San Francisco's Lung Transplant team and especially Dr. Charles Hoopes, who at that time was their Director of Cardiopulmonary Transplantation. Dr. Hoopes, you are without a doubt the most talented, dedicated thoracic surgeon in the field today. You cared about the love of my life as an individual and, in my heart, I believe you felt pain with David through each setback or complication. You allowed him to make a choice when others would not and I will be forever grateful to you.

I also want to thank the doctors and nurses of the Lung Transplant team who wanted to remain anonymous. You laughed with us and cried with us. You were there at 3 a.m. when I needed to call you about his condition. You were there when our Lord took him home. From the bottom of my heart, thank you. Your tireless efforts are so important, not only to the transplant recipients, but to their families.

To the family of Don and Margie Elliott, who have both passed away, thank you for allowing David and me to be part of your family for a short while. We loved Don and Margie as if they were our own parents and I know that Margie is still beating Don playing dominoes in Heaven!

How can I say thank you to my own family? You put your own lives on hold to sit by David's side, laugh with him, and pray for him. You cried with me and helped me when I couldn't eat or sleep or breathe after losing him. I love you all so very much and David did, too.

Thank you to Krisi Keley, my editor with the Scrupulous Scribe, and Linda Boulanger with TreasureLine Publishing for taking a chance on this first-time writer who wanted her late husband's story to reach and inspire people. What a wonderful group of talented authors to be associated with! Linda, you answered every question I had, no matter how silly or repetitive it was. Thank you, thank you.

I need to thank those families who allowed their loved ones to become organ donors. What a blessing you are! In your sorrow and loss, you saw that another life could be saved and you unselfishly let your loved one give that gift of life. If others would only see the life-changing affects that the gift of organ donation gives, perhaps the transplant waiting list would no longer exist.

Finally, and most importantly, I thank God, our Heavenly Father for allowing David to be in my life for almost 25 years He was my soul mate, the spiritual leader of my family, my husband, and my friend. Knowing that he is basking in the warmth and light of our Savior and Lord and that I will see him again keeps me breathing.

❧

ABOUT THE AUTHOR

Author Laura Bichler Hern is a wife and mother of two adult children. She loves the Lord and tries to do His will in her life each day. She has a passion for all genres of music, writing, travel and people. Laura has a B. A. in Non-profit Management and Education and is currently a licensed Insurance Agent for the state of Minnesota. Throughout her career, she has worked as Children's Ministry Director, instrumental band teacher for elementary and high school students, and as a church organist and choir director. She has traveled throughout the United States, Europe, and Singapore, and enjoys learning the history and traditions of different cultures.

An outstanding motivator of people of all ages, from children through adult, Laura also enjoys public speaking and has a keen sense of humor. Her writing touches the soul of the reader and pulls them into the story as if they were actually present. Watch for more stories from Laura coming soon.

For more information about Laura visit: www.laurahern.com